BUDDHISM AMONG THE TURKS OF CENTRAL ASIA

ŚATA-PIṬAKA SERIES

INDO-ASIAN LITERATURES

Volume 626

Reproduced in original scripts and languages
Translated, annotated and critically evaluated by
specialists of the East and the West

Founded by
Prof. RAGHUVIRA *M.A., Ph.D., D.Litt. et Phil.*
Continued by
LOKESH CHANDRA

आचार्य—रघुवीर—समुपक्रान्तं

जम्बुद्वीप-राष्ट्राणां
(भारत-नेपाल-गान्धार-शूलिक-तुरुष्क-पारस-ताजक-भोट-चीन-मोंगोल-मञ्जु-
उदयवर्ष-सिंहल-सुवर्णभू-श्याम-कम्बुज-चम्पा-द्वीपान्तरादीनां)

एकैकेषां समस्त्रोतसां संस्कृति—साहित्य—समुच्चय—
सरितां सागरभूतं

शतपिटकम्

BUDDHISM AMONG THE TURKS OF CENTRAL ASIA

Margit Kőves
University of Delhi

INTERNATIONAL ACADEMY OF INDIAN CULTURE
and ADITYA PRAKASHAN, NEW DELHI

First published: 2009

ISBN 978-81-7742-087-6

Rs. 1250

Published by Aditya Prakashan, 2/18, Ansari Road, New Delhi – 110 002.
email: contact@adityaprakashan.com
website: www.adityaprakashan.com

Printed at Rajkamal Electric Press, New Delhi – 110 033.

CONTENTS

1 . INTRODUCTION

The study of the history of Central Asia has a special importance for those who are committed to research in the field of Sanskrit Buddhism. According to the legends, links to Central Asia existed since the times of Asoka, and the Central Asian route through East Turkestan led many traders and missionaries to China and back. The most accessible route to China led through Central Asia, via Bactria, Sogdiana, Kashgar, Khotan, Karasahr, Turfan, Kuci and Tun-huang. These were the places where great nomadic empires came to life and from where they started their unpredictable movements towards the Black Sea and Europe. In Central Asia Buddhist culture was flourishing. According to a legend Buddhism was founded in Khotan by Asoka's son. In the Uigur manuscripts many places are mentioned by their Sanskrit name: Kuci, Heyruka and so on. When Indians went to Central Asia, Gandhara art was transplanted to the Tarim valley.

Buddhism was a live tradition in this area and these traditions were retained and evolved here even after the decline of their eminent position in India. The realisation of the importance of Central Asian history and literature came about step by step.

First, the importance of the Tibetan tradition was discovered in the study of Indian and Chinese with many features representing Tantrism. Many dhāraṇīs can be found in this version, especially in chapters vi, viii, xii, xiv, xviii and xix, which led many Tibetan authorities, like Mkhas-grub-rje and Situ pan-chen to consider it among the Tantras and not among the sūtras. I-tsing's translation became very popular among the Mahāyāna sects. It served as a base for further translations. Among them are the Tibetan, Uigur-Turkish and Mongolian translations.

Next Csoma de Koros opened new opportunities for further research on the texts of Tibetan Buddhist literature originating in India. The importance of such studies for Indological research was soon recognized by leading scholars of India like S. Ch. Das, the great promoter of Tibetan studies, Rajendralal Mitra and others.

The Uigur translation deserves special attention for various reasons. Though its most extensive manuscript originated in the 17th century, the fragments of the same translation belonging to the ninth century AD were discovered by the Second Prussian Expedition in Turfan. It is also known that the Mongolian and the Tangut translations were made from the Uigur text. A study of the Uigur Suvarnaprabhāsa-sūtra can provide new information on the contacts of Uigur and Tibetan literary traditions, on the position of Sanskrit in the Central Asia of those times, and even on the reconstruction of the Sanskrit text.

The scope for studies on the relationships of the Uigur Suvarnaprabhāsa-sūtra with those in other languages are provided by the results of philological studies carried out on the text in the aforesaid languages. The Sanskrit text was edited by Sarat Chandra Das and Pandit Sarat Chandra Shastri in 1898, by Hokei Idzumi in 1931, by J. Nobel in 1937, and by S. Bagchi in 1967, and it was translated into English by R. E. Emmerick in 1970. Some Chinese and Tibetan versions of the text were published and annotated by J. Nobel. The Uigur text was published and partly translated into German by W. Radloff. Some fragments of the text in Uigur language found in Turfan were published by F. W.K. Mueller in 1908. The availability of the main versions of the text has made it possible now to have a comparative study which has not been attempted so far.

On the basis of the information given in the colophons of the Uigur version, it is generally believed that the Sūtra had been translated from the Chinese. A careful examination of all the colophons, however, shows that this is not true in every case. The colophon of the first chapter discloses that it was translated probably from the Tibetan. The orthography of the names and the dhāraṇīs shows a measure of closeness to Sanskrit forms, which can not be explained with the help of the Chinese or Tibetan versions.

Textual interrelationships can not be clarified without an examination of the historical situation of the given community and period. From the sixth century AD onwards Chinese, Arabic, Tibetan sources refer to the Turks, or different Turkish tribal confederations, like the Qarluqs, the Uigurs, or the Basmyls. Turkish documents relating to those times in Runic and Uigur scripts have been published since the beginning of the 20th century. A systematic account of this period of Turkish history — about the Turkish States on the Orkhon River, the Uigur State after the destruction of the East Turks, their contacts with the Tibetans and Chinese, and after the victory of Qyrqyz over the Uigurs the migration of Uigurs to East Turkistan — has not been given so far. The present study makes an humble attempt at a brief history of Turks on the basis of the Runic and Uigur documents published earlier and the publications and translations in Russian, Turkish, German and English sources.

A study of the history of this area shows that Central Asia was a meeting ground of different cultures, and of different peoples and population groups speaking different languages. These contacts were of a dynamic and sophisticated nature. The picture that emerges from the study of the texts is not simple, but complicated. By comparing various versions of the text in different languages an attempt has been made to find out some facts which contribute to a better understanding of the situation which led to the transmission of canonical texts in a multilingual environment.

Previously on the basis of the opinions of scholars like Max Mueller, Winternitz, it was generally believed that the mantras and dhāraṇīs, as found in various texts, were nothing but combinations of meaningless syllables. The recent researches in the field have approached this question differently and the role of the mantras in initiation and in yogic exercises has been stressed and at the same time the need for an examination of the language of the dhāraṇīs has been expressed by scholars like A. Wayman, M. Eliade, F. Bernhard, Lokesh Chandra, S. C. Banerji and so on.

Under the circumstances it has been decided to investigate the interrelations of different dhāraṇīs, which were transmitted in Sanskrit, Uigur, Tibetan and Chinese versions. The dhāraṇīs are very important as they provide good material for comparison. These are pronounced similarly in all the versions and do not follow other changes of the text. Thus they retain more archaic features than other parts of the text.

For this comparison, all the dhāraṇīs of the Uigur version — 35 dhāraṇīs, from which two are repeated in the same context — have been collected, transcribed in Roman script, and collated word by word with the corresponding Sanskrit, Tibetan and Chinese dhāraṇīs.

At the end of the last century a great revelation was the discovery of a Sanskrit manuscript in Central Asia dating as far back as the 4th century AD, since early Sanskrit manuscripts are not extant in India. Thousands of manuscripts in other languages, many of them translations from Sanskrit, were also found. The archeological excavations led by A.M. Stein started from India, and many Indians were also members of these expeditions.

Rabindranath Tagore also realized the importance of such studies from the point of view of national awakening and did his best to introduce Tibetan, Chinese, Japanese and South-East Asian studies at Santiniketan. P. C. Bagchi's works threw new light on Indian and Chinese relations.

Many Tibetan texts were published by Indian scholars like by R. Sankrityayana, who collected Tibetan and Sanskrit materials in Tibet which are preserved now in Patna. These materials inspired those interested in Mahāyāna Buddhism for further research. The Indian texts translated into Tibetan are related to various branches of Sanskrit literature and the reliability of the Tibetan texts gives considerable help in the restoration of original Sanskrit texts. R. Sankrityayana also recognized the importance of Central Asian Buddhist literature. His book on Central Asia highlights the important historical processes of peoples living in the steppe.

RaghuVira during his stay in China and Mongolia collected Mongolian, Manchurian and Chinese materials. His collections at the International Academy of Indian Culture also contain Japanese and South-East Asian materials. Some of the manuscripts collected by RaghuVira have been edited in the Satapitaka series by his son Lokesh Chandra.

The Calcutta University and the Royal Asiatic Society pursues research on Tibetan and Sanskrit manuscripts. Aloka Chattopadhyaya's name should be mentioned among the eminent scholars working there in the field of Tibetan studies.

The Jawaharlal Nehru University has established a department for studying Central Asian languages and literatures.

The discoveries of the expeditions led by M. A. Stein and the Japanese, German, French and Russian expeditions, highlighted the written culture, art and civilization of the first millennium in Central Asia. The manuscripts uncovered in the area showed that Central Asia was a meeting place of various cultures, and that in the monasteries and settlements Sanskrit texts were translated into Chinese, Khotanese, Tocharian, Sogdian and Tibetan. Not only were the monks and nuns supposed to know Sanskrit and recite their confessions in Sanskrit, but the laymen were also expected to know enough Sanskrit so that the titles of holy works and certain Buddhist terms did not become corrupted. Besides Buddhism, Manicheism and Nestorian Christianity were professed in this area. The Uigur script taken over by the Uigur-Turkish tribes from the Sogdians in the 8th century, became the basis of the Mongolian and Manchurian scripts. Many Mongolian and Manchurian texts along with Tangut texts were translated from Uigur. The translation literature was mainly of canonical character. It consisted of sūtras, dhāraṇīs, avadānas, confession-prayers, stories, tales, prajñāpāramitā texts as well as some extracanonical works.

Manichean and Nestorian texts show the effect of Buddhist literature. However the numbers of fragments are many and the work of identifying little pieces and reconstructing the original text is painstaking. The texts give a great amount of material to the linguists as well as to the philologists. The texts written in the same language but in different scripts give information on minor details of pronunciation of the given languages.

The Suvarnaprabhāsa-sūtra is one of those texts which were translated into several languages like Chinese, Tibetan, Khotanese, Uigur-Turkish, Sogdian, Tangut and Mongolian.

These translations have a special importance because some of them have preserved such contents of the text, which are not available in the original Sanskrit. The first Chinese translation done by Dharmakṣema in the fifth century AD represents the earliest stage of development of the Sūtra. This is the shortest version. The other Chinese and Tibetan translations are based on another version, which is represented by the Sanskrit manuscripts from Nepal belonging to the 17/18th centuries. The text of this version incorporated further discourses on philosophical questions, viz., teachings on the Trikāya, Nirvāna and the Bodhisattva ideal. Some dhāraṇīs were also added. The first Chinese version had only a few dhāraṇīs in Chapter VIII. A further enrichment of the text is represented by the translation of the famous Chinese scholar I-tsing who visited India towards the end of the eighth century. This translation is based on an original Sanskrit text, which is not extant. It incorporates the results of fully developed Mahāyāna Buddhism with many features representing Tantrism. Many dhāraṇīs can be found in this version, specially in Chapters VI, VIII, XII, XIV, XVIII and XIX, which led many Tibetan authorities, like Mkhas-grub-rje and Si-tu panchen to consider it among the Tantras and not among the Sūtras. I-tsing's translation became very popular among the Mahāyāna sects. It served as a base for further translations. Among them are the Tibetan and Uigur translations.

Chapter 1 contains an introduction which deals with the circumstances that have made the research possible in the field, the details of sources and the theoretical problems involved.

Chapters 2-5 contain a comprehensive introduction to the main subject: the Uigur and Tibetan Suvarnaprabhāsa-sūtra. Chapter 2 describes the area where the Uigurs lived i.e. the area of East Turkistan and Kansu.

Chapter 3 gives an account of the exploration of East Turkistan and the expeditions which brought to light the remnants of the civilization and culture of the Central Asian peoples.

Chapter 4 details the history of Turks in Central Asia. This chapter has been divided in accordance with the different stages of Turkish history in Central Asia: (a) history of the First Turkish Empire on the Orkhon River (546-658 AD), (b) history of the Second Turkish Empire (678-747 AD), (c) an account of the Uigur State. It incorporates the history of nomad Uigurs as well as the after their settlement in the area of Kocho and Bisbalyq, (d) history of the Uigurs in East Turkistan and Kansu after the fall of the Uigur Empire. During the 13th/18th centuries East

Turkistan was under growing Chinese and Muslim influence, whereas Kansu was mainly under Chinese supremacy.

Chapter 5 describes (a) the origin and development of Uigur language from the stage of Proto-Turkish, and (b) the history of Uigur literature. It shows, through examples, how Turkish oral literature contributed to the formation of written Uigur literature.

Chapter 6 describes the place of Suvarṇaprabhāsa-sūtra in Uigur literature, details the fragments of the text of the Uigur version, quotes titles of chapters and colophons in Uigur language and gives their English translation.

Chapter 7 describes in details the other versions and manuscripts of Suvarṇaprabhāsa-sūtra in Sanskrit, Chinese and Tibetan languages.

In chapter 8 the significance of dhāraṇīs and mantras in Buddhist literature is described. In Uigur language the mantras are called dhāraṇīs, while generally such passages in Buddhist literature which hold mantras are called dhāraṇīs. So the name dhāraṇī can cover two meanings. Dhāraṇīs have a great relevance for philological and linguistic studies in revealing inter-relations between different versions of a text.

In chapter 9 a list of the Uigur dhāraṇīs of the Suvarnaprabhāsa-sūtra is given along with the corresponding Sanskrit, Tibetan and Chinese versions. It also describes the context in which the dhāraṇīs were presented, the instructions given along with the dhāraṇīs and the god or goddess to which the dhāraṇīs belong.

Chapter 10 explores the rules of some regular correlations between the Sanskrit and Uigur sounds. Attempt has been made to explain some regular correspondences.

Chapter 11 presents conclusions which have been drawn from the proceeding chapters, i.e. the place of the Suvarnaprabhāsa-sūtra alongside other versions in Sanskrit, Chinese, and Tibetan languages. The common peculiarities of the Tibetan and Uigur versions and their interrelation with the Sanskrit version are set forth in this chapter. It also unfolds the scope of further investigation which would widen the researches on other texts of Uigur Buddhism.

2. ABBREVIATIONS

ADAW	Abhandlungen der (Berliner) Deutschen Akademie der Wissenschaft.
ABAW	Abhandlungen der (Berliner) Preussischen Akademie der Wissenschaft.
Alt.	Altayan.
AO	Acta Orientalia, The Hague.
AOH	Acta Orientalia Hungarica, Budapest.
APAW	Abhandlungen der Preussischen Akademie der Wissenschaften. Philologisch-historische Klasse, Berlin.
Aserb.	Aserbaijani.
Bashk.	Bashkir
Bibl. Buddh.	Bibliotheca Buddhica, St. Petersburg / Leningrad.
CAJ	Central Asian Journal, Haag and Wiesbaden.
CC	Codex Cumunicus, W. Bang-J. Marquart Ostturkische Dialektstudien, Gottingen 1914.
Chag.	Middle Turkish dialect of the records written in 10-15 centuries at Timur's Court.
Chuw.	Chuwash
Crim. Tat.	Crimean Tatar
DTSL.	V.M. Nad'elyaev, D.M. Nasilov, E.R. Tenisev, A.M. Scherbak, Drevn'e Turkskiy slovar' (Old Turkish Dictionary), Leningrad 1969.
EUT	A. Caferoglu, Eski Uygur Türkçesi Sözlügü (Old Turkish Dictionary), Istanbul 1968.
Fnd. I	Philologicae Turcicae Fundamenta, Vol. I, Wiesbaden 1962.
Fnd. II	Philologicae Turcicae Fundamenta, Vol. II, Wiesbaden 1965.
FWKM	F.W.K. Mueller, Uigurica I, APAW, 1908.
Gag.	Gagauz
Gen. Turk.	General Turkish
Hak.	Hakas
Hung.	Hungarian

JA	Journal Asiatique, Paris
JRAS	Journal of the Royal Asiatic Society, London.
JSFOu	Journal de la Societe Finno-Ougrienne, Helsingfors.
Kar.	Karachay
Kasg.	Mahmūd al-Kasgari: Divan Lugat at-Turk, edited by C. Brockellmann, Mittelturkischer Wortschatz, Budapest-Leipzig 1928.
Kaz.	Kazakh
Kipch.	Kipchak
Kirg.	Kirgizian
Kkalp.	Karakalpak
Koib.	Koibal
KB	W. Radloff, Das Kutadgu Bilig des Yusuf Hass Hājib (The Kutadgu Bilig of Yusuf Hass Hājib), St. Petersburg 1891-1910.
Liu Mau Tsai	Die Chinesischen Nachrichten zur Geschichte der Ost-Turken (T'u-kue) (Chinese Sources on the History of the Eastern Turks), Vols. I-II, Wiesbaden, 1958.
Mong.	Mongolian
MSFOu	Mémoires de la Société Finno-ougrienne.
Nog.	Nogay
Old Turk.	Old Turkish
Osb. Usb.	Uzbek
Osm.	Osman Turkish
PDTP	S.E. Malov, Pamyatn'iki Drevn'e-tyurkstoy pismennosti (Old Turkish Written Records), Moscow-Leningrad 1951.
rep.	repeated
Russ.	Russian
SBAW	Sitzungberichte der (Berliner) Preussischen Akademie der Wissenschaften.
Skr.	Suvarṇaprabhāsottama-sūtra, Das Goldglanz-sūtra, ed. J. Nobel, Leipzig 1937.
Skr. Bag.	S. Bagchi, Suvarṇaprabhāsa-sūtra, Darbhanga 1967.
TT I	Türkische Turfantexte, SBAW, 1929.

TT II	Türkische Turfantexte, SBAW, 1929.
TT III	Türkische Turfantexte, SBAW, 1930.
TT IV	Türkische Turfatexte, SBAW, 1930.
TT V	Türkische Turfantexte, SBAW, 1931.
TT VI	Türkische Turfantexte, SBAW, 1934.
TT VII	Türkische Turfantexte, ABAW, 1936.
TT VIII	Türkische Turfantexte, ADAW, 1952.
TT IX	Türkische Turfantexte, ABAW, 1956.
TT X	Türkische Turfantexte, ADAW, 1958.
Turkm.	Türkmanian.
Uig.	Uigur
Uig. (in ch.8)	W. Radloff, S.E.Malov, Suvarnaprabhāsa Tekst uygurskoy redakcii (in Russian: Suvarṇaprabhāsa text of the Uigur version), Petersburg 1917.
Uzb.	Uzbek
Yak.	Yakut
ZDMG	Zeitschrift der Deutschen Morgenlandischen Gesellschaft, Leipzig, Wiesbaden.
-	omitted
+	hypothetical (usually) Proto-Turkish form.
>	changes to
<	originates from
~	or

SANSKRIT MANUSCRIPTS

ABG	Cambridge University Library.
C	Leningrad.
DE	Bibliothèque Nationale.
F	Royal Asiatic Society, London.
Chin.	Suvarṇaprabhāsottama-sūtra, Das Goldglanz-sūtra, ein Sanskrit text des Mahāyāna-Buddhism. I-tsing's Chinesische version und ihre Übersetzung, Leiden 1958.

TIBETAN MANUSCRIPTS

Tibetan text	Suvarṇaprabhāsottama-sūtra, Das Goldglanz-sūtra, Ein Sanskrittext des Mahāyāna-Buddhismus. Die Tibetischen Ubersetzungen mit einem Wörterbuch, ed. J. Nobel, Leiden 1944.
Tib. I	the oldest Tibetan version.
Tib. II	second Tibetan version.
Tib. III	latest Tibetan version based on I-tsing's translation.
P	blockprint in Paris
Hs.	manuscript in Berlin
C	blockprint in Cambridge
II Hs.	Kanjur manuscript in Berlin
II BI.	Narthang blockprint
IPP Ming Tripitaka	The Tibetan transcription of the dhāraṇīs of the Suvarṇaprabhāsa from *Sanskrit Texts from the Imperial Palace at Peking in the Manchurian, Chinese, Mongolian and Tibetan Scripts*, Part 2, ed. Lokesh Chandra, from the collection of Prof. Dr. RaghuVira, New Delhi, 1966.

3. GEOGRAPHICAL BACKGROUND

The area we are considering is in East Turkestan and reaches south east including the Kansu area of China. The boundaries of East Turkestan are the Altai range on the north-east, Mongolia on the east, K'un-lun system on the south, Sari-gol and Muztag-ata on the west, and the main range of the T'ien-shan system on the north upto Aqsu. The natural boundary of East Turkestan on the south-west is another area which may interest us and is known as Kansu Corridor or the Su-lo-ho basin[1].

The geography of East Turkestan has been dealt with here as the course of history indicates. The Uigur Turks came to East Turkestan first and some of them later went to Kansu and settled down there. The said area which is also known as the Chinese Sin-kiang (Hsin-chiang) province consists of two regions: Jungaria is the territory between the Altai and T'ien-shan, and Kasgaria is the region of Tarim basin. The former is about 250 sq miles in area and has the character of a great depression. It can be divided into two parts: the first part extends from the slopes of the Altai to the Qara Irtis and Urungu, while the second one comprises of the area right from Qara Irtis to T'ien-shan.

The Jungarian gap which is about six miles wide and fortyfive miles long is the only real break in the masses of mountains between Afghanistan and Manchuria. Though this gap served as a corridor for military operations, but at the same time it is not very convenient for the purpose, as winds blowing through the mountains are so hot in summer and so cold in winder, that they made this invasion route extremely difficult. Other passes over the mountains are generally more reliable and hence more frequently used[2]. The Jungarian gap is so divided that almost half of it falls under China and the rest under the Soviet Union.

The North-Eastern parts of Jungaria have practically no water and it is a desert of red clay covered with a thick layer of dust. The southern parts on the other hand are lower lying and therefore have comparatively more watering. During the period under study the region suited very well to pastoral nomadism. The permanent settlements in the region were in fact established primarily as stations on the northern routes between the East and West. Since the late 18th century, the settlements in this region have tended more to agriculture, under Chinese influence. This region had been a favourite grazing ground of nomadic tribes and therefore it had played an important role in the historical development of East Turkestan.

The other part of East Turkestan, the Tarim basin (Kasgaria), is surrounded by high mountains. It comprises of an area of 450,000 sq miles. The melting snows of the mountains rush down in the

---

[1]W. Samolin, *East Turkestan to the Twelfth Century*, Central Asiatic Studies, The Hague 1964, pp. 8-18.

[2]G.B. Gressey, *China's Geographic Foundations,* New York and London 1934, pp. 183-184.

form of many streams to the central depression. Grazing grounds here are not extensive. Water resources provide the means for a well developed irrigation system and hence large scale agriculture.

First in order are the great southern ranges. The southern system is known as K'un-lun and extends from the junction of the Qara-korum-Himalaya system and the Muztag-ata range. It starts some 200 miles south of the Tarim basin and it proceeds in the eastern direction for about 500 miles. South of Carqyq, the system is divided in two branches: one branch first leans towards Tun-huang, then turns south-east, and the other branch leans south. The two branches surround a high plateau region called Kokonor (Qoqonor) basin. The portion of the northern branch which extends towards the north-eastern direction is known as the Astain-tag, while the other one which turns to the south-east and forms several somewhat parallel ranges is known as Nan-shan and serves as the southern boundary of Kansu. The Nan-shan system forms the traditional boundary between China and the autonomous region of Tibet.

The ranges of Nan-shan which converge slightly towards south-east are all of great height. Its highest point rises from 18,000 to 21,000 ft and are comparable to the main K'un-lun range to the south of Khotan. The Pei-shan on the other hand expands in the western direction joining the T'ien-shan, known as Quruq-tag in Turkish, which means 'dry mountains'.

Some of the geographic names of the Tarim basin can be found in Old Turkish manuscripts, partly in the manuscripts written in Uigur script, and partly in Manichean script. These names are: Üch-Turfan — the old name is *Hecyuka*, Kuca — the old name is *Kuci* but in later manuscripts it is called *Kuysan*. *Hippuka* is a place named in this area. The fact that these names are Sanskrit in origin, means that there were Indian settlers in this area, or devout Buddhists living in these places who gave such names. In the Turfan manuscripts on the other hand Chinese names of places are found in the Uigur script. These names are: Tun-huang ~ *Tu kuvan*, Su-chou ~ *Su-ciu*[3].

Like the K'un-lun and the Qara-korum Himalayan system the T'ien-shan is of Tertiary and Quarternary origin. The organic process is still under way. This region is drained by the Tarim river system. The western extremity of this system is the Yarqand Darya, which begins at an altitude of over 17,000 ft in the Muztag-ata range. Later the Yarkand Darya is joined by the powerful Aqsu Darya to form the Tarim river. The area is usually without rainwater or has very little rain. It has some water from snow in the extreme east.

Thus from the physiography and the climate of the Tarim basin, it is evident that the culture of the region could be neither that of a rain dependent agriculture nor that of pastoral nomadism. It is sustained on the irrigation-based agriculture of the people living in the vicinity of the water sources. Since the water sources are placed at a distance, the settlements had taken the characteristics of oasis communities. The distance between one community to the other was quite considerable and

[3]Annamarie von Gabain, *Historisches aus den Turfan-Handschriften*, AO 1970, pp. 116-124.

therefore the usual political organizations which emerged took the form of more or less independent or semi- independent city states.

Kansu which is 135,000 sq miles in area is of particular importance, because of the Kansu corridor in western Kansu. The Kansu corridor is not only a major route between the Chinese eastern provinces and Turfan, but also a natural passage linking China with Central Asia[4]. This corridor became famous due to the accounts of travelers who passed through it. Prominent among them were Hsuan Tsang[5], who traveled by this route to India, Marco Polo, who came by this route to China, and so on. Chinese silk goods were taken by caravans to Central Asia and Europe through the Kansu corridor, it is therefore known generally as the place where 'Silk Road'[6] started. The Kansu corridor is some 600 km long. It extends from Lanchow, past the Wuhsiao Mountains, then it proceeds further along the foot of the Tsing-ling Mountains and finally reaches the Sin-kiang border. It is surrounded by high ranges that overlook the low-lying valley. It is composed mostly of highlands which are 5,000 feet above sea-level. The main water source of the Kansu corridor is the melting snow of the Chi-lien Mountains which in its turn created the Edsin Gol, that goes northward and joins the Gashiun Nor.

---

[4]Wang Chun Heng, *Simple Geography of China*, Peking 1958, pp. 195-203.

[5]Samuel Beal, *Travels of Hiouen Tsang,* 1951, p. 486-487: "The country of Kie-sha is about 5,000 li in circuit. It has much sandy and stony soil and very little loam. It is regularly cultivated and is productive. Flowers and fruits are abundant. Its manufactures are a fine kind of twilled haircloth and carpets of fine texture and skillfully woven. The climate is soft and agreeable, the winds and rains regularly succeed each other. The disposition of the men is fierce and impetuous, and they are mostly false and deceitful. They make light of decorum and politeness and esteem learning but little. Their custom is when a child is born to compress his head with a board of wood. Their appearance is common and ignoble. They paint (mark) their bodies and around their eyelids. For their writing (written characters) they take their models from India and although they (i.e. the forms of letters) are somewhat mutilated, yet they are essentially the same in form. Their language and pronunciation is different from that of other countries. They have a sincere faith in the religion of Buddha and give themselves earnestly to the practice of it. There are several hundreds of sangharamas with some 10,000 followers, they study the Little Vehicle and belong to the Sarvāstivāda school. Without understanding the principles they recite many religious chants. Therefore there are many who can say throughout the Three Pitakas and the Vibhāṣā (Pi-p'o-sha). Going from their south-east 500 li or so, passing the river Sita and crossing a great strong precipice, we come to the kingdom of Cho-kiu-kia.

Cho-kiu-kia (Chukuka-Yarkiang). Their kingdom is some 1000 li or so round. The capital is about 1011 in circuit. It is hemmed in by crags and mountain fastnesses. The residences are numerous. Mountains and hills succeed each other in a continuous line. Stony districts, spread in every direction. Their kingdom borders on two rivers, the cultivation of grain and of fruit-trees is successful, principally figs, pears and plums. Cold and wind prevail throughout the year. The men are passionate and cruel; they are false and treacherous and in open day practice robbery. The letters are the same as those of K'iu-sa-ta-na (Khotan) but the spoken language is different. Their politeness is very scant and their knowledge of literature and the arts equally so. They have an honest faith however in the three precious objects of worship and love the practice of religion. There are several tens of saṅghārāmas but mostly in a ruinous condition; there are some hundred followers, who study the Great Vehicle.

On the southern frontier of the country is a great mountain with lofty defiles and peaks piled up one on the other and covered with matted underwood and jungle. In winter and all through the year the mountain streams and torrents rush down on everyside. There are niches and stone chambers in the outside they occur in regular order".

[6]L. Boulnois, *The Silk Road*, London 1966, pp. 61-74.

The Hwang Ho (Yellow River) divides the Kansu province into two parts in the east-west direction. From the place where it enters the province, it turns into a torrential stream some 50-70 yards wide, across which boats manoeuvre with the greatest of difficulties.

East of the Alashan (Holan) mountains lies a narrow strip of flat depressed land along both sides of the Hwang Ho, which is called Yinchuan Plain.

Large parts of Kansu are covered by loess. These portions are called Loess Highlands, which constitute almost the entire province of Kansu, and are 4500 feet above sea-level. The loess is concentrated south of the Ordos Desert and the Great Wall upto the Minshan and the Tsing-ling shan. This loess area is divided by the Liu-pan-shan. One of the most striking features of the loess is that it stands vertically high, often very high, several tens of feet above the mountains.

The loess region is almost impassable if one does not keep to the trodden paths. This fact led to the establishment of many passages which were being used for one to two thousand years. The loess is soft and easily cut, so cave dwellings are found everywhere. For example the cave dwellings of Tun-huang are exceptional in beauty and grandeur. The loess would provide a good land for agriculture, because of its ability to hold moisture, if the area had a little more favourable climate. But the climate of the loess highlands is effected by the nearness of the desert. The summer monsoon looses its rain-making capacity, before reaching the north-western provinces, and the winter winds carry no moisture. In Kansu the rainfall is small, and the hillsides remain parched and brown even in mid-summer. The summer temperature is seldom above 27°C (80°F). During winter it has icy winds from Mongolia and the temperature is considerably below freezing point. Therefore only 7% of the whole area can be cultivated even in recent times.

Outside the Tibetan Plateau the Tsingling is the greatest mountain in China. It forms a high and rugged barrier extending from Kansu to Honan. In the west they join the Min Shan (which is known as Amnye Ma-chhen range in Ch'ing-hai province), the elevations rise to 20,000 feet, while in other parts the peaks are 10,000 to 12,000 feet in height. The heart of the range is a wild unexplored country. The Tsingling consists of a series of parallel ridges all tending a little south of east[7].

Between the valley of Han Kiang and the Red Basin of Szechwan is the Tapashan, another rugged mountain forming beautiful ranges, but at the same time they are almost unmanageable for communication. The Tsingling and its associated ranges are of particular geographic significance because of the way in which they divide China into the dust-blown north and the green humid south.

The Nan-shan marks the southern border of western Kansu and does not extend into the central portion of the province, beyond Lanchow. Its eastern extent may be represented in the ranges which encircle the Ordos Desert outside the great bend of the Hwang Ho. The first of these is the Alashan (Holan Shan), which is a narrow range reaching a maximum of nearly ten thousand feet. To the

[7]J.F. Rock, *The Amnye Ma-chhen Range and Adjacent Regions*, Serie Orientale Roma XII, Roma 1956, pp. 114-115.

north-west of the desert are the Karanarin Ula and to its east is a group of mountains known as the Taching Shan. The Taching extends along the borders of Mongolia, following the line of the Great Wall.

During recent centuries China has been traditionally known to consist of eighteen provinces lying south of the Great Wall, together with other territories of Manchuria, Chinese Turkestan and Tibet. Even these provinces had a changing history, for example, during the nineteenth century several pairs of them such as Shensi and Kansu were united and named as Shenkan. Before 1928 Kansu was bigger than what it was in the recent past. Before the establishment of Ching-hai province, parts of Kökö Nor belonged to Kansu.

4. EXPLORATION OF AND EXPEDITIONS TO TURKESTAN

Prior to Christ, Europeans and Chinese knew very little of this region. Kansu was the westernmost part of the Chinese Empire with a changing political status. The main concern of the Empire lay in keeping the nomadic tribes outside the Great Wall.

Nevertheless beginning with Emperor Mu-wang, who visited the Kökö-Nor area, there had been travelers to this area. Traditionally sea-routes from Europe were not much used. It happened that routes mainly passed though Turkestan. There had been three historical routes: "The Silk Road" which passed through Cherchen, Khotan, Yarkand, Kashgar, the *second* one on the west, west of the T'ien Shan along the north edge of the Takla-makan, including cities like Aksu, Kucha, Karasahr, and *third* which is called the North road from Hami to Karakol, Urumchi, Manas, Chugchak and then to areas now in Russia[1].

Record of the Roman Empire indicate that trade goods from China reached Italy in the early centuries of the Christian era. Contacts between the two empires were not strong, because of the Parthians (whose country lay between the Roman Empire and China) and it did not allow them to come closer. Buddhist pilgrims often used the Silk Road in the vicinity of, Yarkand from where they returned southward to approach India from the North. The first of them was monk Tso-ngan who made the trip in 316 AD. Other pilgrims followed him. To name a few: Hoi-sun and Song-yun in the 6th century AD, Hsuen Tsang in 629-645 AD. Hsuen Tsang set out across the Gobi Desert and reached Hami. Proceeding from there he went to the southern slopes of the T'ien-shan and further to the west of Chinese Turkestan. After his travels through the Talas Valley, Tashkent, Samarkand, he proceeded southward and then entered India.

During the same centuries, Nestorian missionaries established posts across Central Asia.

The Mongol conquest by Cinggis Khan and his successors united the whole of Central Asia under one sovereignty. Astonishingly enough, the Mongol rulers took a liberal attitude towards religion, social customs etc., and consequently travels became possible again. As a result, in the 13th century Chinese travelers again started going to the West. Most of these travelers had left accounts of their journeys. Our knowledge of the history of Central Asia during medieval times is mainly based on these accounts.

Marco Polo, the most famous European traveler in this area went through Balkh, the Pamirs and then taking the Silk Road arrived in China after three years of travels. Fortunately the young Marco Polo had learned both the spoken and written languages of the region and then became very well acquainted with the culture in which he lived. He has left an account of his travels. Few of the

[1] L. Boulnois, *The Silk Road*, London 1966, pp. 61-84.

travelers in Chinese Turkestan have left any account of their travels which can be scientifically acceptable to researchers. Due to lack of other works even these may be utilized.

In the 19th, and more so in the very beginning of the 20th century, more and more travelers happened to be scientists, or had at least a scientific training. At first their energies were taken up in tracing political boundaries and locating cities[2]. Only at the end of the nineteenth century they began searching under the surface and in fact those were the great discoveries which brought to light Buddhist and other manuscripts in Brahmi, Sogdian, Sanskrit, Tibetan and Uigur scripts.

With the support of the Russian Imperial Geographic Society, Russian explorers went to Central Asia. In 1859 Golubyov traveled to the Tien-shan, the Altai, Balkash and the Chinese side of the provinces of Ili and Tarabagatai. Captain Valikhanev was in Turkestan around the same time. He described the cities, their size, the walls around them and their population. He found six cities of considerable importance: Kashgar with 16,000 houses, Yanisar with 8,000 houses, Yarkand with 3,000 houses, Khotan with 18,000 houses, Aqsu with 12,000 houses and Üch-Turfan with 4,000 to 6,000 houses.

In 1860 a treaty was signed in Peking between Russia and China. Accordingly the territory between the Ussuri river and the sea was transferred to Russia, the boundary line was redefined in the Turkestan area. The line ran from the Yenisey to the Tien-shan south of Isyk Kul, along the Jungarian Alatau, crossing the Ili river, then following the T'ien-shan to Kokand. From then onwards, in generalized terms, Russian Turkestan became a reality, distinctly separated from the Chinese Turkestan.

Captain Montgomerie made continuous efforts in exploring the area of Tibet. He succeeded in presenting to the Royal Geographical Society 191 sheets of maps covering the area between Nepal and Lhasa.

Around the same time Severtsov, as the head of an expedition, traveled through the T'ien-shan and drew maps of the area where it meets the Tengri Shan and approaches the valley of the Naryn, at Paschi, and at the Ak-sai valley. He took specimens of several birds and stones to Russia.

The Forsyth expedition in 1874 and the Trotter expedition around the same time provided reports on buried cities in the desert, where the sand sometimes uncovered them. Forsyth also reported that a wall had been evidently built to keep the armies out of Khotan and Yarkand. He found traces of such a wall between Sosser and the Karakorum Pass.

In 1878 the Treaty of Livadia transferred most of the area between Jungaria and the T'ien-shan. The Russians received commercial privileges and had permission to travel to China. These circumstances made possible the Potanin and Przhevalski expeditions. Przhevalski drew new maps of the K'un-lun Rangs, gave names to many peaks and reported about several buried cities whose remains he found.

---

[2]J.A. Dabbs, *History of the Discovery and Exploration of Chinese Turkestan*, The Hague 1963, pp. 30-44, 89-117.

Graf Béla Szécheny and Lajos Lóczy of the Geological Department of the Vienna Museum prepared the first report on the caves of Tun-huang. It was Lajos Loczy who informed Aurel Stein of the caves in 1902.

After these expeditions a change in emphasis appeared in the travels. So far the collection of geological and biological specimens, the outlining of the mountains and valleys, and establishment of important features of topography were the main goals. By the end of the 1880's the maps were rather definite and new problems were brought into focus.

The Dutreuil de Rhins Expedition started in 1890. He was joined by Grenard, a scientist and orientalist. The expedition had a bad finish. Dutreuil de Rhins was killed but Grenard succeeded in saving the manuscripts and one thousand photographs which were taken on the expedition. The manuscripts were very valuable documents in Brahmi and Kharoshthi scripts going back to the 6th and 7th centuries AD. A Swedish explorer Sven Hedin, who had been exploring in Iran and was at that time in Kashgar, decided to find out the circumstances of the death of Dutreuil de Rhins. It led to the fruitful series of travels by Sven Hedin.

Towards the close of the 19th century minor travelers came for hunting, catching wild horses and so on. But at the same time the major expeditions resulted in better and more scientific exploration. Thus the Klementz Expedition to Jungaria and Chinese Turkestan could return in 1898 with surveys of the Altai and western Gobi with meteorological observations, as well as zoological and botanical collections. Besides, Klementz also visited ruins of ancient cities near Turfan, Khara-Khoja and Toek Mazar. He found a series of Buddhist temples with well preserved frescoes, ancient manuscripts, and inscriptions in Chinese, Sanskrit and other languages. He examined one hundred and thirty of these cave temples and brought back some of the frescoes and inscriptions besides many manuscripts.

Linguists were more and more involved in further expeditions. Captain Kozlov, with funds provided by the Tsar, was assigned the task to go to Tibet. He included in his party B. Th. Ladyghin, who knew the Chinese and Manchurian languages very well.

The work of Mark Aurel Stein (later Sir Mark) furnished the best example of the combination of geographical and archaeological exploration during this period. M.A. Stein, of Hungarian origin, studied in Budapest and went to Britain for university education. After his education he became Inspector of Schools in the Punjab (India), and continued in the field of Indology and history. Gradually the finds from Turkestan, the scraps discovered by Sven Hedin, paper and palm leaf fragments brought by Bower from his journey through the Turkestan area during 1889-1891, bits of documents which had been sold in various towns of Central Asia, the Klementz expedition, and the several reports of buried cities, all combined led Stein to try his luck in this field of science. In June 1900, on one year's leave from his service, Stein started his first journey. He took with him an Indian expert from Srinagar, named Babu Ram Singh, to map the covered area, who already had been to Central Asia in an earlier expedition with Captain Deasy. They started their expedition through the Kilik Pass to Tashgurgan, Ulugh Rabat, Karakul Lake, Bulunkul, Tashmalik Fort and

Kashgar. They rested in Kashgar for some days, then Stein followed the old road to Khotan and reached there on October 2[3]. His surveyor made an attempt to trace the Yuring Kash river to its source in the Kun-lun. They succeeded in doing so and were able to obtain an accurate survey of the river system.

In the middle of November, they returned to Khotan, and selected Dandan-ulik as the most promising place for excavations[4]. Stein found stucco images, frescoes, wooden tablets, several household items, mostly belonging to an early Indian culture period. He also found Sanskrit manuscripts belonging to the sixth and seventh centuries AD. In January 1901 he moved the work of excavation to the Niya river where he found many wooden tablets with inscriptions in Kharoshthi script. He also found Sanskrit manuscripts, seals and figures that showed Greek influence. From the Niya river he went to the place where once the Ender river flowed. There he found buried houses, stupas and other objects. Stein began his trip back to Khotan with loads of manuscripts and art treasures. After a rest, he started again for the site at Rawak, which is not far from Dandan-ulik. Here he found relics of statues and other pieces of art. In April 1901 he left Khotan and returned to Kashgar where he parted with his companions. Babu Ram Singh and others returned to India, while Stein crossed the Andijan mountains and took the Trans-Caspian railway to Kransnovodsk, crossed to Baku and in July 1902 reached London. Stein's successes aroused immediate activity in other countries. When his reports were published, other countries began to send expeditions to collect what was still un-explored in Central Asia.

A party of Japanese expeditioners started in August 1902. The leader of the expedition was K. Otani who happened to be in England when Stein arrived there. K. Otani set out from England in the company of M. Hori, who studied geography at Oxford. They went by train to Osh, then over-land to Kashgar via Terek-davan. They continued their journey through Tash-kurgan from where they went to Yarkand on yaks and further to Khotan to rest and to study Turkish and Chinese languages. In January they set out again following the Khotan Darya to Aqsu. From Aqsu they returned to Kashgar and set out for Kucha through Aqsu and Bai. This trip took two months. They spent three months at Kucha exploring neighbouring sites. They visited seven temples and excavated them. The collections of manuscripts were valuable finds. Most of these manuscripts are kept in the Museum of the University of Kyoto.

In 1903 German scientists were deputed to Chinese Turkestan: A. Grünwedel and G. Huth his assistant from the Berlin Ethnological Museum. They departed from Berlin in August 1902, entered Turkestan at Kuldja and came south to Turfan where they established their headquarters. They immediately began to work in the vicinity of Turfan. The excavations unearthed a valuable collection and became famous in Germany. Enthusiasm arose for a second expedition. The main

---

[3]M.A. Stein, *Innermost Asia: Detailed Report of Explorations in Central Asia and Westernmost China*, Oxford 1928.

[4]M.A. Stein, *Ancient Khotan*, Oxford 1907.

support for such an expedition came from the Sanskritist H. Pischel, historian Edward Meyer, linguist F.W.K. Mueller, and the orientalist Edward Sachau. Albert von le Coq was placed in-charge. The expedition spent nine months excavating caves and stupas. They found numerous coins and manuscripts in a number of languages.

The second German expedition took to Berlin the Uigur manuscripts of the Suvarnaprabhāsa-sūtra which happened to be an early tenth century translation of the Chinese version. A comparatively small part of the Uigur manuscript was published by F.W.K. Mueller in 1908[5].

In October 1905 Le Coq left for Kashgar where he met Grunwedel. They formed one group and returned to Kucha and Turfan to undertake further excavations. Their efforts were fully rewarded by the quantity of manuscripts and art treasures.

In 1906 the French Academy also decided to send an expedition headed by Paul Pelliot, professor of Chinese at the École Française d'Extreme Orient at Hanoi. He went by Kashgar North-west via Maralbashi Aqsu, Bai through the Tekes valley to Kucha. He worked at Kucha and Kashgar for eight months and dug out the caves and sites already visited by Germans, Russians and Japanese. Inspite of this, Pelliot and his partners found a mass of valuable manuscripts and art treasures. The expedition then proceeded to Urumchi, Turfan, Su-chou and western Kansu for the study of the famous Caves of Thousand Buddhas at Tun-huang. Although Stein had already taken away much of the finds from the caves, Pelliot still obtained a large quantity of manuscripts. The manuscripts were written in Chinese, Mongol, Tibetan, Uigur and Brahmi scripts[6].

In 1906 M.A. Stein went on his second expedition. He started from Khotan, went to the Niya valley and the Pisha valley. Under a large Buddhist temple he found a number of manuscript leaves in Sanskrit, Chinese and Khotanese, wooden tablets in Tibetan and Khotanese scripts. They dated from the 8th century AD. At Niya valley he found wooden tablets with inscriptions, many Kharoshthi documents, coins and fragments of various kinds of cloth. During this expedition Stein went to Miran twice for excavations. At first he found Tibetan manuscripts and other manuscripts in Kok Turkish Runic script, the earliest type of Turkish writing. During this expedition he visited Kansu and Tun-huang when he found evidence of the old Chinese Wall which was quite separate from the famous Great Wall. He went again to Tun-huang where he found manuscripts both in Chinese and Brahmi scripts. Later he set out along the Khotan river for Aqsu from where he went to Kelpin and Üch-Turfan.

In 1908 the Japanese returned to Turfan via Urga, Kobdo and Urumchi. Their leader was Zuicho Tachibana. After some studies and excavations at Turfan, they went to Lob-Nor, from where they made a trip to the north to visit Lou-lan. Manuscripts dating to the 2nd century AD were discovered as a result.

---

[5]F.W.K. Mueller, *Uigurica* 1908, pp.15-35.

[6]P. Pelliot, *Kao-tch'ang, Qoco, Houo-tcheou et Qara-khodja, avec une note additionelle de R. Gauthiot* (in French: Kao-tch'ang, Qoco, Houo-tcheou and Kara-khoja with a note of R. Gauthiot), JA 1911, pp. 579-603.

One of the most successful Russian expeditions was the Oldenburg Expedition in 1909 under the leadership of the outstanding linguist and Indologist S.F. Oldenburg. First they went to Karashahr, visiting Buddhist temples. Thence they proceeded to the Turfan Oasis and studied the ruins of the old city of Idiqut Shahri, which had about a hundred caves. Oldenburg also studied the area of Lob Nor. Finally in March 1910, the expedition returned to St. Petersburg[7]. In 1909-11, S.E. Malov went to Sin-kiang and Kansu for a linguistic survey. He got from a Chinese headman of the village Wun-si-gu (or in Uigur-Turkish: Indjan) the Uigur manuscript of the Suvarṇaprabhāsa-sūtra[8].

In 1910 under the leadership of Tachibana another Japanese group went to try their luck in excavations. He went to Urumchi, Semipalatinsk, then continued to Turfan and later on to Kara-khoja. He found many Buddhist texts there. He also dug at Yar-khoto. He found many Buddhist relics in the Altyn-Tagh. After a very arduous journey through the Takla Makan he followed the caravan route to Tun-huang in Kasu, where he visited the Caves of the Thousand Buddhas and found a few manuscripts which were not taken by Stein and Pelliot.

After the expedition of Tachibana the period of archeological discoveries was almost over. The study and interpretation of the manuscripts which had started immediately after their discovery continues till now, adding immeasurably to the science of history, philosophy, literature and linguistics.

---

[7]S.F. Oldenburg, *Russkie Archeologicheskiye Issledovaniya v Vostochnom Turkestane* (in Russian: Russian archaeological excavations in East-Turkestan), Kasansk 1921, pp. 25-30.

[8]W. Radloff & S.E. Malov, *Suvarṇaprabhāsa-sūtra Tekst uygurskoy redakcii* (in Russian: Suvarnaprabhāsa-sūtra text of the Uigur version), Petrograd 1917.

5. HISTORY OF THE TURKS IN CENTRAL ASIA

5a. The First Turk Empire (546-658)

A study of the history of Central Asia presents special difficulties. So is it in the case of a general summary of the history of the First Turkish Empire (545-658), Kök Turkish Empire (678-747 AD), the Uigur State (747-847), its post-history upto the 17th-18th century, and upto the date of the Uigur Suvarṇaprabhāsa text[1]. These difficulties are due firstly to the lack of original documents of these peoples in their native language, in this case by the Turks themselves. The art of writing history or even the art of writing was not common among the barbarians and the possibility of a survival of the few written documents in a society which was constantly moving was very slender. For this reason the few monuments which have come down to us are of exceptional value. They are precious not only because of their rarity, but also for their particular literary beauty and because they give us an insight into the formation and functioning of nomadic empires[2]. First of all it should be mentioned that the Orkhon inscriptions which are engraved in a Runic script, had to be deciphered[3]. There are some other documents written in the Runic script but slightly different from the Orkhon inscriptions. These are the inscriptions from the valley of Talas river[4], and from the valley of Yenisey river[5]. There are manuscripts found in Turfan, in Miran, in Tun-huang[6] and in Kara-Khoja[7], among whom is a divination book, juritic documents, and small inscriptions on graves.

About the beginning of Turkish history over a long period only one original major historical

---

[1]W. Radloff & S.E. Malov, *Suvarṇaprabhāsa (Sutra zolotogo bleska) Tekst uygursko redakcii* (in Russian: the Sutra of Golden Light: text of the Uigur redaction), Petrograd 1917.

[2]D. Sinor, *Orientalism and History*, Bloomington 1964, pp. 56-69.

[3]V. Thomsen, *Altturkische Inschriften aus der Mongolei* (in German: Old Turkish Inscriptions from Mongolia), ZDMG vol. 78, Leipzig 1924, pp. 121-127.

W. Radloff, Die Altturkische Inschriften der Mongolei (in German: Old Turkish Inscriptions from Mongolia), St. Petersburg 1894, 1895, 1897.

[4]S.E. Malov, *Talasskie epigraphichesskie pamyatniki* (in Russian: Epigraphic monuments from the Talas river), Leningrad 1936, pp. 17-38.

[5]V. Thomsen, *Turcica*, Helsingfors 1916, H.N. Orkum: *Yenisey yazitlari* (in Turkish: Inscription from the Yenisey river), Ankara 1939.

[6]A. von le Coq, *Kokturkisches aus Turfan* (Inscriptions of the Kok Turks from Turfan), Sitz. d.k.Preuss. Akad. d. Wiss. Phil.-hist. Klasses XI, Berlin 1909, pp. 1047-1061.

V. Thomsen, *Ein Blatt in Turkischer Runeninschrift* (in German: One page in Turkish Runic Script), Sitz. d.k. Preuss. Akad. d. Wiss. Phil.-hist. Klasses, 1910 vol. XV, pp. 296-306.

V. Thomsen, Dr. M. A. Stein's Manuscripts in Turkish Runic Script from Miran and Tun-huang, JRAS, London 1912, pp. 181-22.

[7]V. Thomsen, *Fragment of a Runic Turkish Manuscript from Kara Khoja*, MSFOu, 1916, pp. 37-43.

source is available: the Orkhon inscriptions from the time of the Kök Turkish Empire. Rest of the information about the Turks is from sources written by sedentary peoples, who either surrounded the vast territory where the Turks lived and were continuously on the move, or those who perhaps at some stage of their history came into contact with them. This puts not only the scholars of philology, but also the historians, in a difficult position. The problem is not only that one can get mostly hostile information from these sources, but also that in order to solve seemingly unimportant, but actually complicated, essential questions one has to penetrate into Chinese, Tibetan, Greek, Persian, and Arabic philology. Even if sources are translated and published, the Turkish proper names transcribed by a Chinese historian[8] to whom it was previously unknown — become often unrecognizable. Usually the context helps historians to supply the missing elements, but when it comes to identifying the person to whom the events referred to are related becomes complicated.

Till now there has been any synthesis of the early history of the Turks. We shall sum up Turkish history from the beginning to the 18th century.

The origin of Turks is not clear. However, there is a vague hypothesis that their progenitors were living in the western part of Shensi, which was attacked by the Huns in the 4th century. A-shi-na chief of the community had supposedly submitted himself to the Huns. But when the T'o-pa tribes defeated the Huns (Hephtalites) A-shi-na fled to the southern slopes of the Altai hills where they became vassals of the Juan-juans, otherwise called Ju-jus[9]. The origin of the Juan-juans is not clear, but quite definite information is available about them from the 5th century when they were at the height of their power. By that time they controlled an enormous territory which included Mongolia on both sides of the Gobi Desert, the Altai, Jungaria, Kasgaria, the Steppe, the northern part of T'ien-shan, the west of the Siberian Steppe, perhaps as far as the Urals. The Hephatalites (Huns) were originally their vassals, but became more and more powerful and as such gradually took over the actual control of the territories under Juan-juan overlordship. They took over Sogdiana and gradually after some time Kasgaria. The Juan-juans, the Hephtalites and later the Turks, had practically the same type of nomad overlordship.[9] The nomad rulers took little interest in local affairs and depended on their vassals mainly to raise levies for wars.

Speaking about the nomadic type of overlordship, the term 'nomadic empire' should be defined. The Chinese called the nomad 'barbarians of the west'[10]. They led a particular way of life

---

[8]Liu Mau Tsai, *Die Chinesische Nachrichten zur Geschichte der ost-Turken (T'u-kue)* (in German: Chinese sources about the history of the East Turks (T'u-kue), Wiesbaden 1958, p. 3: "Die besonders schwierige Aufgabe der Identifizierung der uberaus zahlreichen historischen Ortsnamen gerade in diesen Randgebieten liessich auf Grund aller Quellen — und Nachschlagewerke in vielen Fallen nicht befeidigend und sehr oft leider uberhaupt nicht losen".

V. Samolin, *East Turkistan to the Twelfth Century*, London-The Hague-Paris 1964, p. 55

[9]R. Sankrityayana, *History of Central Asia*, Calcutta 1964, p. 42.

L.N. Gumilyov, *Drevnie t'urki* (in Russian: Old Turks), Moscow 1967, pp. 22-23.

V. Samolin, *East Turkistan to the Twelfth Century*, London–The Hague–Paris 1964, p. 55

[10]D. Sinor, *Orientalism and History*, p. 58

as they were on the move season by season, year by year in search of grazing grounds and water. The herds provided them with food, home-made clothes and so on. The horses provided them in each case with a weapon which ensured their military superiority over enemies. Thus a limited supply of day-to-day needs due to the small scale economic production led to the nomadic community making use of their military superiority to obtain goods beyond their own production. The surplus was available in the form of booty and ransom. Only in the highest stage of its evolution, did the nomadic society of Central Asia need strong centralized leadership. The centralized leadership was essential in peace time for distribution of grazing land, and a strong leadership was even more essential in war. The nomadic empires organized and unified many tribes, but their interests were not always identical. In order to emerge and achieve success, various tribes had to co-operate with each other. The dissolution of such an empire was even more rapid than its formation. When the leadership of a particular ruling clan, or of the ruling tribe, ceased to be advantageous for the majority, their co-operation disintegrated and consequently the empire ceased to exist. New alliances emerged, paving the way for the seizure of power for such a person or tribe who could offer more advantages and thereby ensure more prosperity for the majority of people concerned. Huns, Mongols, Juan-juans and Turks all followed the same pattern of fusing the nomads into an unity in which national, religious and linguistic differences were comparatively unimportant[11].

In the 5th and 6th centuries the Turks (Tu-chueh) Turkut were under Juan-juan overlordship. First they turned against their own overlord and gradually defeated all their previous allies, and also imposed themselves on some of them.

When the Turks, A-shi-na and his community, first came to the southern slopes of Altai mountains in the 5th century, they mixed with other tribes which, as it might be presumed, originated from the Huns. Since then these people came to be known as Turks. During the course of ages, the word changed its meaning.

In the 5-8th centuries, this name became more of a linguistic definition of people speaking the Old Turkish language. However at the same time, they were surrounded by other peoples who also spoke Turkish and despite this were not called Turks. Arabic writers of history and geography name all the nomads of Central Asia Turks without distinction. Chinese called them T'u-kue or T'u-chiuh and provide detailed information about them during their long and ambiguous relationship[12].

The first official reference to the Turks (T'u-kue) in contact with the Chinese Government was made in 545 AD which says that Bumyn Khagan was reigning over the Turks[13]. It is probably at the time when the Turks were mentioned as a nation, i.e. when the history of the first Turkish Empire started.

---

[11]*Op. cit.* p. 59.

[12]Liu Mau Tsai, *op. cit.* pp. 1-5.

[13]*Op. cit.* p. 1.

History of the First Turk Empire (546-658 AD). In northern China a new war had started. The leader of the Eastern Wei kingdom entered into an alliance with the king of the Juan-juans, A-na-huai and T'u-yu-hun, and together they attacked the Western Wei kingdom. The king of the Western Wei Wen-ti sent an envoy named An-no-p'an-t'o to the T'u-kue (Turk) king Bymyn (T'umen) in 545 AD[14]. "They — the Turks — were very happy and thus spoke to each other: 'our state will become great, because today an envoy from a great state has come to us'". Tu'men sent his envoys with presents to the king of Western Wei, but at the same time he also fulfilled his duty as a vassal of the Juan-juans. When the Toles (T'ieh-le) revolted against the Juan-juans, the Turks helped their overlord (the Juan-juans) and unexpectedly attacked the Toles. The Toles expressed their obedience to the Turks. They became Turkish vassals.

After getting into a strong position the Turks sent an envoy to ask for the hand of a Juan-juan princess. The Juan-juan king refused and sent an envoy to scold Bumyn: "You are my melter (the Turks melted iron for the Juan-juans). How do you dare to come with such a request?"[15] Bumyn executed the Juan-juan envoy, and in 551 he asked for the hand of a Chinese princess, Tschang-lo (Ever-happiness). In the winter of 552 Bumyn unexpectedly attacked the Juan-juans. A-na-huai died and his son An-lo-tschen escaped to Ch'angan, the capital of Western Wei. The Turkish arrived at the same place with a powerful army and demanded that the Chinese deliver the fugitives to them. The Turks killed the Juan-juan ruler and his followers on the spot[16].

After the victory over the Juan-juans, Bumyn took for himself the title *Ili-Khagan* and his wife got the title *K'o-ho-tun*. According to Chinese sources these titles were equal to the old Hiung-nu *Schan-yu* and *Yen-tschi* titles. Bumyn died very shortly after his successes in 552[17]. In Bumyn's life-time his brother Istemi took over the western parts of the state. Such a partition had a historical precedent when the Juan-juans allowed their vassals the Hepthalites to take over the western territories. The same partition had been made by the Hunnic Empire: the dividing line had been the hills of Altai along the Edzin gol[18]. In all these cases the Eastern States were theoretically the senior ones.

The real partition which canonized the two states as two rival powers took place in about 581. This was basically the aim of Chinese policy concerning the Turks, to split the Turks and play one state against the other. Their policy succeeded because of the fact that Istemi the Khan of the Turks of the west was succeeded by the long lived Tardu, while Bumyn was succeeded by his three sons in thirty years. Bumyn's successors were K'o-lo (who died in 553), Mu-han (who reigned 553-572) and T'o-po (who reigned 572-581). As regards the succession to the throne among the Turks, the rule of succession was by brothers in order of age. Thus the sons of the three former Khans had

---

[14]*Op. cit.* pp. 6-7.

[15]*Op. cit.* p. 7.

[16]L.N. Gumilyov, *op. cit.* p. 28.

[17]Liu Mau Tsai, *op. cit.* p. 7.

[18]V. Samolin, *op. cit.* p. 55.

an equal right. First She-t'u, son of K'o-lo became Khagan. Ta-lo-pien, who had the title of A-po and was one of the sons of Mu-han claimed the succession but he had to seek refuge among the Turks of the west. All this helped the Chinese to deepen the rivalry and enmity between the two states. They did not hesitate to interfere in Turkish politics. They sent envoys to Tardu, the Khagan of the Turks of the west and the envoys pointed out that their subordination to the Turks of the east did not correspond to the political realities. They also presented Tardu with the emblem of a wolf's head which was the symbol of supreme authority among the Turks. Tardu revolted against the Eastern Turks, which led to the partition in 581[19].

The Western Turks started attacking the western territories. They attacked and by 559 defeated the T'u-yu[20]. They went as far as Herat in Iran and after long and protracted battles left the place[21]. Although the Turks were finally defeated, but Iran paid for it heavily. Tokharistan revolted and entered into an alliance with the Turks[22]. It was an important event, not only historically and politically, but also culturally. It led to an important contact with Sogdiana and India[23]. This conquest bestowed upon the Turks a huge territory, bigger than the Juan-juans (their previous overlords) ever had.

Shortly afterwards, a scion of the Turkish royal house A-shi-na She-orh[24] started systematic Chinese conquests of Central Asia. He led the Chinese army against the oasis states. These states were originally under Western Turk overlordship, who tried to strengthen their alliances in every possible way. They tried to involve the oasis states into their politics by appointing Sogdian advisers for consultations on state affairs, entering into matrimonial alliances, for instance, the Sogdian king married the daughter of a Turkish Khagan. The contacts with the Central Asian states of Kucha, Turfan and Khotan had economic importance because of their position as trading centres on the Silk Road. These contacts had cultural advantages as well, as the places were transmitting points of religion and art. The Western Turks were engaged in inter-tribal quarrels on the question of inheritance after the death of their Khagan, Kara Churin Bogu, and his son Nili Khagan. Thus they could have only less and less interference in the Chinese operations in East Turkestan. Turfan proposed peace to China in 608, and other states followed: Fergana, Samarkand in 609, Koucha in 610, and sent their envoys to the Chinese[25]. After resistance in varying degrees, Chinese colonization led more or less to the establishment of Chinese rule in East Turkestan[26]. Chinese overlordship was in a sense autonomy for the oasis states and the rule of the kings under the supervision of Chinese officials. At larger cities like Kucha, Kashgar and Khotan, Chinese garrisons were kept and maintained.

---

[19]On the politics of splitting of the Chinese see Liu Mau Tsai, *op. cit.* pp. 396-398.

[20]*Op. cit.* pp. 21-22.

[21]L.N. Gumilyov, *op. cit.* p. 128.

[22]*Op. cit.* p. 128.

[23]*Op. cit.* p. 133.

[24]His biography is in Liu Mau Tsai's above cited book pp. 263-265.

[25]L.N. Gumilyov, *op. cit.* pp. 155-156.

The Western Turks, who had their centers on the Ili and west of Ysyk-köl, tried to intervene in Chinese operations in East Turkestan. First of all they made efforts to come to an understanding with the Tibetans. In the beginning of the thirties of the seventh century, the Tibetans sent envoys to the Chinese Court. But after the victory of the Tibetans over the T'u-yü-hun, whom the Chinese supported and wanted to restore to power, hostilities developed between them. Thereafter the Tibetans started attacking Chinese garrisons in East Turkestan and were able to take over Kucha and Kashgar and thereby the Chinese trade routes as well. During this period, the Turks were in alliance with the Tibetans. At this time the Western Turks were under the domination of the Töles and the Türges tribes[27].

Chinese sources provide ample information about the Turks, though the information is confined to Chinese Turkish contacts only. During periods of alliances, Chinese and Turkish inter-marriages were common. Already King Kao-tsu (206-195 BC) said that he hopes that marrying a Chinese princess to the Schan-yu of the Hiung-nu will make the Hiung-nu friends of China, if not by the time of the marriage, then by the time the son of the Chinese princess sits on the throne. First Bumyn married Princess Tshang-lo and later the two rival Chinese kings asked for the hand of the daughter of Muhan Khagan. King Kao-tsu of the North-Tschou won, and married Queen A-shi-na. Afterwards about seven inter-marriages took place which are mentioned in Chinese sources. Not only the Khagans but also their sons married Chinese princesses. A-shi-na She-Orh married a Chinese princess called Heng-yang and afterwards started serving the Chinese Empire. He played a great role in the Chinese take-over of the oasis states by leading military operations[28].

Generous Chinese gifts and presents on the occasion of marriages and visits of the Chinese envoys gave an impetus to the Turks to go in for more marriages with Chinese princesses. These gifts were generally in the form of silk-rolls and rolls of brocade, several pieces of art, cotton-wool and in one case female singers[29]. The Turks in their turn presented to the Chinese mainly horses, but sometimes sheep, camels and precious stones. However, despite the matrimonial relations during those 130 years the Turks attacked the Chinese for booty about 90 times.

The Chinese were also trading with the Turks. It was Bumyn who first came to the Chinese border to buy some silk and sarsanet. In the case of Turks the trade did not mean trade in terms of money alone, but exchange of horses for Chinese goods. According to an account dated 607, one Turkish horse was worth four and a half rolls of Chinese silk[30].

The Chinese sources also provide some information about the religious life of the Turks[31]. They worshipped the sky as a deity by offering sheep and horses. Their belief was that they originated

---

[26]V. Samolin, *op. cit.* p. 59.
[27]*Op. cit.* p. 59.
[28]Liu Mau Tsai, *op. cit.* pp. 263-265.
[29]*Op. cit.* pp. 453-455.
[30]*Op. cit.* p. 455.
[31]*Op. cit.* p. 459.

from a she-wolf. From anthropological materials collected among Turks by S. Rudenko and A. Gluxov and the archeological finds excavated from the Altai region it is clear that the figure of a wolf had some magical meaning among the Turks[32].

Buddhism became known among the Turks when T'o-po Khagan (572-581) came under the influence of Monk Hui-lin of North Ts'ou. He started building monasteries and sent envoys to the North Ts'ou to get the sūtras translated into the Turkish language. The North Ts'ou king made Liu Schi-ts'ing translate the Nirvāna-sūtra into the language of the Turks and presented it to the Khagan[33].

Monk Jinagupta of Gandhara on his way back home from North Tschou stayed for some time with To'-po. Here he translated the North ts'i sūtras together with eleven lamas[34].

5b. The Second Turk (Kök Türk) Empire (678-747)

Towards the end of the 7th century the Western Turks in the north of the T'ien-shan stopped calling themselves Turks and started taking the name *Ten Tribes* (*On ok* in Turkish). The name could also be translated as *Ten Arrows*. After the victory of the Chinese over their Khagan in 657, these tribal confederacies under the leadership of the Toles and Tūrges became permanent reliable allies of the Chinese in the north-west[35].

In the last decade of the 7th century Wu-tsien, the usurper Empress Wu, directed the affairs of the Chinese state, first in the name of her husband Kao-tsung, and later after her husband's death acted in the name of her son. Thus she was practically the absolute mistress of the Chinese Empire for 55 years. In internal state affairs she overcame all obstacles in the destruction of the mandarins, consolidation of the administrative machinery of the state and so on. She was deeply interested in Buddhism. She ordered the famous rock Buddha image of Lung-men, alongwith Bodhisattvas, monks and guardian kings. On I-tsing's arrival at Loyang in 695 after his long journey and sojourn in India and outer India of as many as twenty-four years in the sanctuaries, Wu-Tsien went to meet him along with her large retinue[36]. I-tsing, who had brought back a large number of Sanskrit texts with him, was provided every facility by her for the purpose of the translation of these texts into Chinese. The great monk scholar on his part dedicated most of his life to this task.

She was not very successful in her relations with the Turks of the new Turkish state established on the Orkhon. The founder of the new Turkish state was Elteris Khagan about whom we get information from the Orkhon inscriptions[37] (circa 682). The new Turkish Empire never attained the

---

[32]*Op. cit.* p. 460.
[33]L. N. Gumilyov, *op. cit.* p. 23.
Liu Mau Tsai, *op. cit.* p. 461.
[34]Liu Mau Tsai, *op. cit.* pp. 461-462.
[35]L.N. Gumilyov, *op. cit.* pp. 259-260.
[36]R. Grousset, *Rise and Splendour of the Chinese Empire,* London 1952, p. 150.
[37]PDTP pp. 54-70.

power of the earlier empire founded by Istemi and Bumyn, but was successful in challenging the majesty of the Chinese Empire. The Orkhon inscriptions give a detailed history of their contacts with the Chinese. It may be cited: "...... to the Tabgac people the noble sons became slaves, the pure girls became servants. The Turk nobles gave up their Turkish names and took Tabgac names and submitted to the Tabgac Khagan for fifty years they gave their work and strength.... The Turk common folk spoke thus: "We were a people with a Khagan, where is our Khagan? So they spoke. And thus became enemies of the Tabgac Khagan. Becoming his enemies, they again became hopeful"[38]. Throughout this period the Chinese were able to use the Toles who were normally vassals of the Orkhon Turks to counterpoise the latter.

In the last decade of the 7th century the Arabs united under the banner of Islam, swept all of Western Asia, and in the 8th century started conquering Bactria and Sogdiana. The Chinese, on the other hand, were more concerned about the Tibetan conquest. The Tibetan were very clever, increasing their influence in this region by way of marriages. As Chinese records suggest in the 8th century "....over twenty countries of the west and north submitted to Tibet"[39].

The main sources of information about the Kok Turks, the Second Turkish Empire are the inscriptions on the tombs of Kul Tegin and Tonyuquq. The monument of Kul Tegin includes a bigger and a smaller inscription. It lies on the bank of the Orkhon river in Inner Mongolia. The other monument of Tonyuquq on the bank of the Selenga river provides information about the Second Turkish Empire. The long inscription of Kul Tegin gives the exact date of the engraving, 732, the year of monkey, seventh month, twentyseventh day[40]. The inscription gives an account of the life of Bilge Khagan, of the fights and events of the life of Turks. The latter part describes the war against the Tanguts in 700, the battle in 715, the victory over the Karluk in 717, the subjugation of the Uigur by the end of 718, the defeat of the Imperial Army in 720, and the following campaigns in 721-722 and 733.

The inscription of Tonyuquq describes the same events as the bigger inscription on the tomb of Kul Tegin. It was engraved earlier in 717-718.

The inscription of Kul Tegin starts with a historical excursus: "When the blue sky was created (above) and the brown earth down, human sons were created in between. Bumyn Khagan and Istemi Khagan started reigning over the human sons". It means that according to the inscription, beginning of the world dates back to the beginning of the 6th century AD. It further describes briefly the history of the First Empire, and the Turkish way of inheritance to the throne: "After the Khagans their younger brothers, then their sons became Khagans". It tells about the enticements used by the Chinese. However, the author blamed only his countrymen for having been tempted so easily and in this way ruining their people. With this it closes the account of the history of the First Empire.

---

[38]PDTP pp. 21-22, 29, 37.

[39]As quoted in V. Samolin, *op. cit.* p. 66.

[40]PDTP p. 27, 33, 43.

The history of the Second Empire and the events related thereto give a fair amount of information about the geographical knowledge possessed by the Turks of the Second Empire. To the south, they knew of two big states: China which they called Tabgac, and the other was Tibet which they called Tuput[41]. They knew some tribes in the east: Kidani[42], Tatabi[43] and the Otuztatars[44]. They knew tribes who were living around the Baykal Lake, the Bajirki[45], the Kurikani[46], the Kirghiz[47] in the western parts of the Sayan Mts. and the Karluks[48] on the Irtish river. It seems they knew most of the western countries. They knew the Sogdians and called them Sogdhak[49], they called the river Syr Darya as Yenchu[50], the Passage Buzgala-Temir-Kapyg as Temir Kapyg[51]. They call the big cities by their name, for example Bukhara[52]. They mention Kurdan[53], the deserts of northern Turkmenia, the Tokhars[54], the Arabs[55], and Purum[56] which actually means Rome, as well as the Byzantine Empire.

Their evolution may be seen by the fact that whereas the Turks of the First Empire did not have any concept of their own chronology, the Turks of the inscriptions had already adopted a calendar in terms of animal cycles.

It seems that after T'a-po's reign Buddhism did not disappear completely. Bilge Khagan, known as Pi-kia in the Chinese sources, built Buddhist and Taoist temples. According to Liu Mau Tsai, Buddhism was probably well known and popular among the Turkish ruling classes[57].

The inscriptions give information about the important military offices in the Turkish Empire on the Orkhon. They had the offices of Yabgu and Shad[58], and the office of the Deputy Khagan who was called A-po[59]. They were chosen from among the brothers and sons of the Khagan. There were *biriya* and *yiraya* "right" and "left" shads who accordingly commanded the right and left sides of the army. Chinese sources also give information about this system[60]. For example Mo-tsho Khagan,

---

[41]PDTP p. 27, 29, 34.
[42]PDTP p. 56, 61, 65.
[43]PDTP p. 24, 31, 40.
[44]PDTP p. 21, 29, 36.
[45]PDTP p. 24, 31, 41.
[46]PDTP p. 21, 29, 36.
[47]PDTP p. 25, 32, 41.
[48]PDTP p. 25, 32, 41.
[49]PDTP p. 60, 64, 69.
[50]PDTP p. 19, 27, 34.
[51]PDTP p. 19, 27, 34.
[52]PDTP p. 27, 33, 43.
[53]PDTP p. 57, 62, 66.
[54]PDTP p. 60, 64, 69.
[55]PDTP p. 27, 29, 36.
[56]PDTP p. 27, 29, 36.
[57]Liu Mau Tsai, *op. cit.* pp. 461-462.
[58]PDTP p. 22, 30, 38.
[59]PDTP p. 19, 27, 33.
[60]Liu Mau Tsai, *op. cit.* p.180.

who reigned in 690-691, made his son, who held the office of A-po, command approximately 40,000 persons, while the other shads had 20,000 persons each under their command[61].

The genealogical tree of the First and Second Turkish Empire in accordance with the Chinese sources and the Orkhon Inscriptions[62]:

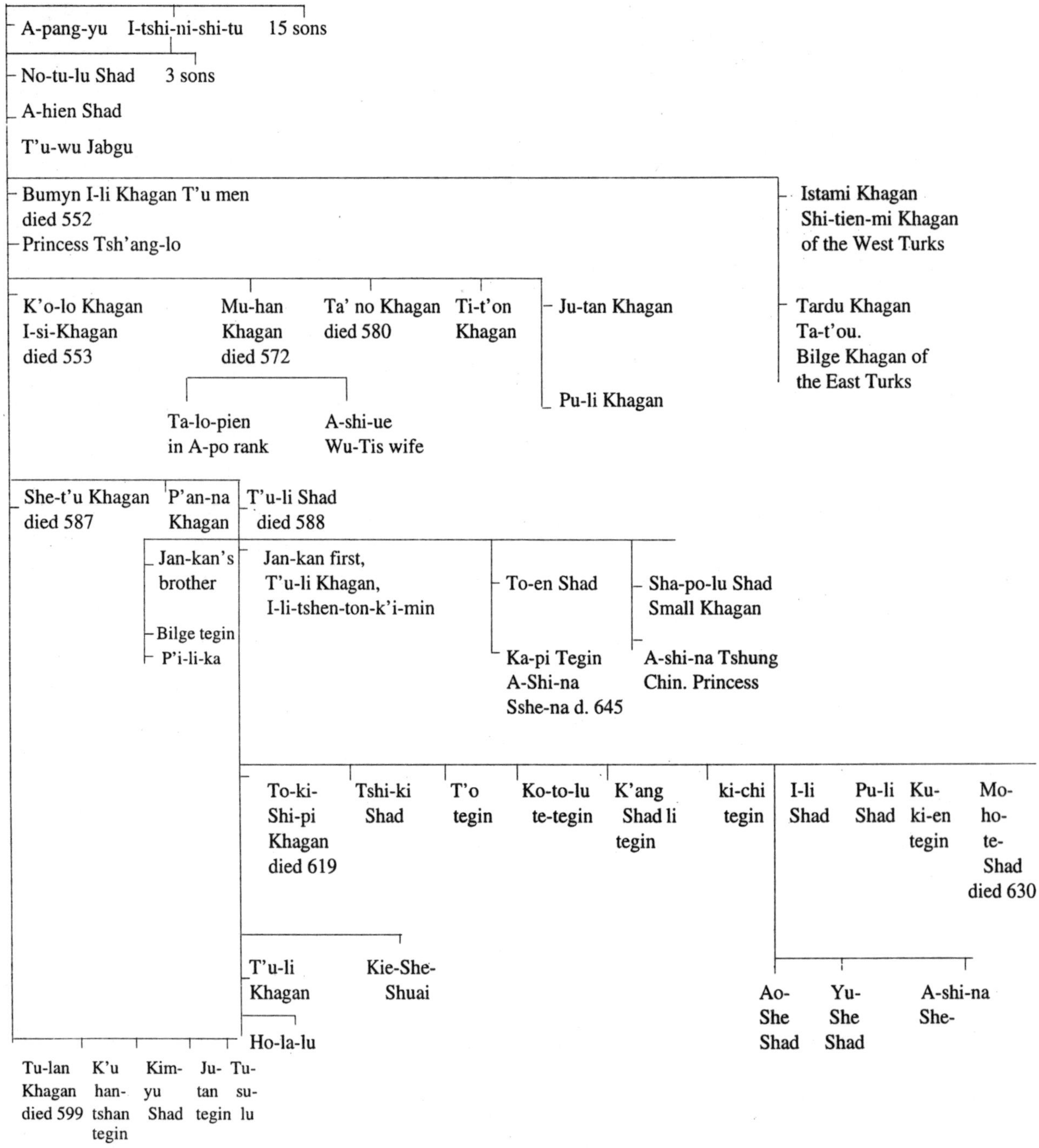

[61]Liu Mau Tsai, *op. cit.* p.218.

[62]Liu Mau Tsai, *op. cit.* index.

5c. The Uigur State (747-14th century)

In 712 the Chinese Emperor Jui-tsung, who was a famous supporter of Taoism, handed over the power to his son Li-Lung-chi[63]. He is remembered now as Hsuan-tsung. He was only twenty-eight years when he succeeded to the throne. His reign was from many points of view, the grand siècle (great age) of Chinese history. He himself was a poet, musician and a patron of arts. Literature and art were flourishing in his time and many of the terracota figures excavated by A. Stein and others in Tun-huang give evidence of the pastimes of Hsuan-tsung's court[64].

During his reign in the forties of the 8th century the Second Turkish Empire was overthrown by some related tribes. This historical event has been described by the Chinese[65] and Arabic[66] sources. According to these sources, the Qarluq tribes who lived at that time under the rule of the Khagan of the Western Turks, rebelled together with the Uigur and Basmil against the Eastern Turks (Kök Türk) and made the Basmil ruler their Khagan. In 744, the Uigur tribes deposed the Basmil ruler and established their rule over the Qarluq tribes as well[67]. Some of the rebelling tribes later left the Uigur territory in 749 and fled to the Qarluq. The Qarluq shifted their alliance to the Western Turks in 745. From this time onwards hostilities between the Uigur and the Qarluq continued till the end of the Uigur Empire[68].

The origin of the name Uigur is not clear. According to Mahmud al-Kasgari's work *Dīvān-i Lugāt-i Turk*[69], a sort of encyclopaedia about Turkish people and their history: "When D'ul qarnayu approached the country of Uigur, the Xaγan of Uigurs sent 45,000 men to him, the wings of their hats were like the wings of gerfalcons, and they shot arrows backward as they shot them forward. D'ul qarnayu was astonished at them and said (in modern Persian) *Inan xwud xwurand*, that is, 'these men provide their own food because game cannot escape them, and they eat as much as they like'. So the country was called Xudxur[70]".

Following this quotation Kasgari describes the phonetic changes through which the word `*xudxur* becomes Uigur. Later on other Turkish authors advanced another theory on the origin of the word Uigur. Yusuf Hass Hajib sums up this theory in his work *Kudatgu Bilig* as follows[71]: "When that country had submitted to Oguz and the sovereignty over it was firmly in his hands, he erected a golden tent and held a great feast, he honoured his kinsmen and subordinates chiefs,

---

[63]R. Grousset, *op. cit* p. 151.

[64]Sir Aurel Stein, *The Thousand Buddhas: Ancient Buddhist Paintings from the Cave Temples of Tun-huang on the Western Frontier of China*, Recovered by Sir Aurel Stein, with an Introductory Essay by L. Binyon, London 1921.

[65]Liu Mao Tsai, *op. cit.* p. 230.

[66]K. Czegledy, *Gardizi on the Uigurs, AOH* 1973, p. 264.

[67]K. Czegledy, *op. cit.* p. 264.

[68]*Op. cit.* pp. 264-265.

[69]As quoted by G. Clauson, *The name Uygur, JRAS* 1963, p. 145.

[70]As quoted by G. Clauson, *op. cit.* p. 146.

[71]As quoted by G. Clauson, *op. cit.* p. 147.

and entertained his troops; those of his uncles and tribesmen who had allied themselves to him he called Uygur, which means in Turkish 'to join and help'".

The same story is repeated in the same book somewhat differently and in the works of other Turkish authors like Rasīduddīn G. Clauson refuted this theory by putting forth the following two reasons. First, the verb *uy* at that stage of development of Turkish language when the name Uigur originated must have sounded *ud* and the deverbal suffix *-gur* is originally a Mongolian suffix which found its way into Turkish much later and is not a part of the original Turkish system of suffixes[72].

The Chinese called the Uigurs Hui-ho[73], the Islamic conquerors of Central Asia called them Toquz-oquz[74], the Tibetans called them Yu-ge-ra[75].

About the group which fled to the Qarluq in the fifties of the 8th century, three famous nomadic chieftains played important roles in the northern part of China: Abuz Yabgu, Ko-shu Han and An Lu-shan. They served the Chinese court at one stage or the other and never really trusted each other[76].

The new Uigur state supported the Chinese not only in principle, but also provided them direct assistance twice at short intervals: once to help recapture Ch'ang-an and Loyang in 757, and afterwards again in 762 on the final expulsion of the rebels. The Uigurs entered Loyang in November 762 and did not leave it until March of the following year. During the occupation of Loyang, the Uigurs met Manichean monks who converted the Uigur Khagan into Manicheism[77].

The Manicheist priests in China were of Sogdian origin. The Uigurs became devoted Manicheists and adopted the Sogdian script for their language. The Sogdian influence was not limited to the adoption of the alphabet by the Uigurs but many technical expressions connected with religion got into the Uigur language. A great number of Sanskrit words were transmitted to the Uigur language through Sogdian.

Manicheism was founded in Persia in the third century. As regards its origin it derived partly from Zoroastrianism and partly from Christianity. By the time the Uigurs came to the territory of the later Uigur State, they had begun to profess Manicheism. According to Gardizi, about three to four hundred persons used to assemble every day at and around the Khan's palace and loudly recited the hymns of Mani. This relates to the second part of the 9th or the first half of the 10th century. The Uigurs professed Manicheism for about a hundred years. It had a considerable impact on all fields of culture.

At that time the Uigurs had already infiltrated the area of Kansu and the Lop region. Probably a group of them had occupied the area before the establishment of the Uigur State on the Orkhon.

---

[72]*Op. cit.* pp. 148-149.
[73]Liu Mau Tsai, *op. cit.* p. 350.
[74]V. Minorsky, Tamim ibn Bahir's Journey to the Uyghurs, *BSOAS* 1949 pp. 225-305.
[75]Sarat Chandra Das, *A Tibetan-English Dictionary*, Delhi 1973 p. 1138.
[76]Liu Mau Tsai, *op. cit.* pp. 267-268.
[77]R. Grousset, *op. cit.* pp. 174-176.

The fact that Aurel Stein found a Turkish Runic document in this area at Miran proves an early Uigur penetration in Kansu[78].

The Qarluq and other Turkish tribes were not satisfied even then with the Uigur rule. They turned to the Tibetans for support and this led to the Tibetan conquest of Kucha, Turfan and the Oasis States. Finally Tibetans took over Khotan also. The Qarluq who were hostile to the Uigurs by that time became masters of Kashgar and other small states along the southern part of the T'ien shan, perhaps upto Aqsu[79].

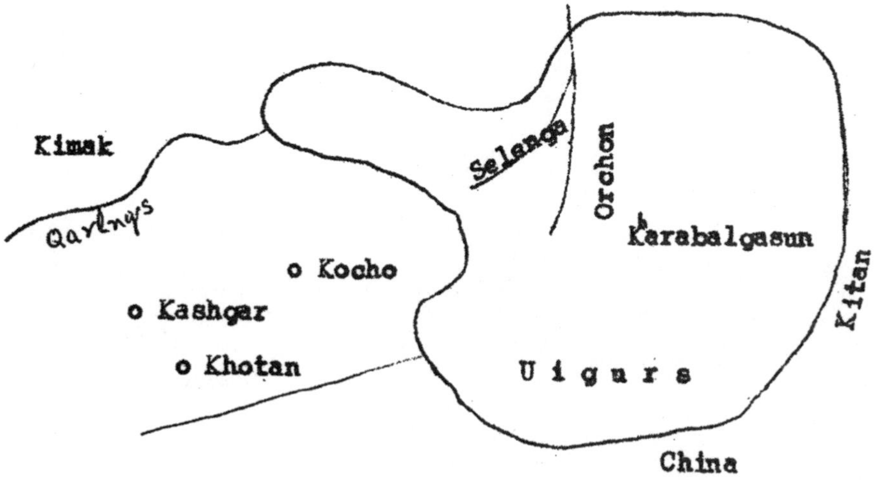

Map of the First Uigur State on the Orkhon[80]

Kharabalgasun was the capital of the First Uigur State. It was famous for its Manichean temples. The original name for Kharabalgasun established in 821 for a Chinese Queen, was Khatun-ch'eng "Queen's City". Archeological excavations around Kharabalgasun uncovered parts of the irrigation system. Probably its population was raising millet and wheat. This certainly gives positive evidence that the Uigurs led a settled life. This tendency was encouraged by the influence of Manicheism and Buddhism. These religions required houses of worship.

In 758 the Qyrqyz were vassals of the Uigurs. In 840 during the winter when the animals died of famine and epidemics started among the Uigurs, the Qyrqyz army attacked the Uigurs and robbed their capital city.

When the Uigur state on the Orkhon was destroyed by the Qyrqyz in 840 the Uigurs started moving south and west, and not towards other grazing grounds, but more to settled areas. They split into two main groups: one moving into the Kansu area, the other into the Turfan-Bisbalyq area. The Uigur heir Mang-li, after the Qyrqyz conquest, first established himself in the Kucha area. In 848 they rose in rebellion at Tun-huang and within two years after that the Tibetans were expelled from Hami and Turfan. The Uigur move into Turfan, Bisbalyq and the Kansu region took

[78]A. Stein, *Serindia*, vol. I p. 471.
[79]V. Samolin, *op. cit.* pp. 68-71.
[80]Copied from L.N. Gumilyov, *op. cit.* p. 370.

place later in the period 866-872. The new Uigur state was based primarily on oasis settlements. The borders of the Uigur state stretched beyond Kucha in the west, Hami in the east, Urumchi in the north and Khotan in the south. The area is partly covered with oasis settlements but it has plains covered with sand in other parts. In 982 in the south-east of the Uigur state came to life the Tangut state of Hsi-hsia. The western part of Kashgaria including Khotan became a part of the Kharakhanid state founded in the 10th century[81].

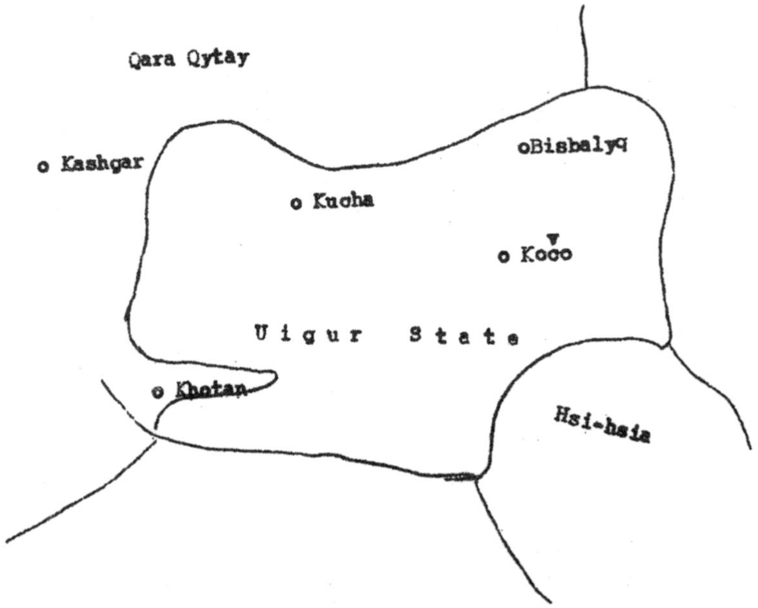

Map of the Uigur State from the 10th upto the 14th century[82]

For the exact location of the Uigur state it is necessary to describe the surrounding people. According to O. Pritsạk[83], the Qarakhanids were the rulers of the Qarluq and assumed their rank of Khagan from the former reigning dynasty. The western expansion of the Qarluq power brought the Qarakhanid into contact with the Islamic world. Pritsak supposes that after 893 Kashgar became the capital of the western Qarakhanids. About the beginning of the 10th century a Samanid prince who was the brother of Ismail Samanid ruler fled to Ogulcaq. He was installed as Governor of a place called Artuc, south of Kashgar. The prince, by name Nasr, showered Ogulcaq with gifts brought from the Islamic countries in order to show his gratitude towards him. After some time Ogulcaq permitted the construction of a mosque in Artuc. Ogulcaq observed the Muslim merchants at prayer. The sight of the praying merchants impressed him so much that finally he visited Nasr to collect more information about Islam. He studied the Quran and became a Muslim. As regards the information about the Qarakhanid-Uigur relationship, the available sources are silent.

[81]L.N. Gumilyov, *op. cit.* pp. 425-433.

[82]Copied from Gumilyov, *op. cit.* p. 378.

[83]O. Pritsak, *Von den Karluk zu den Karachaniden, ZDMG* 1951 pp. 270-300 (in German: From the Karluks upto the Karakhanids).

In 1028 the Uigurs of Kansu became vassals of the Tangut state. The Tangut state, which was called Hsi-hsia by the Chinese, was becoming a great power. It might be that the oasis states along the southern rim of the Tarim basin belonged for some time to the Tangut state. At the end of the 11th century there were three political groups in East Turkestan. The Qarakhanids in the west with their eastern boundary some distance east of Khotan; the Uigur state including the oasis states from Kucha eastward including the eastern portion of the T'ien Shan; and the Hsi-hsia state, which was in possession of the southern settlements east of Khotan[84].

The Qarakhanids had shortly earlier been converted to Islam. They were not orthodox, but whenever the situation so demanded they laid a heavy hand on their opponents. They rose probably in opposition to Buddhism, especially because of the fact that their natural enemies the Uigurs assumed the role of defenders of Buddhism in East Turkestan.

As regards the economy of the Uigur state, two trends were predominant, one was cattle-raising and the other agriculture. Due to the hot climate and scarcity of rainfall, agriculture in the area could be carried out only through an irrigation system. The chronicles give some information about the economy of this area during the times of the Former Han dynasty (206 BC-25 AD). This area was the westernmost part of the Empire, which sometimes belonged to China, sometimes to other powers like the Kushans, the Hsiung-nu, the Hephtalites and the Tibetans. A Chinese chronicle says: "Nearly in all the states of the Western part people live in settlements, have cities, husbandry, cattle-breeding"[85]. One more information about the agriculture from the Kharosthi documents: "Grain is little, they bring grain from Kashgar and Yarkand"[86]. According to the same documents millet and wheat were the basic products of agriculture. In the Turfan basin these two products were cropped twice in a year. In Kharasahr, the inhabitants raised rice, millet, vegetables and grains. Concerning household animals, they reared camels and horses. They also reared silk-worms, not for manufacturing silk but for cotton and thread. In Kashgar there was plenty of rice, millet, vegetables and sesame, and other grain crops. In Urumchi the land was favourable for cultivation as well as for animal husbandry. The earliest sources show that irrigation-based agriculture played a very vital role here. Domestic animals were raised not only for personal use but also for sale. The development in agriculture was retarded due to wars in the area, for instance the channels of irrigation in Kocho and Yar were destroyed in the 14th century after the conquest of the area by the Chagatay reigning house of Uzbekistan. However, when the Turks conquered the agricultural oasis in the area from Hami to Kucha most of them adapted themselves to the new mode of economy under the pressure of new circumstances. The Uigur tribes living in the north and west of Urumchi could continue with their nomadic cattle-breeding. The author of the work *Hudud al-alam* in the

---

[84]See the earlier map on p. 35.

[85]D. I. Tichonov, *Chosyaystvo i obsestvenniy story uygurskogo gosudarstva*, X-XIV vv. (in Russian: Economy and social system of the Uigur State in the 10-14th centuries), Moscow-Leningrad 1966, p. 60.

[86]As quoted by D.I. Tichonov, *op. cit.* p. 61.

10th century[87] and Gardizi[88] in the 11th century have provided reports about the economy of the Uigurs. Their reports say that those Uigurs who lived in cities and villages occupied themselves with agriculture, and those who lived in the north of T'ien-shan, where wonderful grazing lands were available, could "stick" to their nomadic cattle-breeding. For the history of Uigur settlements in Turfan, the report of the Chinese envoy who came to Turfan records in 981[89]: "This country has five kinds of grains but there is no buckwheat". The Chinese envoy suggests through this information how rich the people of that land were, that they did not even need this inferior kind of wheat. Gardizi gave an account of the vegetables grown in the Turfan area: "In this area there is plenty of fruits, plenty of wheat, it is abundant with barley, pumpkin, sesame, lemon, fig, and silk. They use silk in their garments; they have very many mulberry trees, sometimes as many as that one person owns 2,000 tress. They have in the same amount grapes and pears of different kinds"[90]. It seems that agricultural production did not change much after the Uigur conquest. The same areas remained agricultural centres — Hami, Liang-chou, Turfan, Kharasahr and Kucha. It seems from the documents published by Radloff[91] and Malov[92] that in the agriculture of the Uigur state vine-growing played the most important role. The state took tax from the vine-growers in kind. The state could give exemption from this tax to monasteries. According to Gardizi[93], the Uigur king had around 1,500 servants at his court, and "the servants drink wine three times a day; they produce wine from grapes". In accordance with the change of climate and soil they grew different sorts of grapes. The main tools were the plough and the hack. They used plough on the fields and hack in the gardens. They yoked camels to the ploughs for tilling fields. In the Uigur state use of manure was very well known and they are known to have used cow-dung for the purpose and residue in the channels was also used. For grinding grains they had hand and water mills. The water mills showed a high level of technical development which is similar to the more modern form of flour production.

The Uigur state followed the Turkish tradition of rearing horses. Horse-rearing was important for trade with China, and also for their own military purposes. They used horses for communication and transportation e.g. for the movement of envoys, for collection of taxes and duties and for the exchange of state officials. Monasteries and some individuals owned a large number of horses and live-stock. However, the poor peasants had to rent cattle for domestic work. On the other hand, the richer middle class peasants kept their cattle in their stalls and in the monasteries, and prepared feeding stuff for the cattle[94].

---

[87]D. I. Tichonov, *op. cit.* p. 62.

[88]D. I. Tichonov, *op. cit.* p. 64.

[89]*Op. cit.* p. 69

[90]*Op. cit.* p. 70

[91]W. Radloff, *Uigurische Sprachdenkmaler* (in German: Uigur documents), Leningrad 1928, Doc. 26, 69, 91, 121, 126.

[92]PDTP, pp. 200-207.

[93]D.I. Tichonov, *op. cit.* p.70.

[94]*Op. cit.* pp. 60-85.

Industry, in this case it is more handicraft, was connected with the towns of the state. The Uigur state had very many flourishing towns like Miran, Niya, Dandan Oylik which were destroyed partly by natural calamities and partly by historical events from the 14th century onwards. On the other hand, towns like Kocho, Yar, Kharasahr, Kashgar, Yarkand and Khotan developed on the ruins of the Uigur state. The archeological excavations conducted by A. Stein[95], the Prussian[96] and other expeditions uncovered iron and finished metal objects belonging to the period of the Uigur kingdom. They used iron for manufacturing plough-fans, hacks, bits, stirrups, knives and so on. In the Uigur state, semi-precious stones were available which were processed by their own craftsmen.

Craftsmen were further needed for building, construction, especially for their decoration. Kocho and Yar had many temples and monasteries which had panels relating to events of Buddha's incarnations and earthen figures of Buddhist saints. Burnt bricks were used for building temples. In some rare cases they did use stone as well.

As regards different branches of handicrafts, weaving in the households played the most important role. They produced cotton cloth for their own use and also for sale. However, these materials and some thicker ones were produced not only in their house-holds, but also in small factories. Among these materials the latter ones were used for making clothes, sacks, beddings, etc. Silk materials were also made in the small factories which were given to the state as tax in kind.

Pottery occupied an important place in this respect. The potters produced burnt bricks for building purposes, dishes for house-holds and vessels for rituals. In the period of 10-14th centuries small-scale industry was developing in the towns of the Uigur state[97]. From the 14th century onwards, when the Uigur state was conquered by the Chagatay ruling house of Uzbekistan, this industry of the Uigur state lost its level of development[98] that it had attained.

The Uigur state availed itself of the opportunity of its position on the Silk Road and having the traditional trading centers in its territory. They had trade with China, where they sold jasper, horses, camels, sheep and furs of animals, like sable, fox, squirrel and ermine. Cheap cotton materials had a good market in China[99].

Besides China, the Uigur state had regular trade contact with the Khitans. In the beginning of their history the Khitan was a tribe of the north-eastern frontier of China which later played an important role in Chinese history. They had wars with the Hsi-hsia state, and as a result were allied to the Uigurs. In the interim war periods they also had trade with the Hsi-hsia, but many times the Tanguts stopped the Uigur caravans on their way to the Chinese Court, took away what was to have

[95]A. Stein, *Innermost Asia*, Oxford 1928.

[96]A. von le Coq, *Chotscho Königliche preussische Turfanexpedition* (in German: Kocho: The Prussian Turfan Expedition), Berlin 1913.

[97]D.I. Tichonov, *op. cit.* pp. 79-91.

[98]Emel Esin, *Islamiyetten onceki Tuk Kultur Tarihi ve Islama Giris* (in Turkish: The history of Turkish culture before Islam, and at the time of embracing Islam), Istanbul 1978, p. 277.

[99]C. Mackerras, *Sino-Uigur Diplomatic and Trade Contacts*, *CAJ* 1962 pp. 218-222.

been presented at the Court, imprisoned the envoys and later sold them for horses and bulls. The way of trade in the Khotan oasis of the Uigur state is described in one of the sources: "The trade here is barter trade, and the tax is paid in kind. The main objects of trade are exchange of calico, silk and wheat. The value of other goods was determined by their quantity. People numbering upto 20,000 meet and exchange their goods on Fridays"[100]. From the fact that payment was made in exchange of goods in kind suggests that the class of traders did not gain real importance in that society. They played a more important role as mediators in other spheres of exchange. In the inner market the traders worked through their agents. They gave the goods on credit to their agents, telling the exact price, which the agent had to give to the owner after selling the goods. If he could not sell the goods, he had to return them.

With the emergence of the class of traders, usury also started taking shape. The documents published by V. Radloff give detailed information about usury[101]. In one case silver is given in usury. For 4 satir silver all together a person had to pay 1 bakir per 1 satir silver, which means 4 bakir for one month. In another case for 1 satir silver one had to pay 1.5 bakir a month, and the borrowed silver was all together 6 satir. It seems that the rate of usury in the case of silver was very arbitrary.

Sesame oil which was one of the basic necessities of a houshold was very often taken on loan by the poor peasants. If a person took it on loan for six months, he had to return twice as much as he had taken originally[102]. Other items in this regard were wine and cloth materials[103]. In case of the former the rate of return was 100% more.

The peasants who were divided into various communities had to do labour conscription. The types of labour conscription were, according to the documents, *alban, basik, bert, kabas, kab, kalan, kupcur, kurut, saliq, sakin, tintsuj, tutun* and *yasak*[104]. The main problem with these terms is that it is difficult to distinguish between the labour done for the state and the individual property owners. Of the said taxes *kupcur* is one which is mostly known[105]. It is a kind of tax which was paid by the nomads as well as the settled population of the Uigur state. They were paying it in kind or in money (in silver). The other extremely common kind of tax is the *kalan*[106]. It was given for the State. In some cases it seems to have the same meaning as *kupcur* with the difference that it had to be paid sometimes, say, in kind. In some cases it was paid in cloth material or in horses. *Kalan* was mainly taken from the peasants. Another kind was *yasak*. Unfortunately its meaning is known only from the sources of much later times, i.e. from the times of the Golden Horde. At that time it meant a kind of tax which had to be given by the subjugated peoples. It was one tenth of the crops.

---

[100]D.I. Tichonov, *op.cit.* p. 88.

[101]W. Radloff, *Uigurische Sprachdenkmaler* (in German: Uigur documents), Doc. 47, 52, 18, Leningrad 1928.

[102]*Op. cit.* Doc. 7.

[103]*Op. cit.* Doc. 4.

[104]D.I. Tichonov, *op. cit.* p. 101.

[105]W. Radloff, *Uigurische Sprachdenkmaler*, Doc. 9, 54.

[106]*Op. cit.* Doc. 14.

In the documents such terms like *kupcur-kalan, kalan-yasak, kalan-alban* are also found. In essence all these terms are the taxes which were paid to the state. They suggest their collection method as state taxes.

The *tutun*[107] was yet another kind of tax. It was a kind of household tax which had to be paid in kind, for example, in the form of home-made material they possessed. It is usually mentioned with some other kinds of taxes like *kurut* and *kabin*. It can be further established that most of the said taxes were paid in kind. The tax-payers had to give special taxes to the revenue officers. Most of these taxes survived in the Mongol era[108].

By studying Uigur and other documents it comes to light that there was state ownership of lands in the Uigur state. There were lands belonging to the Idiq qut (the Supreme ruler), to the monasteries, monks, traders and to the peasants.

Before going into the details of different types of land-ownerships in the Uigur state, it is worth mentioning that in the neighbouring Tibetan country the state owned big lands and the same were given for temporary use to the peasants[109]. Likewise the State transferred lands for use also to the feudal lords. There were also lands owned by the monasteries. In the Hsi-hsia state too there were lands belonging to the state, to the emperor and to private owners. Though there is no definite evidence proving the existence of monastic land-ownership, E.I. Kychanov finds it very probable that there were lands of this nature[110].

Uigur documents mention that the state confiscated lands. The right of the state over the confiscated land was manifested in the person of the *Induq qut*. The Chinese documents found in the territory of Sin-kiang and published by A. Maspero give more information about state owned lands[111]. According to them the state owned waste lands, forests, pastures, gardens, irrigation channels and confiscated lands. The state was entitled to give the right for construction of channels for irrigation.

Most of the peasants owned lands, which they got from the state for hereditary use. This class of small holders had a great importance for the state, because of the fact that they were the tax-payers. From the documents it is evident that the land belonged to the *Induq qut* and on account of this the peasants had to pay tax. The tax was collected by revenue officers. According to some documents the small holders of the village were divided into ten people. These ten persons owned the responsibility for the other's debts in the case of their deaths. The question arises as to what sort of rights did a person have to the land in use? The small holders had the right to sell the piece of land under their possession along with the water which was meant for irrigating that land, their houses and the court-yard around them. The small holders were also entitled to sell their vineyard or lease

[107]*Op. cit.* Doc. 21.

[108]D.I. Tichonov, *op. cit.* pp. 101-110.

[109]V.A. Bogolovskiy, *Ocherk istorii tibetskogo naroda* (in Russian: An essay on the history of the Tibetan people).

[110]E.I. Kychanov, *Gosudarstvo Si Sya (982-1127)* (in Russian: The Hsi Hsia State), Moscow 1962 pp. 11-12.

[111]L. Maspero, *Les documents chinois* (in French: Chinese documents), London 1953, Doc. 332, 335, 337.

out their land either wholly or partly. The lease of land carried different conditions, say, they could share the work and also the expenses connected with the rented piece of land and then share the crops. In some cases the land-holder, while in other cases the lease-holder, paid the tax of the land. The time of lease was very short, just one season[112].

The documents further suggest that the *Induq qut* and his family owned special property called *qoriq*. The word *qoriq* was also used in the Mongolian language and it meant the property which was forbidden for any outsider. It connoted not only the palaces and gardens belonging to them, but also the cattle, the grazing lands and the water which irrigated those grazing lands[113]. Only those belonging to the close circle of the *Iduq qut* knew about these places, and their exact location used to be a secret. Special people looked after *qorig* lands.

Another term which occurs quite often in the documents is *inju* lands. *Inju* lands were owned not only by the *Induq qut* and his close people, but also by the landowners of smaller status. The institution of *inju* was well known in Iran and in the Caucasus region. But in Iran the holders of *inju* lands did not have to pay tax, while in the Uigur state some of the owners of *inju* lands had to pay tax. Initially *inju* lands were offered by the ruler for the services rendered to him. Naturally at the same time, a part of the *inju* lands were not taxable. The holders of *inju* lands had full rights over the lands, so much so that even the non-taxable lands could be sold. The sale of the said land also implied non-payment of tax as earlier[114].

The Buddhist church too became a big landowner in the Uigur state and had active participation in the multi-sided economy of the state. Certain monasteries had their own hayfields and corn-farms. A Chinese document published by A. Stein gives information that the duties of monks also included looking after the agricultural work on the fields belonging to the monastery[115]. Tibetan documents also contain important information about monastic lands[116]. According to them the monasteries in the Khotan-T'ien Shan area rented out lands to the peasants. The rent was used for the maintenance of the monks and the monastery. The peasants working on the monastic lands were not supposed to be free in moving out of the monastic lands.

The *sanghin* lands did not have to pay tax. During Mongol times this trend strengthened further. The Mongolian Khans not only supported the right of the Buddhist church to hold lands without paying tax for them, but also presented lands to the church with the right not to pay tax. Under these circumstances the church and the monks played a very active part in usury. For instance, a monk named Kin-Yung from Hukoi monastery gave away money on loan and did receive monthly interest of 10% for it[117]. For money given on loan a monk had a woman in

[112]D.I. Tichonov, *op. cit.* pp. 120-126.
[113]*Op. cit.* pp. 127-128.
[114]*Op. cit.* pp. 162-168.
[115]A. Stein, *Ancient Khotan*, Oxford 1902, Doc. 16.
[116]F.W. Thomas, *Tibetan Documents Concerning Chinese Turkestan*, vol. V. p. 259.
[117]A. Stein, *Ancient Khotan*, Doc. 5.

mortgage[118], while a third held a stock of grains in mortgage[119]. With the help of usury, slowly all the lands around the monasteries became their property. The monasteries became big landowners and consequently very often fighting emanated due to the possession of lands[120].

In the Uigur state there existed a land-owning class which was free to sell lands along with water. A special trading class emerged which occupied itself with buying and selling of lands[121]. Thus many traders bought lands for themselves and became big landowners. Gardens of walnut trees (sometimes with 2,000 trees), apricot trees and pomegranate trees used to be sold and purchased[122].

The special mention of water for the house or fields proves the fact that water was equally precious in the Uigur state, as all over Central Asia.

The Social System of the Uigur State

The top functionary of the Uigur state was the *Iduq qut*. He had all the civil and military powers in his command. It was not only power that was concentrated in his hands, but also the biggest properties of the country were under him and his family's possession. According to Wan-yan-de: "The emperor, the empress and their heir had cattle and grazing lands in plenty, though nobody could tell their real number"[123]. Gardizi gives information about the *Iduq qut*'s court. He wrote: "There are about one thousand persons who are the bodyguards of the king and who could eat and drink in the king's presence"[124]. The *tarxan*-s also belonged to the close circle of the king. They were usually envoys to the Chinese or Tibetan Court. Later on, during Mongol times, the Mongol Khans appointed *daruga*-s[125] or high officials. During the times of Mongol invasion the names of Mongolian office bearers appear along with those of the Uigur officials. The owners of medium sized landholdings were called *elci*. The lowest stratum of the ruling class was called begi. In the documents data are given about the different strata of peasants. Peasants were known as *qadas, qalanci, inju, qul, tutuq* and *quvaq* based upon their relative dependence upon the ruling class. Although these names occur quite often in the documents, but no information is available about the details of their respective positions.

In the beginning, the word *quvaq*[126] meant a kind of tax which had to be paid in kind i.e. in the form of grains. Later on it became a kind of socage. During the Mongol times, say from the 13th century onwards, the number of people taxed in socage increased and the big landowners had the right to inherit the labourers as well. After the 14th century the word *quvaq* is not mentioned in any

[118]*Op. cit.* Doc. 10.
[119]*Op. cit.* Doc. 11.
[120]D.I. Tichonov, *op. cit.* pp. 142-144.
[121]*Op. cit.* p. 145.
[122]*Op. cit.* p. 146.
[123]As quoted by D.I. Tichonov, p. 148.
[124]As quoted by D.I. Tichonov, *op. cit.* p. 149.
[125]*Op. cit.* p. 150.
[126]W. Radloff, *Uigurische Sprachdenkmaler*, Doc. 43, 55.

document. On the other hand, another word *urliq*[127] occurs in its place very frequently. Another category *qalanci*[128] is mentioned above, which probably connoted a similar position. The peasants who were unable to pay the tax called *qalan*, had to do labour for the state instead of the tax. A section of the state peasants slowly became socemen of big landowners.

Inju was a well known name in Central Asia, viz. in Azerbaijan, Iran etc. When it reached here through the Mongolian conquests it was of much later origin than in the Uigur state[129]. In the latter the lands and the people living on it were named *inju* lands and *inju* people respectively[130]. *Inju* consisted of mainly vine-yards and fruit-gardens and the labourers who worked on them. It seems that cattle breeders were also known as *inju* men. However, no evidence is available so far to substantiate it.

Taking loan was a way to become a socman in the Uigur state. While borrowing silver one had to mortgage his son or brother. The text of such Uigur documents reads[131]: "I (the name follows) took silver (the quantity follows) on loan and for this I make my son (name follows) a *tutuq*[132] to stay with (name follows) for (number follows: usually three) years". The documents on the *tutuq* system belong to the 7th-8th and 10-14th centuries. A similar system existed in Russia during the middle ages which was termed serebrennik. The same system is known to have found its existence in Mongolia. If the loan was not paid back, the person mortgaged became a socman, and consequently the mortgagee was free even to sell him.

The word *qadas*[133] occurred very often in the Turkish texts belonging to the 6th century onwards. In the Orkhon inscriptions it means a close relative or friend, but its meaning changed in the Uigur documents. In the latter it connoted a person who engaged himself in work with another under an agreement. Many times even the relatives took up jobs with each other[134].

In the Uigur state thralldom was a well-known institution. Thralls were called *qul*[135]. They were fed and were well provided with clothing by their proprietors. They had no right to even marry without their permission. They could be sold, but could also be set free on payment of money, which was named *bert*. The word *qul* was also termed *qarabas*, which after the Mongolian conquest was replaced by a Mongolian word *kuq*. In one of the documents, a contract records the information that a person sold his son for sixty pieces of gold[136].

In the monasteries the lowest class of monks were called *sal*. In one of the Sanskrit-English

---

[127]*Op. cit.* Doc. 21.

[128]*Op. cit.* Doc 77.

[129]D.I. Tichonov, pp. 163-164.

[130]W. Radloff, *Uigurische Sprachdenkmaler*, Doc. 21.

[131]D.I. Tichonov, *op. cit.* p. 169.

[132]The verb *tut* means 'to hold, to keep something or somebody', from this word generates the noun tutuq. Cf. DTSl. p. 591.

[133]DTSl. p. 401.

[134]D.I. Tichonov, *op. cit.* pp. 172-177.

[135]PDTP, p. 23, 30, 39.

[136]D.I. Tichonov, *op.cit.* p. 181.

dictionaries, the word finds mention with the meaning "domestic servant"[137]. They had to do most of the manual jobs in the monasteries, in vine-yards and in gardens. Their main dependence was on the monks[138].

The Manicheist monasteries had a strict hierarchy, on the top of which were placed high priests who were served by all the lower priests. Every month two assemblies used to meet in the monastery with the provision of special food stuffs on the occasion. Many men worked in the monasteries as wood-cutters, doctors and so on. The monasteries also utilized the services of contractors for cotton materials and wool, which used to be distributed in accordance with the rank of the monks.[139]

From the facts given in the documents it seems that most of the peasants in the Uigur state in the 9th century were paying tax to the state for using the land. Some of the peasants had to pay their rents to the monasteries or to private owners but their number at that time was not very large. From the 12th-13th centuries onwards the number of peasants under landowners and monasteries increased on account of transfer of *inju* lands to them.

Buddhism became the dominant religion in the Uigur state because of its economic power. The monasteries owned big tracts of land for which they had not to pay any tax. They had their own band of serfs, who were bound to the monastic lands. In the monasteries a special class of low-rank monks, the *sanin*-s used to perform heavy work. The church played a role in the economic life of the State. The monasteries are reported to have resorted to lending money, silver and wheat.

After the period of Mongol invasions, the Uigurs were called to the courts of the new masters of Inner Asia to teach Buddhism and its arts. On account of their being scribes in the Mongol Empire, the Uigurs exercised a considerable amount of cultural influence all over Central Asia, in China and in the Muslim world[140].

5d. The History of East Turkestan and Kansu, after the fall of the Uigur State

Cities like Yar-khoto, Kocho and Bisbaliq belonged to the center of the Uigur State (the area of Turfan). They were occupied by the Mongols in 1209. As it can be seen from the documents of that era, the Mongol occupation did not basically change the economic system, the *Iduq qut* still had his role as the head of the Uigur state. The only change was that Mongol officials were appointed to some posts with a view to function together with Uigur officials. The area of Kucha, Karasahr and some parts of T'ien Shan were annexed by the Mongols in the 13th century. In the 14th century, the Chagatay ruling house conquered these cities and after a period of a hundred years thereafter

[137]Monier-William, *Sanskrit English Dictionary*, Oxford 1899, p. 1042.

[138]D.I. Tichonov, *op. cit.* pp. 181-183.

[139]P. Zieme, *Ein Uigurisches Text uber die Wirtschaft Manichaischer Kloster im Uigurischen Reich* (in German: An Uigur text about the economy management of affairs of Manicheist monasteries in the Uigur Empire), Researches in Altaic Languages, 1975 pp. 331-338.

[140]E. Esin, *The Turkish Baksi and the Painter Muhammad Siyah Kalam, AO.* 1970, pp.81-114.

embraced Islam and became dedicated Muslims. The area of Fergana and Kashgar had already come under Muslim influence in the 11th century. Kashgar became the first center of Muslim literature in Turkish language. Khotan on the other hand was occupied in the 13th century[141].

The most important dates in the history of East Turkestan are:

1. 1347 When Tughlaq Timur founded the new eastern branch of the Chagatay Empire. Their winter capital was Kashgar, Yarkand or Aksu. Their summer residence was in the north of the T'ien-Shan.
2. 1361-1362 Tughlaq Timur conquered Samarkand.
3. In the beginning of the 15th century Buddhism was still predominant in Turfan and Hami. It lasted here till about the end of the century.
4. After 1533 the power of the Chagataids declined. Hodsha Machdumi A'zem ruled in Kashgar. Under his sons, Muhammad Emin and Muhammad Ishaq the split between the sects the 'White Hill' (Aqtaglig) and the 'Black Hill' (Qarataglig) took place. From these times started the political power of the religious leader (the hodsha) against the civil (state) power.
5. In 1677 Hodsha Apak was expelled from Kashgar by Ismail Khan. He went to the Fifth Dalai Lama Ṅag-dbaṅ-blo-bzaṅ-rgya-mtsho for help, who on his part arranged the help of the Khan of the Dsungars, Galdan Khan.
6. In 1678-1679 Hodsha Apak, with the help of Galdan Khan expelled Ismail Khan from Kashgar and established his power of the 'White Hill'. So the real power went to the Dsungars.
7. In 1696-1697 the suppression of the Dsungars by the Chinese[142].

Buddhism still existed in Hami and Turfan in the 15th century. However Buddhism had no real role in the territory of the previous Uigur state. The history of East Turkestan was dominated by the collisions of different Muslim sects and of the gradually growing Chinese influence.

The centers of Uigur culture, after the collapse of the Uigur state, remained the monasteries of Kansu, some monasteries of Shensi and Tibet, where composition and copying of Buddhist works in Tibetan, Chinese and Uigur language went on till the 18th century[143].

This was the period of the Ming dynasty and the Manchus in China. In the beginning of the 14th century national uprisings against the Mongolian Yuan dynasty became more and more frequent. These uprisings culminated in 1368, when Chu Yuan-chang, a former Buddhist novice drove out the Mongols and founded his own dynasty which he called the Ming dynasty.

---

[141] E. Esin, *Islamiyetten önceki Türk Kultur ve Islama giriş* (in Turkish: Turkish culture before Islam, and introduction of Islam), Istanbul 1978, pp. 117-143.

[142] W. Eichhorn, *Kolonialkämpfe der Chinesen in Turkestan während der Ch'ien-lung* (in German: Colonial wars by the Chinese in Tukestan during Ch'ien-lung), ZDMG pp. 262-266.

[143] *EUT* pp. VII-XI.

The Mongols were expelled from the whole country and the Chinese empire was restored. The control over Kansu passed to the Ming emperors and so also that of Tibet[144].

The Chinese knowledge of Tibet had become more detailed during the Ming dynasty. The old practice which was frequent during the reign of the former Yuan dynasty was retained by the Ming emperors. Tibetan lamas were invited frequently to the Chinese Court to renew their appointments and to get new titles. The rulers of the Ming dynasty appreciated the importance of the official support for the religious sects in Tibet. The earlier Yuan dynasty gave its support to the Sa-skya-pa sect (founded in 1073). Under the Ming dynasty it was the Karma-pa sect founded in the 12th century with its center at Mtshur-phug monastery west of Lhasa, which was singled out for special imperial favour and support. However, while Karma-pa monks were by far the most frequent visitors to the Ming Court, monks from the other sects were also invited to pay their tributes. These constant comings and goings were so frequent and involved so many people that they sometimes caused problems to the local administration. In 1569 an imperial decree was issued to reduce the frequency of the tribute missions to once in three years and to limit the number of participants[145]. The Ming Emperors were the first to develop contacts with European Christianity and trade. They has built many grandiose palaces[146].

In Tibet there was a vigorous struggle among the various Lamaist sects. Among the rival sects and groups there emerged Tson-kha-pa (1357-1419) with his reform of the Tibetan Church. He founded a new sect, the Dge-lugs-pa, which stressed strict disciplined pure conduct and deep philosophical education. The Dge-lugs-pa sect was destined to get in the following centuries the position of the Sȧ-skya-pa sect both in the religious and the political spheres[147]. After Tsoṅ-kha-pa's death, the sect was controlled by two authorities, viz. the Dalai Lama and Panchen Lama.

In the early period of its existence the Dge-lugs-pa increased its numerical strength and political influence. Though Yung-lo the Ming Emperor(1403-1424) took interest in the new sect and in the person of its founder and invited him twice to Peking in 1408 and 1413, the sect never could really win the full support and favour of the Imperial Court.

The Dge-lugs-pa sect finally became a political power by the support of the Mongol rulers. When both the Chinese emperors and the Tibetan kings were cool in their attitude towards the Dge-lugs-pa, Bsod-nams-rgya-mtsho (1543-1588), Tsoṅ-kha-pa's fourth successor as the head of the Dge-lugs-pa sect, entered into friendly relations with the Ordos Mongols whose Altan Khan (1543-1583) invited him to visit the Ordos. On his arrival in 1578, Bsod-nams-rgya-mtsho converted the Mongol Khan to the Dge-lugs-pa sect. In return Altan Khan awarded him the title of 'Dalai Lama Vajradhara' (Vajradhara is a Sanskrit word which means the Holder of the

---

[144] J. Kolmas, *Tibet and Imperial China*, Canberra 1967 pp. 29-32.

[145] *Op. cit.* p. 32.

[146] R. Grousset, *op. cit.* pp. 258-271.

[147] S.C. Das, *Contributions on the Religion and History of Tibet*, New Delhi 1970 pp. 145-149.

Thunderbolt). Thus under new circumstances and under a new set-up, the former Tibetan-Mongol alliance which had existed in the thirteenth century was renewed in the sixteenth century.

In 1642 the Fifth Dalai Lama became the spiritual and secular head after defeating the Gtsag-pa kings and broke the power of the Karma-pa sect with the aid of the Qosot Mongols. He had to share his power with the Panchen Lama. For his services the title of "King of Tibet" was bestowed on Gusri Khan and a part of his army was stationed permanently in the vicinity of the Tengri-nor Lake north of Lhasa[148].

The Manchus began to conquer China in the sixteenth century. In 1644 they captured Peking from the Ming emperor. This was possible only because of the anti-Ming rebellion in China and also because of the fact that Ming generals sought Manchu help against the Chinese rebels. Once the Manchus were in Peking they refused to leave and established their dynasty on the Chinese throne[149]. The Manchu ruler and the Dalai Lama established good relation but this had only a minor effect on the relationship of the two states. Military power in Tibet remained in the hands of the Mongol kings.

Sans-rgyas-rgya-mtsho (1679-1705) shared power with the Dalai Lama in the newly established office of the regent. His attitude towards the second Manchu ruler of China Emperor K'ang-hsi (1663-1722) was openly hostile. The regent sided with the opposition of the Manchus in China. The K'ang-hsi emperor (1662-1722) who was the most capable among the Manchu rulers supported cultural activities. He commissioned many literary undertakings like the official history of the Ming dynasty or the K'ang-hsi Dictionary which was in use for more than 200 years. The hostile attitude of Sans-rgyas-rgya-mtsho was revealed when he refused in 1699 to support the Emperor in the latter's struggle against the Oirat Dsungars. Galdan Khan wanted to reunite the Mongols and thus establish a new Mongol Empire. However, Galdan Khan was defeated and the Buriats and the Khalkas came under Chinese supremacy. He was killed by Lha-bzan Khan, who was Gusri Khan's fifth successor as the King of Tibet (1697-1717). It was a service on his behalf to the Emperor K'ang-hsi[150]. After that Lha-bzan Khan deposed the Sixth Dalai Lama on the pretext of misconduct. The alleged misconduct of the sixth Dalai Lama Tshaṅs-dbyaṅs-rgya-mtso was that contrary to his norm of conduct he wrote love-songs, which are still extant. Lha-bzan Khan's interference was resented all over Tibet and in the neighbouring A-mdo. Thus his position in Tibet became very weak. In 1714 his opponents turned to Tshe-dbaṅ-rab-bstan (1697-1727), Galdan's nephew and successor and the leader of the Oirat Dsungars, for help. The Dsungar army crossed the un-inhabited land of north Tibet and occupied Lhasa in ten days. In 1717 Lha-bzaṅ Khan was killed. Thus the Mongol dynasty of the Kings of Tibet (1642-1717) was overthrown and the Dsungars temporarily gained control over Tibet.

---

[148]L. Petech, *China and Tibet in the early 18th century*, Leiden 1950 p. 221.

[149]R. Grousset, *op. cit.* pp. 279-283.

[150]L. Petech, *op. cit.* p. 9.

The Uigur were geographically and historically so placed that different cross-currents of cultures converged with them. Thus the Indian, Iranian, Tibetan and Chinese cultures exercised considerable influence on Uigur culture. The relative degree of influence of each of the aforesaid cultures depended mainly on the turns of historical or political events in that region. After the 14th century, the Uigurs came under the authority of the Chagatay ruling house. Chinese and Tibetan cultures exercised considerable impact on Uigur literature, art, religious ideas, way of life and even on economic and social development.

6. ORIGIN AND DEVELOPMENT OF THE UIGUR LANGUAGE AND LITERATURE

6a. Language

It is a well known fact that every language over the centuries undergoes considerable changes with the passage of time. The old phenomenon is followed by the new. With time a series of changes take place, which finally manifest themselves in the latter. Students of linguistics should not only record the said phenomena, but also give a picture of their origin and development[1].

Concerning the history of the development of Uigur as one stage of the development of Turkish languages, a general introduction to the old and new Turkish languages is needed. Philipp von Strahlenberg was the first to propound the theory which connects the so-called Uralian languages with the Turkish languages. He spent as many as fourteen years in Siberia and studied not only the languages of that region but also the social system of the Turkish people living on the banks of the Volga on the basis of anthropological and ethnographical facts about them[2].

Thus he classified the languages into six groups:

1 Finn-Ugor: Hungarian, Finn, Vogule, Cheremissian, Votyak, Ostyak.
2 Turk-Tartar: Tartar, Yakut, Chuwash.
3 Samoyedic.
4 Mongolian-Manchurian: Kalmuck, Manchurian, Tangut.
5 Tungusic: Tungusic and some other Siberian languages like Kamasin, Arin, Koryak and Kuril.
6 Languages which are spoken by people living between the Black Sea and the Caspian Sea.

Though the theories of Philipp von Strahlenberg are outdated, but the information provided by his book on Siberian languages is a well-established fact which is highly appreciated even two hundred and fifty years after its first edition. Moreover, Strahlenberg had published a Kalmuck-Mongolian dictionary with German explanations, which is still a much appreciated work for the Mongolists[3].

The famous linguist and philosopher Leibnitz paid special attention to the Turkish-Tartar and Finno-Ugrian languages. Through this he also attracted the minds of his contemporaries towards

---

[1]G. Hazai-P Zieme, *Zu einigen Fragen der Bearbeitung Turkisscher Sprachdenmaller* (in German: Some remarks on the research on Old Turkish literary records). *AO* 1970 p. 125.

[2]Ahmet Caferoglu, *Türk dilitarihi* (in Turkish: The history of Turkish language), Vol. 1 Istanbul 1970 pp. 10-14.

[3]As quoted by A. Caferoglu, Ph. Strahlenberg: *Vocabularium Calmuck-Mungalicm* (in Latin: Kalmuck-Mongolian Dictionary 1730).

the comparative study of Uralic and Altaic languages. With the aim of comparative investigation of Uralic and Altaic languages, in 1770 a Hungarian scholar, J. Sajnovits published a book in Latin entitled *Demonstratio idiome Hungarorum et Lappnonum idem esse.* Sajnovits was the first to compare the Hungarian language with the Lapp language. In the same century another Hungarian, J. Gyarmathi wrote a comparative study based on Strahlenberg's work[4].

Nearly a hundred years after the edition of Strahlenberg's work, R. Rask from Denmark published a comparative study of the languages spoken in North Africa, Greenland, Asia and the Caucasus. It was an important initiative because till then mainly Indo-European languages had been compared. He established a new theory of Paleo-Asiatic (Old Asiatic) languages. Under this name he included not only the old Indo-European languages but also the Tungusic, Mongolian, Turkish, Finno-Ugrian languages. Later the same idea of kinship between Paleo-Asiatic languages was put forward by Wilhelm von Humbolt.

Comparing the structure, the morphology and the vocal harmony of the same languages, Max Mueller introduced the theory of 'agglutinating' languages. To the group of the so-called 'agglutinating' languages belonged Siamese, Tibetan, South Indian, Malay and Turkish languages. Max Mueller also named this group as Turani Languages. The idea of kinship of languages belonging to different geographical regions was supported by many scholars who identified themselves with Max Muller's ideas, such as Lassen, Leipus and Gladwell.

The idea of kinship between the Ural-Altaic languages and East Asian languages was put forward by a number of scholars in the 19th century. J. Hoffman and H. Winkler in their books supported the theory of a Japanese and Ural-Altaic kinship on the basis of agglutination. The question of the relatedness of Japanese language was described in many books by Boller, Winkler, Grunzel and Prohle[5]. Till recently (1941) the question of Old Japanese and Old Turkish languages remained unsolved until J. Ramstedt refuted it on the basis of the history of the Japanese language[6].

Some scholars in the 19th century took up the idea of kinship between the Turkish, Sumerian and Akkad languages. Eber-Schrader, Fr. Hommel and Fr. Lenormant based their theories on the similarity of the vowel-systems among the three languages. In view of the fact that Sumerian and Akkad are dead languages and due to lack of necessary information about their vocal system, it may be suggested that this hypothesis was unfounded.

---

[4]As quoted by A. Caferoğlu: J. Gyarmathi, *Affinitas linguae hungaricae cum linguis fennicae originis grammatics demonstrade* (in Latin: Grammatical demonstration of contacts between the Hungarian and Finnish languages), Gottingen 1799.

[5]As quoted by A. Caferoğlu: Boller, *Nachweis dass das Japanische zum ural-altaischen Stamme gehört* (in German: Proof that German belongs to the Ural-Altaic Family), Wien 1875. H. Winkler: *Japaner and Altaier* (in German: Japanese and Altayese), Berlin 1894.

[6]G.F. Ramstedt, *Uber die Geschichte des Japanischen* (in German: On the history of Japanese), Helsinki 1942.

[7]As quoted by A. Caferoğlu: M. Castren, *Reiseberichte und Briefs aus den Jahren* 1845-49 (in German: Travel-accounts and letters of the years 1845-1849), St. Petersburg 1856.

In fact, it was the Finnish scholar M. Castren who first based the theory of Ural-Altaic kinship on linguistic facts. He established the relationship among Samoyedic, Finnish and Turkish languages[7]. Basing themselves upon Castren's excellent works, his contemporaries started describing and examining the languages of the Ural-Altaic family.

FAMILY OF URAL-ALTAIC LANGUAGES

- Uralic Languages
  - Finno-Ugrian: **IB** **IA**
  - Samoyedic: **II**
- Altaic Languages
  - Turkish: **III**
  - Mongolian: **IV**
  - Manchurian-Tungusic: **V**

The details of the chart given above are as follows:

I. Finno-Ugrian group has two main branches:

A. Ugrian branch: 1. Ostyak 2. Vogul 3. Hungarian

B. Finn branch: 1. Original Finn, Suomi language 2. Estonian 3. Liv 4. Karelian 5. Lapp 6. Votyak 7. Zuyen 8. Cheremissian 9. Mordivin (to this group belong the Permi and Volgian languages).

II. Samoyedic group

III. Turkish group:

1. Yakut
2. Chuwash
3. South-Siberian Turkish languages: (a) Karagas (b) Kamasin
4. Abakan Turks: (a) Kizil (b) Kach (c) Koybal (d) Sagay (e) Beltir
5. Chulim Turks
6. Northern Altaic languages: (a) Kumandi (b) Lebed (c) Tuba or Kara Orman (Turkish) (d) Shor
7. Original Altaic languages: (a) Altaic ones (b) Form Dvoye (c) Teleut (d) Kalmucks from the Altai
8. Turks living in Mongolia: (a) Uryanhar (b) Baraba
9. Turks living on the Irtish and Tobol: (a) Tara Turks (b) Tobol Turks (c) Turks from Tobol and Tumen
10. Kara Kirgiz
11. Kazak Kirgiz
12. Turks from East Turkistan: (a) Taranchi (b) Kashgar (c) Hami Turks
13. Turks from West Turkistan: (a) Uzbek (b) Kurama (c) Karakalpak (d) Turkmanian
14. Volga Turks: (a) Bashkir (b) Kazan Turks (c) Misher (d) Tepter

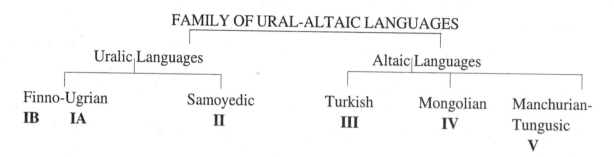

15. Turks from the Northern Caucasus: (a) Nogay (b) Kundur (c) Kumuk (d) Karachay (e) Balkar
16. West Turks: (a) Turkey's Turks (b) Azerbaijans.
17. Crimean Turks: Crimean Karaims
18. Litvanian Karaims
19. Gagauz
20. Balkan Turks
21. Syria's and Iraq's Turks

IV. Mongolian group:

1. Buryatian 2. Kalmuck 3. Oryat 4. Halha

To this group belong Mongols from Afghanistan, Dagurs from Manchuria and the Mongors living in Tibet and China.

V. Tungusic group: 1. Manchurian 2. Lamut 3. Tungusic dialects.

The five main groups of Ural-Altaic languages established by M. Castren are divided into different languages, which are marked by numbers and sub-groups marked by letters in alphabetical order. The letters and numbers mark the geographical situation as well as the degree of relatedness.

In the wake of Ural-Altaic language-theory Schott, who was a supporter of the purely Altaic language family increased the speed of research by bypassing the Uralic languages and focussing all his attention on the Altaic languages. He examined the closeness and relationship between the Turkish, Mongolian and Tungusic languages and published his results in 1836 in a book entitled: *Versuch über tatarische Sprachen*[8]. In his book he studied the degree of relatedness among the Altaic languages, which he called 'Tatar'languages. He examined the languages from the phonetic point of view, checking the words and roots of verbs. Thus he discovered a very important basic feature of the Altaic languages, elaborated later on by others, that in the common words of Turkish and Mongolian against Turkish *z* is to be found Mongolian *r*; and against Turkish *š* there is Mongolian *l*.

In the last century the scholars who sided with the purely Altaic language theory made many important investigations in comparing Turkish, Mongolian and Tungusic languages. H. Winkler, however, took up the task of comparing Tungusic languages with Finno-Ugrian and Samoyedic languages[9]. He connected the Manchurian language with these languages through the Japanese language. He held the opinion that Japanese and Manchurian languages have some basically similar features.

The question of Tungusic language has not been forgotten by the linguists. Many scholars have concluded that Tungusic does not belong to the Altaic family. Though we can not give an absolutely certain answer on the question of the relatedness of Tungusic language, the more recent

---

[8]W. Schott, *Versuch uber tatarischen Sprachen* (An attempt for a summary of the Tatar languages), Berlin 1836.

[9]H. Winkler, *Tunguzisch und Finnisch-Ugrisch* (German: Tungusic and Finno-Ugrian), JSFOu XXX p. 9.

researches of Schmidt, Ramstedt and Pelliot conclude explicitly that Tungusic language belongs to the Altaic family.

From the point of view of syntax an Estonian scholar F. Wiedemann had already published a work in German in 1838[10]. After comparing the typical features of the two groups, he held the opinion that the two language families must be related. After F. Wiedemann a number of scholars worked on the syntax of Uralic and Altaic languages. The best modern studies in this field are those of Ö. Beke[11] and D. Fuchs[12].

In the 19th century, with the increase in comparative studies in Finno-Ugrian languages, Budenz, Donner, Szinnyei and others explored the morphological, lexical and syntactical features of these languages. In this sense the studies of Turkish languages lagged behind during the same period. Among the Altaic languages attention was paid mostly to the Yakut and Chuwash languages.

G.J. Ramstedt was a pioneer in this field. He started fresh investigations into the Turkish language with the study tools of modern philology and with exhaustive knowledge of Mongolian languages. By this time more materials had been published on the phonology of the Turkish languages. The deciphering of the Orkhon inscriptions, the publication of documents in Uigur, etc. threw new light on the earlier stages of the development and history of Turkish language and provided new data for research.

G.J. Ramstedt reviewed Schmidt's idea of Mongolian *r* correlated to Turkish *z*, a feature called rhotacism; and Mongolian *l* against Turkish *š* to which he gave the name lambdaism. He realised that rhotacism and lambdaism were really general features except in Chuwash language. This language showed the same changes as Mongolian, e.g.[13]

1. Rotacism: Gen. Turk. ***öküz*** 'ox' Chuw. ***vōkār*** Mong. ***ükür*** 'animal with horns'.

Gen. Turk. *buzagu* 'calf' Chuw. *peruporu* Mong. *biragu* 'weaned calf'.

2. Lambdaism: Gen. Turk. *kašik* 'spoon'Chuw. *kajek* Mong. *halbaga*.

Gen. Turk. *taš* 'stone' Chuw. *tsul* Mong. *čilagun*.

Apart from rhotacism and lambdaism, there are a number of rules and regular changes which are the characteristics of the Altaic languages:

I. Mong. *u<i* Gen. Turk. *a* (in the first stressed syllable) Chuw. *u<a* Yak. *a* For example: Mong. *sira* 'yellow' Gen. Turk. *sari sarig̃* Chuw. *šure* 'white'

---

[10]As quoted by A. Caferoğlu : F. Wiedemann, *Uber die früheren Sitze der tschudischen Völker und ihre Sprachverwandschaft mit den Völker Mittelasiens* (About the position of the Finno-Ugrian languages and their relationship to the Central Asian Peoples) 1838.

[11]Ö. Beke, *Türkische Einflusse in der Syntax des finnisch-ugrischen Sprachen* (Turkish influence on the syntax of the Finno-Ugrian languages), KSz XV pp. 1-77.

[12]D. Fuchs, *Ubereinstimmungen in der Syntax der finnisch-ugrische und turkischen Sprachen* (in German: Correlations in the syntax of the Finno-Ugrian and Turkish languages), FUF XXIV pp. 292-322.

[13]G. J. Ramstedt, *Zur Frage nach der Stellung der Tschuwassischer* (in German: About the position of the Chuwash language), JSFOu XXXVIII.

Mong. *nirai* 'fresh, new' Gen. Turk. *yaz* 'spring' Chuw. *sur*

Mong. *bui* 'goes' Turk. *ba-r* 'goes' Chuw. *pur* Yak. *bār*

II. The Turkish –*ğ*- sound is retained exactly in Mongolian. For example:

Gen. Turk. *buzağu* 'calf' Mong. *bizağu*

Gen. Turk. *ariğ* 'clean' Mong. *ariğun*.

III. The phonologic system is very similar. The vowel system is rich while the consonant system is relatively poor in all the Altaic languages.

IV. Generally in the languages of the Altaic family short and long vowels can be differentiated.

V. In the agglutinative system all the Altaic languages are in harmony.

VI. From the point of view of agglutination the suffix system is rich.

VII. The Gen. Turkish **a** in the first syllable correlates with Mong. *i~u*, and in some dialects Mong. **a** Gen Turk. *i~u* For example:

Mong. *sira* 'yellow' Gen. Turk *sari*

Mong. *altan* 'golden' Gen. Turk. *altun altin*

Mong. *katagu* 'hard' Gen. Turk. *katiğ*

Mong. *dalay* 'sea' Gen. Turk. *taluy*.

On the basis of these rules and changes, N. Poppe drew up the following picture of the separation of the original Proto-Altaic languages[14]:

PROTO-ALTAIC LANGUAGE

- The times of the common Mongolian-Turkish languages
  - Common Mogolian language
    - The Oldest Mongolian dialects, the formation of the base of the written Mongolian language
      - 12-15 centuries, the formation of the Middle Mongolian dialects
        - New Mongolian dialects, the formation of the Halha dialect.
  - Common Turkish language
- Common Tungusic language

[14]N. Poppe: *Der altaische Sprachtyp* (in German: The Altaic type of language), Handbuch der Orientalistik V, 1964 pp. 1-16.

The foregoing chart gives the oldest stage of the Altaic languages, when the Turkish, Mongolian and Tungusic languages were not separated. There was another stage of development of these languages when they participated and separated in rotacism and lambdaism but were one common language after the separation of the Tungusic language.

PROTO-ALTAIC LANGUAGE (*r* and *l* languages)

- Proto-Mongolian language (*r* and *l* language)
- Proto-Chuwash-Turkish language (*r* and *l* language)
  - Proto-Chuwash language (*r* and *l*)
    - Chuwash dialect (*r* and *l* language)
  - Proto-Turkish language (*š* and *z* language)
    - Modern Turkish language (*š* and *z* language)

In view of the description of the characteristics of the Altaic languages, the origin of the Turkish languages becomes clear. While systematizing the different periods of the development of Turkish languages, the first period in this case is identical with the second period of Altaic languages. There is no written evidence substantiating the details of the first stages of Turkish languages. About the period of common Turkish-Mongolian language and about the Proto-Turkish language most of the information is provided by the comparative studies of Mongolian, Yakut and Chuwash languages.

A. Caferoğlu divided the history of Turkish languages into seven main periods:[15]

1. Altaic period — the time of common Turkish-Mongolian languages
2. The oldest Turkish period — the time of Proto-Turkish language
3. The primary Turkish period
4. Old Turkish period
5. Middle Turkish period
6. New Turkish period
7. Modern Turkish period.

Concerning the third period, the period of primary Turkish language, some documents are in existence. In chronological terms this stage of development of Turkish languages took place sometime before and after the birth of Christ. The languages of Sabirs, Avars, and Pecheneks are supposed to be classified with this period. Unfortunately their language and history remains unknown to scholars until now. The language of the two main groups of Bulgars, the Volga

[15] A. Caferoğlu, *op.cit.* pp. 51-52.

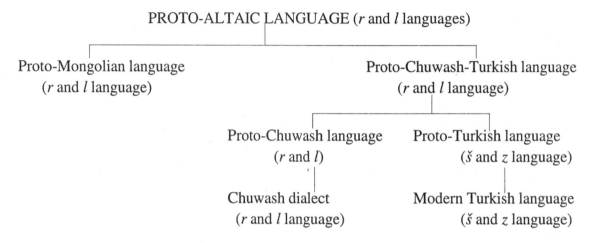

Bulgars, and the Danube Bulgars, also belongs to the third primary Turkish period of development of Turkish languages.

The Bulgars near the Volga river lived in what was called Bulgaria Magna and the country of Bulgars on the Danube was called Bulgaria Minor. Arabic writers give some information about the Bulgars, but there are only two groups of written documents. The first document supposed to have been written in the 8th century AD in Greek language, is a chronology (list) of rulers of Bulgars. Names of animals and persons appear in this document. The names of animals are: *hulgana* 'brown rat', *uhir* 'ox', *bar* 'leopard', *tuulay* 'hare', *luu* 'dragon', *mogoy* 'snake', *mor* 'horse', *hon* 'sheep', *mici* 'monkey', *tahia* 'hen', *nohoy* 'dog', and *gahay* 'pig'. According to J.J. Mikkola these names of animals show that the language of the Bulgars living on the Danube river had features similar to those of the modern Chuwash language[16]. A later group of documents are the records on the tombs of Volga Bulgars from the 13th/14th centuries. These records on the tombs were written in Arabic script and the words therein also show features similar to those of the Chuwash language.

The fourth, Old-Turkish period, includes the records written between the 6th and 7th centuries, mainly the documents in Runic script and the first Uigur documents.

The Uigur Suvarṇaprabhāsa-sūtra together with other texts belongs to the fifth period which lasted from the 10th to the 17th century. To this period belong the monuments of Chagatay literary language, and documents of Kipchak and Oguz languages.

The new Turkish period lasted from the 16th century to the present day.

The history of Uigur language belongs to the fourth and fifth periods of the general history of Turkish languages.

The second period of the Turkish language is the Proto-Turkish period. This era of development of the Turkish language is marked on the above chart by the first separation of Altaic languages. At this stage of development the Proto-Chuwash and Proto-Turkish languages had not yet parted company. Written documents are not available about this period. But on the basis of comparison of the Turkish languages and dialects, the hypothetical system of the Proto-Turkish vowel and consonant system was worked out by N. Poppe, J. Németh and others[17]. In this context it is necessary to discuss the Proto-Turkish vowel and consonant system with a view to evaluating the recent developments of modern Turkish languages[18].

The Proto-Turkish plosives were in initial position: *b-*, *t-*, *k-* and *g-*. The initial plosive *b-* usually remained *b-* in most of the modern Turkish languages. In Chuwash it changes into *p-*. In Osman-Turkish and in Aserbaijani it changes into *v* or it drops. Example: *ber-* 'to give': Old Turkish, Uig. *ber-*, Osm. As. *ver-*, Tat. Bashk. *bir-*, Yak. *biar-*, Chuw. *par-*.

Initial *b-* changes sometimes into *m-* especially when there is a nasal vowel in the word.

[16]J.J. Mikkola, *Die Chronologie der türkischen Donaubulgaren* (in German: The chronology of the Turkish Danube-Bulgars), JSFOU pp. 1-25.

[17]N. Poppe, *Vergleichende Grammatik der altaischen Sprachen* (in German: Comparative grammar of the Altaic languages), Wiesbaden 1960.

[18]A. von Gabain, *Das Alttürkische* (in German: Ancient Turkish language), Fnd. I pp. 21-45.

But many times the original sound in Proto-Turkish cannot be decided, because an *m-* also changed into *b-* in Turkish. Example: *min* 'thousand', Uig. *min*, Osm. *bin*, Tat. Bashk. *men*, Chuw. *pin*, Mong. *minağan.*

+mun +bun 'sorrow', Orch. *bun*, Uig. *mun*, Osm. *bun*, Tat. *mon*, Yak. *mun*

Initial *p-* did not exist in Proto-Turkish and Old Turkish. In some of the modern Turkish languages *p-* came into existence from *b-* through denasalisation: **mun** as in Chuwash. In other languages initial *p-* can be found only in loan-words. However, in the loan-words occasional initial *p-* changes into *m-*.

In the middle of the word, the sound *-p-* gets voiced in a number of languages. In Yakut it changes to *-m-* which could be the result of a longer process when *p-* changed into *b-* and later to *m-*. Example: Hung. *koboz* 'lute', Uig. Osm. *kopuz*, Tat. *kubïz*, Yak. Χomus, Chuw. *kuoas.*

There is a trend of spirantisation of *b-* to *v-* in the Orkhon inscriptions, and in the oldest Uigur monuments. *-b-* can be found in intervocal position. But in some words *-b-* change to *-v-* in the oldest monuments. Examples: *+tabar, tavar* 'product': Uig. *tabar, tavar, tivar*, Osm. Turk. *davar* 'animal' Yak. *tabaar.*

+tabiškan 'hare': Orkh. *tabiškan*, Uig. *taviškan*, Osm. *tavšan, davšan*, Yak. *tabisχan.*

There is a change of intervocal *-b-*, *-p-* to *f* in some Turkish languages: Examples: Hung. *apro* 'very little', Uig. *ufrağ*, Osm. *ufak*, Tat. *anak.*

In the end of a word *-b* gets spirantized and changes to *-v*. Examples: *+sub* 'water': Orkh. Uig. *sub*, Osm. *su*, Tat. *sū*, Bashk. *hiu*; Yak *nu*, Chuw. *šiv.*

+ab 'house': Orch. Uig. *ab*, sometimes Uig. *av*, Osm. *av*, Tat. Bashk. *oy.*

In many cases *-b* becomes unvoiced. In the Osman-Turkish language there can be only *-p* at the end of the word. Example: *mektup* 'letter', *kasap* 'butcher', *jep* 'pocket'

The Old Turkish explosives: *t d k g q* and *ğ* undergo different changes. Initial *t-* usually survives the changes. In some of the languages it changes to *d-*. In Chuwash language it changes to *tč* and *š*. Examples: *+till, til* 'tongue': Old-Turkish, Middle Turkish Uig. *til,* Tat. Bashk. *tel,* Yak. *til,* Chuw. *čalχe.*

t- changes to *č-* in Chuwash: Gen. Turk. *taš* 'stone' Chuw. *čul.*

In an intervocal position *-t-* changes into *-d-*. As Turkish languages have postfixes it happens that a word ending in *-t* becomes *-d-* after adding a suffix. Examples: *+ātağ* 'island': Osm. *ada*, Bashk. Tat. *adau*, Chuw. *utə.*

Osm. at 'name', *adï* 'his name'.

Osm. *ot* 'fire', *odu* 'his fire'.

In intervocal position *-t-* can change into *-č-*; or it can change into *-št-*, or in Yakut *-lt-* can change to *-lj-* or -lǰ-. Examples: *χut* 'paper' > *χuč* 'his paper', *pul-* 'to be'> *pulčə* 'he was', Turk. *itik* 'sharp' Turki *ištik, ilt-* 'to improve' Yak. *iljar, ilǰār*

During the simplification of consonant groups *-t-* and *-d-* drop. Examples: Gen. Turk. *emti* 'now' Kirg. *emi*, Gen. Turk. *gündüz,* 'daytime' Aserb. *günüz*, Gen. Turk. *menden* 'from me' Kaz. *menen.*

The Old Turkish *-d-* between other sounds underwent many changes. Already in Old Turkish and in early Uigur monuments *-d-* was changed. Kāšğari described the differences among the Turkish dialects in the 11th century and mentioned that the *-d-* sound in the word developed differently among them[19]. The monuments in Brahmi script mark the alternate sound *t~dh*, this shows the aspiration of the sound. In Modern Turkish languages and in the Oguz (Osman. Turkish, Asherbaijani and Turkmenian) languages *-d-* corresponds to *y*, in the Altayan language it becomes *z*, in Yakut *t* and in Chuwash it changes to *r*. Examples:

+adaq 'leg': Old Turkish Uig. *adaq*, Middle Turkish *adaq*, Oguz *ayaq*, Altayan *azaq*, *azaχ*, Yakut *ataχ*, Chuwash *ura*.

+qudruq 'tail', Kāšğari *quoruq*, Oguz. *quvruq*, Tat. *qoyrïq*, Altaian *χuzurüχ*, Yakut *quturuχ*, Chuw. *χure*.

Many of the suffixes have *-d-* or *-t-* as the first sound of the suffix. Such suffixes are the suffix of locative ablative *-dan*, *-den*, *-tan*, *-ten*, the suffix of past tense *-tï*, *-ti*, the auxiliary suffix *-tir*, the suffix of the causative verb and so on.

In the Uigur language the suffixes *-t-* and *-d-* occur interchangeably. In modern Turkish languages it is usually assimilated to the preceding consonant. After voiced consonants the suffix starts with *-d-* and after unvoiced consonants the suffix starts with *-t-*.

About the Proto-Turkish suffixes conclusion may be drawn from the modern Chuwash suffixes. In Chuwash the suffixes of locative ablative are: *-ra*, *-rä* and *-ran*, *-rän*. The suffixes of past tense in Chuwash are *-ra* and *-rô*. Exceptional endings are *da* and *dža* after *-n-*, *-l-* and *–r-*. Examples: *utra* on 'horse', *utran* 'from horse', *aka* 'sowed'.

Most probably the original suffix started with *-d-*. Another evidence for the original Proto-Tukish *d* is the Yakut suffix of locative ablative: *-tan*. The Turkish monuments in Arabic script have for the suffix of past tense *c* which also proves that originally for past tense Proto-Turkish and Old Turkish had *-d-*.

Words ending *-d* changed to *-t*, *-t* remained *-t*. As a result of this process Turkish has only *-t* at the end of words. The process of change of word ending *-d* to *–t* was very strong in the 16th-17th centuries. The Arabic scripts did not show this change, mainly the loan-words prove this fact. The two versions, *-t* and *-d* are interchangeable in many cases. Examples: Bagdad ~ Bagdat, Ahmed ~ Ahmet, Dervend ~ Dervent.

In the case of combinations of consonants with final *-d* and *-t*, they drop at the end of words. Examples: Osm. Turk *dost* 'friend', in the other Turkish languages *dos*. Persian *aχond* 'lord' Turkish *aχon*. Persian *ustād* 'master' Turkish *usta*.

In Proto-Turkish the palatal and velar explosives were: *k, g, q* and *ğ*. Initial *k-* changes in some of the Oguz languages to *g-*. It changes in some Kipchak languages (Kumuk, Balkar, Karakalpak)

[19]C. Brockelmann, *Mitteltürkischer Wortschatz: Mahmūd al-Kāšğarī: Dīvān Luğat at-Turk* (in German: Middle-Turkish Vocabulary: Mahmūd al-*Kāšğarī*: Dīvān Luğat at-Turk), Budapest-Leipzig 1928.

also to *g*- Examples: *kör-* 'to look': Old Turkish, Middle Turkish *kör*, Gag. Turkm. Osm. *gör-*, Aserb. *kör-*, Tat. Bashk. *kür-*, Yak. *kör-*, Chuw. *kur-*.

The initial *k*- participates in other changes: *k*- > *č*- in Turki, for instance: *kim* > *čim* 'who'

k- > *χ*- in Kirgisian, for instance: *köl* 'lake' > *χöl*

k- > *k'*> *t'* in some Osman-Turkish dialects, *t'öpek* 'dog'

k changed into *h* and that into ∅ in Karaim language, for instance: *kem* 'who' > *hem* > Kar. *em*

The initial *q*- usually remains in most of the Turkish languages. In some Turkish languages there is no difference between the palatal and velar *q*- and *k*-. These languages are the Kumuk, Osman-Turkish, Misher and Karagas. In Aserbaijani and Turkmen *q*- > *k*-, in Chuwash, Hakas and Yakut before *-a* and *-o* it changes *q*- > *χ*-. In Chuwash sometimes it changes to *y*-. Examples:

+qiš 'winter': Old Turkish, Middle Turkish *kiš*, Aserbaijani, Turkm. *qïš*, Tatar, Bashk, Kirg. Kumuk *qïš*, Yak. *kïs*, Chuw. *χal*.

In some cases in Osman and Aserbaijan languages *q*- > *h*-. Examples: Aserb. *hanqi* 'which', Aserb. *hačan* 'when', Aserb. *hani* 'where'

In some of the Osman dialects initial *q*- drops: *qačan* > *χačan* > *hočan* > *ačan*.

qaya > *χaya* > *haya* > *aya*.

It (*q*-) gets usually voiced when placed in between vowels. It is similar to the trend in the Turkish languages wherein *-p-* becomes *-b-* but is not so frequent. Whether -q- becomes voiced or not seems to be based upon the quality of the vowels it is surrounded by. It seems that in between original Proto-Turkish long vowels *-q-* becomes voiced, while between the original short vowels it does not become voiced. Examples:

bāqa 'frog': Kāšğ. *baqa*, Osm. *bağa*, Turkm. *bāğa*, Kipch. *baga*, Usb. *baqa*, Yak *bağa*.

eke 'sister': Uig. Kāšğ. *eke*, CC *egeči*, Turkm. *ekeǰi*.

tükel 'perfect': Chag. *tükel-*, Osm. Turkm. *tüken*, CC *tükel, tüqel*.

Many suffixes start with *g, k* ~ *ğ, g*. The suffix of dative in Old Turkish was *-qa*, *-ke*, the suffix of accusative was *-g*. In defining the place from which someone or something originates, the suffix *-gï* was added. In most of the modern Turkish languages it works according to the rules of vowel-harmony: words having palatal vowels get a palatal suffix and words having velar vowels get a velar suffix. In the Oguz languages in a number of cases *-g-* disappeared and at the end of the words it changed to *y*, for instance: the suffix of dative *-ğa*, *-ğe* > *a, e*, the suffix of participle *-ğan*, *-ğen* > *an*, *-en*, the suffix of optative *ğay*, *ğey* > *-a*, *-e*.

At the end of a word *-q* usually remains. It drops in Chuwash language. In Yakut it remains after *i, u, ü*, otherwise it changes to *χ*. Examples:

adaq 'leg': Alt. *hak*, *azaχ*, Yak. *ataχ*, Chuw. *ura*. In all the other languages it is *-q* or *-k*.

Some examples showing dropping of *-q* in Chuwash: *qudruq* > *χüre* 'tail', *barmaq* > *purne* 'finger', *baliq* > *pulā* 'fish'.

Some examples denoting the changes in Yakut: *oχ* 'arrow', *irgäχ* 'man' (from *ärkäk*), but *balïk* 'fish', *bisik* 'cradle', *bük* 'curved'.

In the dialects, it is likely to change *k* > *χ*, *ǧ* > *ǵ*, *k* > *q*, *q*> *χ*.

In Old Turkish and Middle Turkish (except for the Codex Cumanicus), in the Oguz languages, in Hakas, in Tuvai and in Turki *g* and *ǧ* remain. In some laguages *g* and *ǧ* assimilate to the vowel preceding it. Examples: *toǧ* 'to be born': Uig. Kāšǧ. Chag. *tog-*, CC *toǧ-*, *tuv-*, Oguz *doǧ-*, Tat. *tu-*, Bashk. Kaz. Kirg. *tū-*, Ozb. *tuǧ-*, Chuw. *tu* ~ *tav*.

teg- 'to reach': Orch. Uig. Middle Turkish *teg- tev-*, Osm. Aserb. *dev-* (*deg-*), Turkm. *deg-*, Tat. *tiy-*, Bashk. *tey-*, Kum. *tiy-*, Kas. Kirg. *tiy-*, *tī-*, Ozb. *teq-*, Yak. *tī*, Chuw. *tiv-*.

Labiodental *f* and *v* originally did not exist in Turkish, they came into being in a secondary way. Initial *v* in some Osman-Turkish words originated from *b-* like in *var-* and *ver-* ('to go' and 'to give'). Some initial *v*-s originate from loan-words: *vapur* 'ship' and *vali* 'a governor of a province'. But initial *v* in loan-words can be replaced by *b* and *p*, as in: Tat. *baǧat* 'time' Ar. *waqt*. Sor. *pes* 'the whole' Russ. *veś*. In the middle of words, it often came from *b*: Osm. *tabïškan* > *tavïškan* 'hare'. Sometimes one faces the reverse trend, when foreign *v* changes to *b*: *ǰubap* < *ǰevab* 'answer', *χayban* < *hayvan* 'animal, living creature'.

Intervocal and word-ending *v* which originate from *ǧ* in some of the Turkish languages change to labial *w*. Such languages are Bashkirian, Tatar and Aserbaijani alongwith many dialects. Examples: Kirg. *suw* 'water', *tow* 'hill'. Aserb. *owa* 'the wild animal' (in genitive).

Intervocal *v* becomes a semi-vowel in some of the dialects. Examples: Osm. *davar* 'flock' in a South Osm. dialect *dauar*.

Initial *f-* originates from loan-words only. Examples: *firtïna* 'storm' (the original word was Italian). *Ferman* 'imperial edict' (the original word was Persian).

In an intervocal position *v* changes to *f*. Example: Osm. *ufak* 'small' < *upak*.

The *s* sound usually remains, except in Bashkirian, in the Turki dialects and in Yakut. It changes to *h* in an initial position in Bashkirian. In Yakut first it changed to *h*, and then it disappeared. In Chuwash it remains but in a number of cases it changes to *š*, that is what the Hungarian loan-words coming from Chuwash reflect. Examples for initial *s*: *sub* 'water': Old Turk. Uig. *sub*, Kāšǧ. *suv*, Osm. Aserb. *sū*, Turkm. *suv*, Tat. *sū*, Bashk. *hiu*, Osb. *suv*, Yak *uu*, Chuw. *šïv*.

Occasionally in Chuwash there can be a zero correlation. Chuw. *əs* 'to draw water', Osm. *sus*.

Under the effect of assimilation and dissimilation *s* can change to different sounds: *sač* 'hair': Tat. *čeč*, Bashk. *ses*, Kirg. *čač*, Kas. *cac*, Sor *šaš*, Yak. *as*, Chuw. *süs*.

In intervocal position, the -*s*- becomes voiced -*z*-. Examples: *yasa-* 'to command, order': Orch. Chag. *yasa-*, Osm. *yasak* 'forbidden', Altayan *yaza*, Sor. *caza*.

In Chuwash -*s*- in an intervocal position chages to -*z*-. Example: *uzδ* 'necessary' < *asiǧ*.

During conjugation when it (*s*) gets into an intervocal position, it gets voiced: Examples: Osm. *domus* ~ *domzun* 'pig', Osm. *horos* ~ *horozun* 'rooster', Osm. *atasi* Bashk. *atahi* 'his father'.

In Yakut *s* changes to *z* and *ž* to *t*+. All the suffixes originally starting with -*s*- show this change. Examples: *iti* 'warm' < *isiǧ*. *utaχ* 'thirst' < *susak*.

In Chuwash the possessive suffix changes from *s* to *š* or *ž*. Example: *amāžā* 'his father'.

Initial *z* can stand only in foreign loan-words, such as: *zor* 'hard', difficult, fatiguing (from

Persian); *zahmet* 'trouble, difficulty' (from Arabic). *ziyan* 'lose, damage' (from Persian).

The final *-z* changed in Altayan, Yakut and Hakas to *-s*. Example: Generally Turkish *köz* 'eye' Alt. Hak *kös* Chuw. *kus*.

Generally Turkish *kāz* 'goose' Alt. *kas* Hak. *χas* Chuw. *χur*.

Generally Turkish *kïz* 'girl' Alt. *kïs* Hak. *χis* Yak. *χās* Chuw. *χur*.

In the middle of words *z* can change to *s* in Yakut and Karagas. In Yakut *z* can chamge to *t*. Examples: Osm. Turkish *kïzar-* 'to become red', Yak. *kitar-*. Osm. Turkish personal pronoun *biz*, Yak. *bit*. Osm. Turkish personal suffix *-ğiz*, Vak. *-it*. Osm. Turkish negative aorist *-baz*, *-maz*, Yak. *-bat*.

In Bashkirian final z changes to δ. Examples: Yak. *biδ* 'we', Yak. *gaδ* 'goose', Yak. *qiδ il* 'red'. We find the same change in a Turkmenian dialect.

When speaking about the development of Proto-Turkish *z*, attention should be paid to the process of rhotacism. According to earlier opinions, the general Turkish *z* Chuwash *r* and Mongolian *r* correlated with Proto-Altaic *z*. After Radloff and Gombocz, Ramstedt was the first scholar who set up the theory according to which the general Turkish *z*, Chuwash and Mongolian *r* correlate to a Altaic *r*[20]. L. Ligeti too supports the later. However, some scholars persist in the theory of original Altaic *z*. Very many of the Old Turkish loan-words have the *r* sound in Hungarian. Some of these words can be traced in Mongolian language. In Mongolian and Chuwash correlation the *r* sound is to be found. There are some Hungarian loan-words with *r* which can be traced to modern Chuwash language only. Some of the Hugarian loanwords having *r* can be traced only in Mongolian while another group of loanwords with *r* cannot be traced either in Chuwash or in Mongolian. The Hungarian language in the course of its history had contact with one Turkish language or perhaps a group of Turkish languages. As a result of this a large number of words which constitute an important basic part of Hungarian vocabulary, present evidences for the history of Turkish languages[21]. For instance such words are: Hung. *borjú* 'calf', *iker* 'twine', *ír* 'to write', *ökör* 'ox', *sár* 'mud, slush', *harang* 'bell', *gyűrű* 'ring', *író* 'buttermilk', *szérű* 'barn', *szűr* 'long embroidered felt cloak of a Hungarian shepherd', *térd* 'knee', *görény* 'fitchew', *tűr* 'to endure, to tolerate', *gyarló* 'frail', *karó* 'stake', *sárkány* 'dragon', *tenger* 'sea' and so on.

Originally initial *š* did not exist in Old Turkish. The present initial s sounds exist in words of foreign origin. Such are *šarap, šah, šehir, šeker* 'sugar'. There are some initial *š*-s which came to existence in a secondary way like *šu* 'this' from *ošu*, *olšu*, or in some imitative words: *šïngïr* 'noise imitating the breaking of glass' or *šapïrda* 'to make a smacking noise'.

In final position *š* changes to *s* in Kasak and Hakas languages, and to *ś* in Chuwash and Yakut languages. Examples: *baš* 'head': Kas. Karakalpak *bas*, Hak. *pas*, Yak. *baś*, Chuw. *puś*.

tïš 'tooth': Kas. *tis*, Hak. *tis*, Yak. *tis*, Chuw. *sāl*.

In the middle of the word *š* changes to Altayan *ž* in Sor and Hakas *z*. Example: *tiši* 'female',

[20]G.J. Ramstedt, *op. cit.*

[21]About the oldest Turkish loan-words in the Hungarian language see Lóránd Benkö-Samu Imre, *The Hungarian Language*, Budapest 1972 pp. 178-181.

Altayan *tiži*, Hak. *tizi*, Sor *tïzï*

From the point of view of Altaic languages the correlation of general Turkish *š* to Chuwash *l* and Mongolian *l* is very important. This correlation is called lambdacism. Examples for the correlation of general Turkish *š* ~ Chuwash *l*: Gen. Turk *beš* 'five' Chuw. *pil-lak*, Gen. Turk *qiš* 'winter' Chuw. *χal*, Gen. Turk *taš* 'stone' Chuw. *čul*, Gen. Turk *tiš* 'tooth' Chuw. *sāl*. In this case, as in the case of rotacism where the Hungarian loanwords showed a similar trend as the Chuwash and Mongolian word, the Hungarian loanwords show *l* against General Turkish *š*.

What complicates the matter in the case of lambdaism is that the Hungarian language has the corresponding Chuwash word in one case only. Hung. *süllő* 'pike-perch', Gen. Turk. *tiš*, Chuw. *šāl –lə* 'pike-perch'; Hung. *dél* 'noon', Gen. Turk. *tūš* 'to fall', Chuw.-; Hung. *dől* 'to fall', Gen. Turk *tüš-* 'to fall', Chuw.- Hung. *kölyök* 'kid', Gen. Turk. *köšek* 'young animal', Chuw. —.

The *ž* sound is alien to the Turkish languages. It can be found in loanwords and in original Turkish words as a secondary development. However, in Altayan, Chuwash and Sor languages there is a trend of *š* changing to *ž*.

Initial *y-* must have existed in Proto-Turkish. It is there in the monuments of Old Turkish language. In Oguz Turki and some of the Kipchak languages it (*y-*) remains, whereas in some Kipchak languages it changes to *ǰ*, *ž* (*z*). In Altayan language it changes to *d'* and *č*, in Yakut it changes to *s* and in Chuwash to *ś*. Examples: *yaz* 'to write': Old Turkish monuments, Uig. *yaz*, Oguz *yaz*, Tat. Bashk. Nog. *yaz-*, Kirg. *kaz*. Kkalp. *žaz*, Karach. *ǰaz*, Balk. *zaz*, Turki *yaz*, Osb. *yoz*, Alt. Yak. *suruy*, Chuw. *šïr-*.

yer 'place, earth': Old Turkish monuments, Uig.*yer, yir*, Oguz *yer*, Bashk. Kum. Nog. *yer*, Tat. *yer*, *ǰir*, *žir*, Kirg. Kaz. KKalp. *žer*, Karach. *ǰer*, Balk. *zer*, Turki *yer*, Alt, *d'er*, Hak. *čir*, Tuvai *čer*, Yak. *sir*, Chuw. *śar*.

In some of the Kipchak languages, *d* can correlate with *y*, and in other Turkish languages *č* can correlate with *y*. Examples: Kaz. *düz* 'hundred', Osm. *yüz*; KKalp. *dastik* 'pillow', Osm. *yastik;* Balk. *dulduz* 'star', Osm. *yulduz*; Chag. Osm. *čilek* 'strawberry', Turkm. *čigelek*, Nog. *čiglek*, Alt. *yilek*, Chuw. *śirla*.

In the Altayan language *y* changes to *n, ṅ* when a nasal consonant exists in the word. Example: Alt. *naṅi*, Hak. *nā*, *navï*, Karach. *ṅā*, Osm. Turk. *yanī* 'new'.

In Chuwash language *ś* correlates with *y* in most of the Turkish languages, which is probably due to the development of original *y* to *d* from *d'* through *j* to *š*. Most of the Turkish languages kept the original *y*. The List of Princes of the Danube Bulgars belonging to the 6th or 7th century shows the second stage of development of *y* to *d'*. Example: Osm. Turk. *yïlan* 'snake', D. Bulg. *d'ilam*, Chuw. *śələn.*

The inscriptions on the tomb of the Volga Bulgars from the 10th through to the 13th century show the next stage of development to *ǰ*.

In Hungarian loan-words the initial Proto-Turkish *y-* correlates with g' (which is written in Hungarian with *gy-*) and this is probably in connection with the second stage of development of

Proto-Turkish *y-* as described above. The original *y* could also drop in Hungarian or develop into *ś* (marked in Hungarian with *sz*). Examples: Gen. Turk. *yaz-* 'to write', Hung. *ír* Chuw. *śir*; Gen. Turk. *yüzük* 'ring', Hung. *gyűrű,* Chuw.—; Gen. Turk. *yel* 'wind', Hung. *szél* Chuw. *śil*; Gen. Turk. *yilok* 'grapes', Hung. *szőlő*, Chuw. *śirla*. These differences in the correlations may be explained on the basis of differences among the different Old Chuwash dialects.

In Uigur a *y-* sound before vowels came to being. Examples: Uig. *yïğač* 'tree', *ēm*, and *yem* alternately 'medicine'; *ïğla* ~ *yïğla* 'to cry', *ïr* ~ *yir* 'song, music'; *inčka* ~ *yinčhe* 'fine'.

In some of the modern Turkish languages the aforesaid underwent the same development: Chuw. *yal* 'village', Gen. Turk. *el*; Chuw. *yāva* 'nest', Gen. Turk. *uva*, *yuva*; Chuw. *yivəś*, *yāvās*, Gen. Turk. *ağač*.

In Karachay and Gagaus a *y-* occurs in front of palatal vowels. Examples: Kar. *yešik* 'door', Gen. Turk. *ešik* 'doorstep'; Kar. *yögüz* 'ox', Gen. Turk. *ögüz*; Kar. *yüč* 'three', Gen. Turk *üč*; Gag. *yem* 'to suck', Old. Turk. *em*.

However, *č* in intervocal position changed to *s* in Yakut, Bashkirian and Hakas languages, changed to *ś* in Chuwash, to *š* in Kipchak and to *ǰ* in the Oguz languages. Examples: *ačiğ* 'bitter': Old-Turk. Uig. Kāšğ. *ačiğ,* Osm Aserb. *aǰi*, Turkm. *āǰi*; Tat. *āča*, Bashk. *asï*, Kirg. *ačun*, Kum. *ačū*, KKalp. Nog. *aššï,* Kaz. *ašči*, *ašši* Usb. *ăči,* Chin. Turki (modern Uigur) *ačïğ*, Alt. *ačïn-* 'to become bitter', Yak. *ahī* < *asī*, Chuw. *jüśa.*

Mainly in the Oguz languages, but occasionally also in some other languages, one can trace a *č* ~ *ǰ* alternation. Examples: *očak* ~ *oǰak* 'furnace, oven', *geče geǰe* 'night'; *agač* ~ *agaǰa* 'tree' in the latter case in dative case. Osm. Turk *güz* 'eye', Chu. *koś* in dative case *koža*. Osm. Turk *öč* 'three', Koib. *us* or *utar* in the sense of 'all the three'.

In front of other consonants *č* changes to *s* in Osman, Aserbaijani and in Turki languages. Examples: *gečti* 'passed trough' changes in Osman to *gešti, kačdi* 'ran' changes in Osman to *kašti.*

. The final -*č* changes to -*s* in Hakas, Yakut and Baskirian, to -*ś* in Chuwash, and in some of the Kipchak languages to -*š*. Examples: *ač* 'to open': Uig. *ač*, Oguz *ač*, Tat. Kirg. *ač*, Bashk. *as*, Kas. KKalp. Nog. *aš*, Uig. *ač*, Usb. *oč*, Alt. *ač*, Hak. *as*.

The *h* sound disappears in some of the dialects. Examples: Osm. *siya* 'black' from *siyah*, Osm. *kave* 'coffee' from *kahve*.

Among the affricates *č* existed in Proto-Turkish. The initial *č-* has different correlations: in Hakas, Yakut and Bashkirian *s*, Chuwash *ś*, and it sometimes changes in Kasak, Tuvai, Sor to *š*. Examples: *ca* 'to beat': Kāšğ KB *čap-*, Oguz *čap-*, Tat. *čab-*, Bashk. *šab-*, Kaz. *šap-*, Turki *čap-*, Usb. *čop-*, Alt. *čab-*, Hak. *sap-*, Sor *šap-*, Chuw. *śup*.

In Karachay the *č* sometimes becomes aspirated *č*; in some of the other languages like Balkar, Karaim, Misher and Toba *č* becomes a double consonant *ts*, in the Soyot language *č* becomes palatalized like: from *čekmen* 'a kind of dress' to *t'epken*.

Loan-words which originally began with *č* entered the Hungarian language in different periods. Accordingly some of the loan-words start with *č-* (which is transcribed in Hungarian with *cs*) as in the words: *csalán* 'nettle', *csat* 'clasp, snap', *csipa* 'gum'. In other phonetic positions, in the middle of the word, and as a final, *č* changes to *š* (which is written in Hungarian with *s*): as in the words *késik* 'is late', *kis* 'small', *kos* 'ram', *kőris* 'ash', *borsó* 'pea', *koporsó* 'coffin'. Probably the Hungarian correlation is connected with a stage of Old Chuwash *č* > *ś* development.

Old Turkish kept the Proto-Turkish *č* in the intervocal position.

The palato-alveolar voiced spirant *ǰ* did not exist in Proto-Turkish. In the monuments of Old Turkish and Uigur languages it has no marking, the marking of this sound is not homogeneous even in the monuments in Arabic script. However, the monuments of Brahmi script have two different marks for denoting *č* and *ǰ* separately. In many loan-words of Arabic and Persian origin, we find *ǰ*: like *ǰende* 'ragged, tattered' from Persian, *ǰale* 'poet' from Persian and so on. Instead of initial *y*, *ǰ* often appears in the Kipchak languages and in Turki.

Nasal sounds existed in Proto-Turkish language. The *m* sound at the end of the word and in the middle of the word remained unchanged, but it alternates with *b-* in an initial position in many words: *men* ~ *ben* 'I', *mun* ~ *bun* 'sorrow'.

The dental nasal sound *n-* does not usually occur in an initial position except for the interrogative word *ne* 'what' or in words where *n-* is of secondary origin. However we can find *n-* in some loan-words like *nahire* 'the first day of the lunar month' (of Arabic origin), *nağme* 'tune, song' (of Arabic origin), *nahemvar* 'unequal, uneven' and so on. The *-n-* remains in the middle of the word or in a final position. The only exception is Chuwash language where *-m̃* correlates to general Turkish word-ending *-n*. Examples: *san* 'to count': Old Turkish monuments, Uigur, Osm., Turkm., Kipch., Turki Alt. *san-*, Bashk. *han-*, Usb. *son-*, Aserb. *say-sana-*, Chuw. *sum*.

Some of the Hungarian loan-words coming from Turkish show the same rule of change as the Chuwash language. Such words are: Hung. *gyom* 'weed', Gen. Turk. *yon*, Chuw. *śum*, Hung. *szám* 'number', Gen. Turk. *san-*, Chuw. *sum*.

The *-n* sound especially in *-nč-* group of consonants drops usually in Yakut, and in some dialects. Examples: *sanč-* 'to pierce, to thrust': Kašğ Uig. *sanč-*, Bar. *cac*, Alt. *sas-*, Hak. *čač-*, Sor *šaš-*, Yak. *as-*.

Gen. Turk. *birinč* 'first', Yak. *biris*.

Gen. Turk. *üčünč* 'third', Yak. *üsüs*.

Gen. Turk. *bilen* 'with', dial. *bile*, *ile*.

In the Proto-Altaic language most probably there was a palatalized *n'* sound. In the Runic monuments on the banks of the Orkhon river, in the monuments near the Yenisey river and in some early Manicheic monuments besides the letters denoting *n* and *y* there is a third letter which denotes *m'* sound. In certain words one can find the mark denoting this sound plus the sign of the *y* sound. On the basis of this fact A. von Gabain distinguished two main Uigur dialects the *n'* and *y* dialects. Some examples for the two dialects: *an̈ïğ* ~ *ayïğ* 'evil, wicked'; *ciğan̈* ~ *ciğay* 'poor'; *kön'* ~ *köy* 'to flame'; *qon'* ~ *qoy* 'sheep'.

The *n* dialect has *-ta*, *-da* not only in the locative but also in the ablative. The *y* dialect has *-tan*, *-dan* in the ablative.

The text of the Uigur Suvarṇaprabhāsa-sūtra belongs to the *y-* dialect

The sound of the old *n'* dialect remained only in Yakut and in some Misher words. In the other Turkish languages the corresponding words have *n* or *y* sounds.

The Old Turkish *n* sound occurs only in the middle of the word or in a final position. In the middle of the word it changes in Osman-Turkish and Aserbaijani to *n* or in some cases to *m*. In Chuwash *n* also changes to *m* or *n*. Examples: *teniz* 'sea': Kašğ KB *teniz*, Osman-Turk. Aserb. *deniz*, Turkm. *deniz*, Tat. Bashk. *dinez*, Kaz. *teniz*, Kirg. *deniz*, Balk. Karach. *tenniz*, Usb. *dengiz*, Turki *tengiz*, Alt. *tenis*, Yak. Chuw. *tinəs*.

In Chuwash, Aserbaijani and Osman-Turkish the process of change from *n* to *ṁ* or *n* is comparatively recent. The old Hungarian loan-words from Chuwash show the earlier stage of development, for instance: Hung. *tenger* 'sea' < Old-Chuw. *tener*. The Arabic script still showed the *n* sound, but the more recent group of Hungarian loan-words from the sixteenth and seventeenth centuries showed *m* or *n* in place of *n*.

The *n* underwent other changes in some cases, *n* > *y*, *n* > *w*, *n* > *m*. Examples: *sönjük* 'bone': Uig. Kašğ. *sönük*, Osm. Azerb. *sömük*, Turkm. *sünk*, Tat. *söyak*, *söyek*, Bashk. *koyak*, Kas. Kkalp. Nog. *süyek*, Kirg. *söök*, Kar. *süwāk*, Usb. *suyak*, Turki *sunek*, Alt. Hak. *söök*, *sök*, Yak. *unuoχ*, Chuw. *šāmādial*. *šānā*.

The *n* > *g* change occurs in some suffixes: *sünükig* ~ *sünükün* 'your bone'.

The final *-n* remained everwhere, except in Osman, Chuwash, Hakas and Karai where it changed to *-n* or *n'*. Examples: *min* 'thousand': Osm. *bin*, Kar. *miṅ*, Chuw. *pin*, Hak. *mun'*.

In all the other languages the final *n* remained *n*. Similarly to the palatalized *n'* sound there might have existed a palatalized *n'* sound. It does not have a separate mark but in some words there is an alternate *n* ~ *y* change and this shows the possibility of the existence of a palatalized *n'* sound. Examples: *münüz* 'horn': Uig. *münüz*, *müğüz*, *müyüz*, Kāšğ. *münüz*, Chag. *bünüz* ~ *mügüz*, Osm. *boynuz*, Aserb. *buynuz*, Turkm. *buynuz* ~ *buynïz*, Tat. *mögez*, Bashk. *nögoδ*, Kaz. Kkalp. Nog. *müyiz*, Kirg. *müyüz*, Kar. *muvuz*, Usb. *muguz*, Turki *munuz*, Alt. Hak. Sor *müs*, Yak. *muos*, Chuw. *māyra*, *myraaa*.

Initial *l-* did not exist originally in the Turkish languages. In modern Turkish languages, however, there is an initial *l-* sound but it came to existence either in a secondary way, in the way of dropping the first syllable of the word. For example: Osm. *lar-* 'to sit' < *olur-* < *toltur-*. The reverse trend can also be seen in Turkish languages when an extra vowel appears in the front of *l-* in loan-words, as in: Osm. *limon* becomes in some languages *ilimon*, it is a loan-word from Italian. Osm. *lazim* 'necessary, requisite' becomes in some languages *ilâzim*. It is a loan-word from Arabic.

The *l* in the middle of the word remains. However in some cases the *l* dropped out. Mostly it happened in front of other consonants, very often in Chuwash and in the Khipchak languages. Examples: Gen. Turk. *al* 'to take, to get, to procure', Chuw. *izε*~ *alsa*; Gen. Turk. *kelgen* 'coming' Tat. *kigan*.

The *-l-* changed in some languages to *d* and *t* as the first sound of a suffix: Aserb. *därsdär-*, Osm. *därslär* 'lesson, class, lecture', Aserb. *išdär*, Osm. *išlär* 'work, service, affair'; Aserb. *gözdär*, Osm. *gözlär* 'eyes'.

The same process took place in Altayan, Hakas, Bashkirian and Yakut. Examples: Bashk. *billimdär* 'sciences', Osm. *bilimlar*; Kas. *andar* 'they', Osm. *onlar*.

The trilled *r* sound did not exist originally in the Proto-Turkish words as an initial sound. It developed in a secondary way by dropping the initial vowel as in Balk. *ra-* 'to move away' from *ïra-*. Otherwise we find initial *r-s* in loan-words, as in: *reng* 'colour, hue' (from Persian), *resen* 'cord, rope' (from Arabic), *rind* 'jolly, unconventional, humorous' (from Persian) and so on. In many loan-words there is an epenthetic vowel in front of *r*. These loan-words may have a literary variant without the epenthetic sound, for instance: *Rum* 'Rome' in colloquial use *Urum*, *rub* 'quarter' (from Arabic) in colloquial use *urup*.

In the middle of the word Proto-Turkish *r* usually remains. In some cases, mainly in consonant groups, it sometimes drops, as in Osman-Turkish, Aserbaijani, Bashkirian, Tatar, Yakut and Turki. Examples: Kar. *bolumu*, Osm. *bolur-mu* 'is it'?

Yak. *otto*, Osm. *orta* 'the middle of something'.

Turki *kigur*, Osm. *kirgür-* 'to introduce'.

In a final position *-r* remains. However, in some cases it might also drop, or change to *-l*. Examples: Aserb. *olulla*, Osm. *olurlar* 'are'. Aserb. Kum. *inǰil* 'quick', Osm. *inǰir*.

The Proto-Turkish vowel system presumably contained nine vowels: *a*, *ï*, *o*, *u*, *ä*, *i*, *ö*, *ü* and *e* and their long equivalents. Among the different groups of Turkish languages the Oguz languages kept the old Proto-Turkish vowel system most faithfully. Osman-Turkish and Aserbaijani preserved all the vowels but not their long equivalents. Turkmenian retained not only the nine vowels but also their long equivalents.

We do not have the same amount of information about the process of vowel changes as about consonant changes. The main reason for this is that the old scripts, especially the Arabic, were not consequent in marking vowels. The most reliable monuments in this respect are those in Brahmi and Uigur scripts. The monuments in Uigur script often do not reflect the short vowel, but usually are very exact in marking the long vowel. The monuments in Uigur script usually mark the long vowel by doubling the sign of the sound. Examples: Suvarṇaprabhāsa-sūtra 617[3] *yīl*, *yēl* 'wind'. Suvarṇaprabhāsa-sūtra 624[16] *ōt* 'fire'.

Among the modern Turkish languages only Turkmenian and Yakut keep the original length of vowels. In some other languages there are also traces of the original length of the vowels. For instance in Osman-Turkish there are a great number of words which are homonyms in the modern language but had alternately long and short vowels in Proto-Turkish. Examples: (in the examples the original short and long vowels are marked). *āt* 'name' ~ *at* 'horse', *āč* 'to be hungry' ~ *ač-* 'to open', *bār* 'there is' ~ *bar-* 'to go', *bāš* 'wound' ~ *baš* 'head', *kōk* 'blue' ~ *kok* 'root', *ōt* 'fire' ~ *ot* 'grass', *tāš* 'stone' ~ *taš* 'exterior'.

Some examples for the modern Turkish equivalents: *āt* 'name': Kāšǧ. *āt*, Osm. *at*, *adï* 'his name', Aserb. *ad*, Turkm. *aat*, Tat. Bashk. Kirg. Alt. Turki Hak. *at*, Usb. *ot*, Yak. *aat*, Chuw. *yat*.

at 'horse': Osm. *at*, *atï* 'his horse', Aserb. Turkm. Tat. Bashk. Kirg. Kas. Turki Hak. *at*, Usb. *ot*, Yak. *at*, Chuw. *ut*.

Vowel harmony is a significant feature of the Ural-Altaic and Altaic languages. In all these languages the assimilation of vowels is progressive: the endings adjust to the vowels of the basic word. In Old Turkish and in Uigur originally there were three pairs of suffixes: *a* ~ *e*, *ï* ~ *i* and *u* ~ *ü*. (It did not have an *o* ~ *ö* suffix because *o* and *ö* were present originally only in the first syllable of the word). These pairs of suffixes gave scope for a palatal and velar assimilation of suffixes. Examples:

1. *a* ~ *e* *-lar* ~ *-ler*, *-da* ~ *-de* *bašda* 'in the head', *yïšda* 'in the forest', *ebde* 'in the house', *közde* 'in the eye' (the suffixes of plural number, and the suffix of locative).

2. *ï* ~ *i* *-tï* ~ *ti* (the suffix of past tense), *aldï* 'took', *geldi* 'came', *öldi* 'died'
-čï ~ *-či* (suffix expressing profession) *balïkčï* 'fisherman', *eskici* 'rag-and-bone man'.

3. *u* ~ *ü* *-duk* ~ *dük* the suffix of participial past tense *barduk* 'went', *tegdük* 'reached', *bertük* 'gave'.

Originally the suffixes had only two alternate versions, and existed in the use of palatal and velar assimilation of suffixes. After some time there emerged labial and illabial suffixes in most of the Turkish languages and this enriched further the scope of assimilation. Labial and illabial suffixes were not present in all the languages and not in all types of suffixes.

1. The *a* ~ *e* suffix is preserved in most of the Turkish languages in its original shape. However, in Yakut and Kasak the same group of suffixes containing *-a-* and *-e-* sounds also took the suffix containing the labial sound *-o-*. Examples: Kas. *bašta* 'in the head', Kas. *žigitte* 'with the boy', Kas. *köldö* 'in the lake'.

2. To the illabial type of suffixes containing *-ï-* and *-i-*, a further *-ü-*, *-u-* type was added, containing labial sounds.

3. To the type of suffixes containing labial *-u-* *-ü-* suffixes were added containing *-ï-* and *-i-* illabial vowels. Thus in both the last two groups of suffixes all together four types of suffixes had developed providing the possibility in almost all the Turkish languages not only for palatal and velar, but also for labial and illabial assimilation of suffixes. The four forms of assimilation took their final shape in about the 18th century. However, the Arabic script does not reflect this change. The aforesaid four forms of assimilation do not exist in Turkmanian, Nogay, Usbek, Turki, Altayan and Chuwash.

Vowel harmony is a very strong feature of the Turkish languages. However, there are some examples which do not show harmony. In Osman-Turkish, there exist exceptions from the rule of vowel harmony in words of Arabic and Persian origin, like: *asker* 'soldier, army' from Arabic, *vüǰud* 'body' from Arabic, *višak* 'handsome slave' from Persian. In Usbek exceptions came into existence under the influence of Tadjik language, in Aserbaijani under the influence of Persian, in Karaim and Gagaus languages the exceptions came about under the influence of Slavonic languages.

Among the changes in vowels there are some older and some newer trends such as the addition of a vowel usually *ï-* or *i-* in front of *l* and *r*. Here some examples may be cited: *limon* ~ *ilimon* 'lemon', the alternate use of coll. *Urum* and *Rum* 'Rome', in case of loan-words. A vowel is usually added to avoid the combination of too many consonants. It is often added in the case of loan-words, like: Russ. *stakan* 'glass' ~ Tat. *istakan*, Russ. *krest* 'cross' ~ Tat. *kires*. In the middle of a word vowels are added to avoid combinations of consonants, like: Ar. *waqt* 'time': Osm. *vakït*, Tat. *vakət*, Chuw. *vəχət*.

Dropping of vowels is also a typical tendency in the Turkish languages. Examples: Tat. *vokla-* 'to sleep' < *+uyukla-*, Crim. Tat. *sitmä* 'fever' < *+isitmä*, Osm. *Stanbul* < *Istanbul*.

In the middle of the word unstressed vowel sometimes drops. In Uigur we find a number of examples for this trend: Uig. *oğur* 'occasion', *oğrïnta* 'at that occasion'. Many times the Mongolian words which are of common Altaic origin kept a vowel at the end of a word. It seems that Mongolian, in these cases, kept the original final vowel while the Turkish languages dropped it. Examples: Mong. *köke* 'blue, Gen. Turk. *kök*; Mong. *konu* 'to put', Gen. Turk. *kon-*; Mong. *baraga* 'speciality', Uig. *bark*.

In the case of haplology a whole syllable drops. This tendency existed already in Uigur, like: Uigur. *sürči* 'shepherd' *sürügči*, Uigur. *ärkän* 'being' *+äzürkän*. The changes were observed only in comparison with modern developments.

Though there are a number of monuments, they do not give much scope for following the developments of vowel changes. In the monuments of Runic script there is one mark denoting *o* and *u*, one mark for denoting *ö* and *ü*, and one for denoting *ï* and *i*. It has a special mark for *e*. As regards the consonants, the different kinds of *s*, *ś* and *š* cannot be recognized very easily in the Orkhon inscriptions. There are marks for consonant groups: *nč*, *nt*, and *it*.

In the Uigur script there is no difference in marking *b* and *p*, *k* and *g*, *s* and *š*. The later monuments do not mark difference between *q*, *ğ* and *χ*. In Brahmi script the signs for *n* and *t*, and of *ğ* and *v* are very similar to each other.

6b. The formation of Uigur literature

The term literature comprises here records of oral tradition and written documents. From the historical point of view the history of Turkish literature is divided into three main periods: the pre-Islamic, Islamic and modern. These terms correspond more to cultural cycles than to actual chronological periods. All Turkish literary manifestations generally covered these periods except isolated episodes like the Codex Cumanicus[22] or during more ancient times, the literature of the

[22]G Györffy, *Autour du Codex Cumanicus* (in French: The author of the Codex Cumanicus), Budapest 1942.

Qaraim Turks[23], who professed Jewish religion and used Hebrew characters, or the literature of the Turkish speaking Armenians in Armenian characters[24]. Some Turkish people, who did not profess the Islamic religion, produced written literature only in recent times.

The greatest collection of Old Turkish manuscripts and block-prints is in Berlin in possession of the German Academy of Sciences while a smaller part of it is now in Marburg/Lahn. Most of these manuscripts were brought to Berlin by the Prussian Turfan expeditions under the leadership of A. Grünwedel and A. von Le Coq from East Turkistan[25].

The Asiatic Museum in St. Petersburg also possesses a collection of finds discovered and taken to St. Petersburg by W. Radloff, S. Malov, Djakov, Klementz, Krotkov, from Turfan area, Urumchi and Su-chou (North-west China)[26]. The finds discovered by Sir Aurel Stein are kept in the British Museum in London. They originate from Tun-huang (North-West China) and Miran (in East Turkistan)[27]. In the Bibliothèque Nationale in Paris are kept the manuscripts found by P. Pelliot in Tun-huang. The ones bought by J. Hackin probably in Turfan are kept in the Bibliothèque Nationale in Paris. The Sven Hedin collection in the Ethnographic Museum at Stockholm has some pages of Old Turkish texts[28]. Huang Wen-pi brought some manuscripts to Peking, which are kept in the Academy of Nationalities. The finds of the Otani Expedition are kept in Kyoto[29]. A few pages of manuscripts are in the possession of the Ethnographic Museum in Ankara[30]. A few pictures with two or three lines of Uigur text are kept in the Stein collection of the Archeological Survey of India.

The material of the manuscripts was paper in most cases. The historical origin of paper in possession of the Turks is revealed by the origin of the word. The Old Turkish word *kağda* comes from the Persian. *kāğād* is derived from the Chinese word for paper. There are some inscriptions on poplar wood, bronze coins with some Uigur words, and pictures with short inscriptions on walls or on silk. The manuscripts were written with brush, on different types of book forms. Some books were of the European type with the European style of fastening the book. This kind of book was not well-known to the Chinese but widespread among the Sogdians and Syrians. Many kinds of big and small books in pothi format were in use. Folding books and book rolls were also well known.

The manuscripts are written in different kinds of scripts: Runic, Sogdian, Uigur, Estrangelo

[23] A. Zajanczkowski, *Die Karaimische Literatur* (in German: The Qaraim Literature), Fnd.II pp. 793-801.

[24] H. Berberian, *La Litterature Arméno-Turque* (in French: The Armenian-Turkish literature), Fnd.II pp. 809-819.

[25] A. Grünwedel, *Bericht uber archeologische Arbeiten in Idikutschari und Umgebung im Winter 1902-1903* (in German: Report on the archeological work in Idikutshari and its surroundings), A. bayr. Akad. d. Wiss. 906.

[26] A. von Gabain, *Alttürkische Schreibkultur und Druckerei* (in German: Old Turkish manuscripts and prints), Fnd. II p. 171.

[27] *Op. cit.* p. 171.

[28] *Op. cit.* p. 171.

[29] *Op. cit.* p. 171.

[30] *Op. cit.* p. 171.

(which is a mixture of Uigur and Sogdian scripts), Manicheic, Brahmi (notes in this script are found in some manuscripts), and a small number of texts in Tibetan script have also been found[31].

The most ancient period of Turkish literature is prior to the conversion of the Turks to Islam in about the 10th century. The geographical background of this literature, as mentioned above, pertains to Mongolia, the Tarim basin and North-West China. There are, clearly two distinct groups: a more ancient epigraphic literature of the pre-Islamic period, and secondly a later literature which is mainly religious pertaining to Buddhism, Manicheism and Nestorian Christianity.

The Orkhon inscriptions are the only literary testimony which has come down to us from the Kök Turk Empire from Mongolia. The existence of other literary works i. e. songs and translations, are certain. A translation of the Parinirvāṇa-sūtra and other Sūtras were made during the times of Northern Tsi dynasty, contemporary of the Kök Turk Empire[33]. The existence of myths and legends which were probably transmitted in the form of an oral tradition can be assumed. The Orkhon inscriptions, the inscriptions of Tonyuquq[34], Kül Tegin[35] and Bilgä Khagan[36], together with some other minor inscriptions (like the Sudǰi inscriptions or some of the inscriptions from the area of Yenisey river) seem to have developed from primitive funeral texts, where it apparently seems as if the deceased is talking in the first person. They are considered as literary documents notable for their variety of content and form with the epic narration prevailing, with the celebration of personalities to whom the monuments are dedicated. They (Tonyugug Bilgä Khagan and Kūi Tegin) are regarded as heroes fighting for an ethico-political ideal: the power and the prosperity of the Turkish people. This ideal is displayed in the inscriptions. It was not only the aim of the hero but it was also the aim of the cosmic order intended by the deities of the cosmic pantheon. In all the three main epigraphic texts devoted to the above-mentioned three personalities the subordination of the historic graphic and oratorical element to the epic is evident. Important historical events like, the military expedition to Sogdiana or the battle of Ming Sha which are emphasized by Chinese sources as very important historical events, are put on the same level as other minor military adventures[36]. Particulars of the historical narration, which are rare, have the function of underlining the difficulty of the action and thus put a stress on the physical energy invested in it. The attention is drawn to the figure of the hero, the horse ridden by him, the wounds inflicted on him, and the enemies killed by him. The quarrels and discussions are dramatically represented. The most important teaching, that is spiritual testament of the inscriptions, is the integrity of nomad spirit in defending national sovereignty against the enticements of sedentary life[37].

---

[31]DTSI p. 290, PDTP p. 392, EUT p. 102.
[32]A. von Gabain, *op. cit.* pp. 172-176.
[33]Liu Mau Tsai p. 461.
[34]PDTP pp. 56-70.
[35]PDTP pp. 19-43.
[36]PDTP p. 27, 33, 43.
[37]PDTP p. 56, 61, 69.

The style of the inscriptions shows features which seem to be related to a strictly Turkish tradition. The same tradition remained alive and vital in the course of centuries in the oral and partly in the written tradition. Its style seems to draw attention to single concrete facts, with a remarkable variety of verbal forms. One can observe this from the idiomatic phrases of a descriptive character, or from the actual and concrete figures of speech expressing abstract figures, often repeated, as it is in epic language. For example: *ärur barur*[38] 'who comes and goes', represents the concepts of 'liberty'. *adaq qamšatti*[39] 'shook their feet' means 'rebellion'. *közi yogaru körti* 'their eyes rose' means 'relief'. *ičrä ašïz tašra tonsuz*[40] 'inside sober outside naked' means 'poverty'. *tün udïmadïm küntüz olurmadim*[41] 'at night I did not sleep, at day I did not sit down, 'untiring work'.

The images have form of similes: *otča borča kälti* 'he came like fire and storm'. *örtče qïzïp kälti*[42] 'he came flaming like fire'. *yagïmïz tägrä učuq täg ärti*[43] 'our enemy around seemed as if they were flying away'. *qanin subča yügürti sünükün tagča yatti*[44] "your blood flowed like a river, your bones lay like mountains".

A proverbial saying reflects the wisdom of Tonyuguq, which says that it is difficult to judge from afar as it is difficult to distinguish a fat bull from a lean one at a distance. Synonymic tautologies are noted in the inscriptions with nouns and verbs, for instance: *iš / küč*[45] 'work', *qut / ülüg*[46] 'fortune', *öl- / yit-*[47] to perish'. *ämgät- / tolğat-* 'to afflict', *sïgta-/ yogla-* 'to bewail'. *ičik- / yükün-* 'to submit', *tut- / it-* 'to put in order'. *it- / yarat-* 'to organize', etc.

Expressions with alliteration are worth noting: *yabiz yablaq*[48] 'contemptuous', *yadaqïn yalïnïn*[49] 'on foot naked'.

A prominent feature of the style is the parallelism with repetition of a smaller or larger part of the sentence with the variation of a few words only. The parallelism has often the function of giving persuasiveness and solemnity to the discourse thus representing an element of the epic style, which is also observed in Mongolian epic poetry. The following examples can be distinguished:

1. synonymic parallelism:

ädgüti äsidi, qatïgdï tinlä 'listen well'
qutum bar üčün, ülügüm bar üčün 'because I am fortunate'
yanduru saqïndim, qatiqdi saqïndim[50] 'I grieved very much'.

[38]PDTP p. 25, 32, 41.
[39]PDTP p. 26, 33, 42.
[40]PDTP p. 24, 31, 39.
[41]PDTP p. 56, 61, 65.
[42]PDTP p. 59, 63, 69.
[43]PDTP p. 57, 61, 65.
[44]PDTP p. 23, 31, 39.
[45]PDTP p. 22, 29, 35.
[46]PDTP p. 24, 31, 40.
[47]PDTP p. 24, 31, 40.
[48]PDTP p. 24, 31, 40.
[49]PDTP p. 24, 31, 40.
[50]PDTP p. 27, 33, 43.

2. antithetic parallelism:

üzä kök tänri, asra yağïz yir[51] 'above the blue sky, below the grey earth'

ïraq ärsär yablaq aği birur, yaguq ärsär ädgü aği birür[52] 'when he is far away he gives bad presents, when he is near he gives good presents'.

3. enumerative parallelism:

inisi ičisintäg qïlïnmadïq ärinč, oğli qanintäg qilinmaduq ärinč[53] 'the younger brothers had not been created like the older brothers, the sons had not been created like fathers'.

bäglig uri oglun qul boldi, silik qiz oglun kün boldi[54] 'your noble son became a slave, your pure daughter became a slave'.

4. parallelism with variations:

sabi süčig, ağïsï yimšaq ärmis[55] "his words were sweet, his presents were nice"

öltäči budunug tirgürü igitim yalin budunug tonlug bay qildim, az budunug üküš qïltim[56] 'I reanimated and restored the people who were going to perish. I clad the naked people, I made the poor people rich, I made numerous the few people'.

The researches of R. Jacobson and others have made it clear that in the frequent parallelisms a search for rhythmical formulas is inherent. The symmetrical structure of the two cola and the homoteleuta are elements which represent a direction towards poetic forms. In some cases a parallelism of caesuras within two cola is noted, in particular in two examples it is noted that a formula 4 + 3 is repeated which appears later as a regular metrical scheme: 1. *körür közüm körmäz tag/bilir bilgim bilmäz täg* 'my eye which saw as if it did not see/my knowledge which knew as if it did not know'. 2. *qizil qanïm tüketi/ qara tärim yügürti* 'my red blood was exhausted, my black sweat was shed'.

To this group of monuments written in the Runic script belong some archaic books of fortune-telling. One of them was translated from I-tsing[57]. This book of divination is full of parallelisms and has rhymes at the end of lines. This divination book, though a translation, has all the features of original Turkish poetry.

Another especially archaic divination book gives a great amount of information about the beliefs of nomad Turks[58]. The main subjects of divination in this book are cosmic powers, demons, the power for ruling the community and mercantile interests. The demand occurs three times: *yirkä tngrikä sevinč tut* 'give sacrifice to the earth and the sky'.

---

[51]PDTP p. 21, 26, 36.
[52]PDTP p. 21, 28, 34.
[53]PDTP p. 21, 29, 36.
[54]PDTP p. 21, 28, 37.
[55]PDTP p. 18, 28, 34.
[56]PDTP p. 18, 28, 34.
[57]W. Bang & A. von Gabain, *Bruchstucke eines Wahrsagebuches.*
[58]PDTP pp. 80-92.

An example for the style of the divination book[59]:

üzä tuman turdï	There above stood the fog
asra toz turdï	Underneath lay the dust
quš oğli uča aztï	The nestling flew away
kiyik oğli yügürü aztï	The cub ran away
kiši oğli yoriyu aztï	The man's young ran away
yana	Then:
tngri gutïnğa	From the grace of the sky
üčünč yïlta	In the third year
qop äsän tükäl kärüšmiš	Everything became very good
qop ögirär säbinur	Everything is happy and glad
tir	That means:
iňcä bilinglar	Be aware:
ädgü ol	It is all good.

In the above cited part of the divination book we first find antithetic parallelism, and then enumerative parallelism. Regular verbal rhymes occur at the end of the lines. The later divination books belong to Buddhism and there is also one divination book used by Christians.

Another important genre of the oral tradition is the songs preserved in collections of narrative texts. These songs have stanzas consisting of four lines, where the beginning of each line alliterates with the next one in the body of a stanza. Each line of the stanzas has 7-10 syllables, and after the fourth syllable there is usually a caesura. The same kind of songs were popular among the Turkish peoples and are retained orally even today. Besides love-songs and dirges, tales and stories were also popular, and these had more religious connotations.

Most of the Buddhist, Manicheist and Christian literature was translated from various languages and was more intended for religious than artistic purposes. However the religious hymns suggest love songs, typical for instance is the poem of Manicheist origin which is a song of a person called Aprin Čur Tigin. The expressions used in this poem, and *qašï körtläm* 'my beloved one with the beautiful brows', *közi qaram* 'my beloved one with the black eyes' although, *yaruq tenrilar* 'bright gods', and *küčlüg brištilar* 'strong angels' are invoked[60].

Though Manicheism was a short-lived religion among the Uigurs, which started in the 8th century, it was popular mainly among the Turks living in the area of Kashgar and Talas, but what is surprising is that the number of texts is very large. Unfortunately only fragments have been left behind by the Turkish Manicheists. It is important to mention in connection with Manicheism that it was considerably influenced by Buddhism and Christianity and they took over many elements from the earlier Persian Mithra cult. In one of the Manicheist confessions there is the mention of sin

---

[59] PDTP p. 81, 86.

[60] ZDMG 1925 pp.261-267.

which would be to harm the place of the Buddha, the Śākyamuni (*azu vχ'da šakimun burχan yirin artatđim ärsä*).[61]

The **Manicheist texts** might be classified into the following genres:

1. Stories and tales which are called by the word *azant, azand*[62]. The Manicheists explained prayers through stories and this led to the popularization of parables. Sometimes original Buddhist tales were included in Manicheist collection of tales.

2. Prayers and hymns The word in Uigur for hymn is *küd* or *baš, bašta, bašik* which could be connected with the Middle-Iranian word *bašah* 'hymnus'. A long hymn of Mani (TT III)[63] is composed of 123 quatrains according to the editors but not all are preserved. The lines of each quatrain begin with the same vowel, or with the same consonant and vowel (without distinguishing between *o/ö* and *u/ü*). In some quatrains all lines of groups of two or three lines show a rhyme of a grammatical type produced by the final syllables *-tiniz*. This ending is the second person plural of the past tense. The individual lines do not comply with definite schemes, the number of syllables varies from 7 to 15. The same irregularities in the number of the syllables of each line occur in the two *küg* of Aprin Čor already mentioned (p. 49).

Two short hymns dedicated in Persian to the "Goddess of Morning" and to *bag rōšan zāwar zīrīft* "God light force wisdom" do not represent the defined schemes.

3. Textbooks were written in the form of questions and answers: the questions of the student *titsi* and the answers of the teacher *ǧošti*. Some fragments in the same form of questions and answers describe the characteristic features of a great man, another one the features of a wise man, actually of the Buddha, as he is called in the text the mahāpuruṣa[64]. This is also a formal borrowing from Buddhism. The lakṣaṇas or thirtytwo physical signs, are described in the same way as in the Buddhist texts.

4. As in Buddhism, confessions were well-known to the Manicheists. The most popular confession-prayer was the *Chuastuanift*, which has one manuscript in London and one at St. Petersburg.

There are four fragments of Christian origin. The biggest of them was published by W. Bang, a passion of St. George[65]. As A. Gabain mentions it, Latin and other sources of this text were set forth. It is similar to a Buddhist text in certain features: as in invocation and in formulation.

1. In **Buddhist literature** a very popular genre was the stories. The stories usually had a moral teaching which expressed the ethical standards of Buddhism. Besides stories of Indian origin, there

---

[61] A. von Le Coq, *Chuastuanift ein Sündenbekentniss der manichäischen Auditores* (in German: Chuastuanift a confession-prayer of the Manicheist believers), ABAW 1910. W. Radloff, *Chuastuanift ein Bussgebät der Manichäer* (in German: Chuastuanift, a confession-prayer of the Manicheists), Petersburg 1909.

[62] A. von Gabain, Fnd II p.231.

[63] W.Bang & A. von Gabain, *Der grosse Hymnus auf Mani* (in German: Mani's Great Hymn), TT III, 1930.

[64] TT VIII.

[65] W. Bang, *Türkische Bruchstücke einer nestorianischen Georgs-passion* (in German: Turkish fragments of a Nestorian Georg-passion), Muséon 1926 pp. 41-75.

are stories of Sogdian, Śaka and Turkish origin. The Daśa-karma-buddhāvadāna[66] is a translation from the Tochar *(Toχri)* language, but it is not mentioned whether it originally came from Chinese or Sanskrit. The frame story is set in the form of questions of a student and the answers of the teacher. As can be seen from the wall-paintings published by A. Grünwedel, A. Gabain, E. Esin from Turfan the stories were often performed.

Turkish Buddhist literature has an immense amount of Jātaka tales and some Pañcatantra stories, which unfortunately are very fragmentary. Most of the stories reached Turkish literature through the avadānas from Chinese, though the origin of many is not known. Among the texts of the Uigurica there is a story about the elephant who lets himself be shot by a hunter. The hunter's dress suggests the dress of the coming Maitreya. Without showing his anger (because showing anger is one of the three main sins) he allows his six tusks to be taken out. In the sky the Gods contemplate about why the elephant showed such great qualities: did he want to have Brahmā's or Indra's throne? Unfortunately the fragment is unfinished.

Another story from the third volume of the Uigurica narrates the story of a king who was born from a tigress and a man and became a man-eater. He became tame after a king who kept his word and went to him in order to be eaten up by him. As he told him the name of Buddha, the man-eater started learning about the cause of all things[67].

The second volume of the Uigurica[68] has a story about Buddha's fight against the Yaksa Āṭavaka. Āṭavaka was a man-eater whom Buddha convinced through his magic powers, and thereby put him on the right path. Another story published in the same book describes the kidnapping of the daughter of a Yakṣa by Arjuna. This tale probably originated from Brahmanical tales.

A story from the fourth volume of Uigurica narrates the Hare'jātaka, about the craving of a hare and his friends[69] for good. The *Tišastvustik* (the Diśā-svāstika-sūtra) published by W. Radloff has notes in Brahmi script. It narrates the story of Buddha meeting the merchants Trapuṣa and Bhallika[70]. The text also incorporates a magic formula for defending travelling merchants. Kubera is mentioned in the text as the guardian deity of Khotan. Several times tales are incorporated in the Sūtras, like the story of the Hungry Tigress in the Suvarṇaprabhāsa-sūtra.

A relatively late Pañcatantra story is that of Kalyāṇaṃkara and Pāpaṃkara[71]. It seems that the

---

[66]As quoted by A. von Gabain, Fnd II p.222.

[67]F.W.K. Mueller, Uigurica III, ABAW 1922.

[68]F.W.K. Mueller, Uigurica II, ABAW 1910.

[69] F.W.K. Mueller, *Uigurica IV,* SBAW Berlin 1931 pp. 675-727.

[70]This text is discussed later among the works of Sūtra literature. Here it is mentioned in reference to the story it incorporates.

[71]E. Chavannes, *La version ouigoure de l'histoire des princes Kalyāṇaṃkara et Pāpaṃkara* (in French: The Uigur version of the story of the Princes Kalyāṇaṃkara and Pāpaṃkara), *Toung Pao* 1914 pp. 492-494. J.R. Hamilton, *Le cont bouddhique du Bon et du Mauvais Prince et version ouigour* (in French: A Buddhist story of the Good and Bad Prince in the Uigur version), Paris 1971. P. Zieme, *Ein uigurisches Turfan-Fragment der Erzahlung vom guten und vom bosen Prinzen* (in German: An Uigur Turfan fragment of the Good and Bad Princes), AOH 1974 pp. 263-269.

Uigur version of this story originated from Tibetan.

The *Maitrisimit* is an important story of Turkish Buddhist collection of tales. It was enacted in ancient times. It is a text of the Vaibhāśika school, which describes the life of Bodhisattva Maitreya. The text was published many times but it was first published fully by S. Tekin in 1960. It used to be performed as a drama.

2. Confession prayers *kšantis* must have been used by the monks and nuns, however not many of them are extant. The reason for the lack of confession prayers could be that some of the texts were not translated into Uigur and were recited in Sanskrit as they were not meant for lay people.

A well-known confession prayer is the *Kšanti qilğuluq nom* which is a translation of the Chinese *Ts'u-pei-tao-ch'ang ch'an-fa,* which was already translated into Chinese in the second century AD by a monk called An Shih-kao from Bukhara.

3. Magic texts like *Sarva-durgati-pariśodhana-uṣṇīṣavijayā-dhāraṇī* or the *Sitātapatrā-dhāraṇī* represent another group of Uigur literature. F. W.K. Mueller published a number of Tantric texts and quite recently a few other texts have been published by G. Kara and P. Zieme in Berlin.

4. Rahmeti Arat has published a number of Budhist hymns[72]. Mostly the origin of the hymns is not clear or the texts are not available. The translations of hymns show a great deal of the specialities of Turkish poetry. Many similarities can be found between Turkish and Chinese or Turkish and Iranian, sometimes Turkish and Tibetan versification respectively. At the same time Turkish versification shows peculiarities which seem to be independent of foreign models. It is possible, as proposed by T. Kowalsky, that the basic rules of Turkish versification developed as a dichtom form from parallelisms (see examples for the types of parallelisms earlier).

The initial alliterations, which are so typical of Turkish, are not found anywhere else, except in Mongolian. They might have been influenced by Turkish poetry. Initial alliterations and rhymes can also be explained as an effect of parallelism. However the rhymes and the scheme of seven syllables with caesura seem to be an evolution of a process.

The documents of Uigur Buddhism are unfortunately very fragmentary. Only small pieces of incomplete manuscripts have been preserved. It is a difficult task to decipher, analyze and identify the fragments line by line by comparison, to bring sometimes 100 or as in the *Säkiz yükmek (Türkische Turfantexte* VI) 500 pieces into correlation[73]. Many outstanding scholars like F.W.K. Mueller, W. Radoff, S. Malov, A. von Le Coq, W. Bang, A.Gabain, R. Arat, S.Tekin, P. Zieme and G. Kara have participated in this work but still their work is not complete. On the basis of identifications achieved it seems to be evident that, however fragmentary and scattered the monuments are, they represent a wide range of literary works originating from a highly sophisticated Buddhist culture.

[72] R.R. Arat, *Eski Türk Şiiri* (in Turkish: Old Turkish poetry), Ankara 1965.

[73]A. von Gabain & G.R. Rachmati, *Das buddhistische Sūtra Sakiz Yukmak* (in German: The Buddhist Sūtra Sakiz Yukmak), TT VI SBAW 1934 pp. 93-192.

A selection of the available texts is given below which might give some idea about the various texts the Uigurs translated or re-translated. It should be mentioned, that the notion of translation as comprehended by the Turks has a wide range of works: from word to word translations to free adaptations.

In the Uigur texts usually there are two words in use for translation, one is *ävirmiš* which means translation word by word, the other is *yaratmiš* meaning a more free composition. Source languages of translations are mentioned: *änätkäk* 'Indian', *tavğač* 'Chinese', *toχri* 'Tocharian', and *tüpüt* 'Tibetan'.

The translated texts include jātakas, avadānas, tales from the Pañcatantra, sūtras, and after the 13th century tantric texts. After the discovery of the manuscript of the Suvarṇaprabhāsa-sūtra in 1909 it became clear that composition and retranslation of Uigur texts went on till about the 17th century. In the monasteries of Kansu simultaneously with the composition and translation of Tibetan, Chinese and Mongolian works the work on Uigur texts went on.

A selection of the available texts is given below.

1. *Tängrili yirlidä säkiz vükmäk yarumīš yaltïrmïš ïduqdarnï tak vip atlï sudur nom bitig*. It is supposed to be a translation of the Chinese: *Fo-shuo-pa-yang-shen-ch'ou-king* (Taisho vol. 8 pp. 1422-1425). Publ. Bibliotheca Buddhica XIV pp. 93-95; Radloff: *Altuigurische Sprachproben* pp. 68-69. The Tibetan version was partly published: Weber-Huth: *Das Buddhistische Sutra der acht Erscheinungen* (in German: The Buddhist Sutra of the eight viṣayas).

2. *Yitikän sudur nom erdini* The Great Bear Sutra. R. Rachmati, *Turkische Turfantexte* VII Nr. 12 pp. 23, Nr. 40 pp. 48-51.

3. *Tängri tängrisi burqan yarlïqamïs garba barimančanï atlï sudur nom bitiq*. Radloff, *Uigurische Sprachdenkmale* No. 102 pp. 180-186.

4. *Maitrisimit nom bitig* F.W.K. Mueller & E. Sieg, *Maitrisimit und 'Tocharisch'*, SPAW. 1916. I, 410-417, Uigurica II pp. 7-14. Ş. Tekin, *Maytrisimit, Burkancilarin mehdisi Maitreya ile buluşma uygurca iptidai bir dram,* Ankara 1976 (In Turkish: Maitreya, the Messiah of the Buddhists, a primitive drama).

5. *Saddharmapuṇḍarīka-sūtra,* translation of the 25th chapter from Chinese, which correlates to the 24th chapter of the Sanskrit version. *Uigurica II* pp. 14-20; *Türkische Turfantexte* V pp. 20-28.

6. *Kim-og-ki atli nom ärdini.* Unpublished, contains 54 lines of a poem. A version of the Vajracchedikā Prajñāpāramitā.

7. *Saṃyuktāgama Sūtra.* These pages with Chinese notes.

8. *Ari-a-rača avavadaka atli mahayan sudur.* Ārya-rājāvavādaka-mahāyāna-sūtra, Bibliotheca Buddhica Vol. XIV pp. 69-90; F.W.K. Mueller, *'Toχri und Kuišan'* in SPAW 1918 I. p. 585.

9. *Aria aparimiti ayurnama mahayan sudur-a,* Uigurica II p. 51. Translated from Tibetan.

10. *Mahamayur sudur.* Mahāmāyūrī-sūtra, Bibliotheca Buddhica Vol. XII p. 95. Radloff, *Uigurische Sprachdenkmale* p. 109 no. 60.

11. *Amita ayusi sudur.* Amitāyuṣ-vyūha. Radloff, *Uigurische Sprachdenkmale* p. 148 no. 89.

12. *Tišastvustik sudur ardini.* Diśāsvāstika-sūtra. It remains an open question whether it was translated from Chinese or from a Sanskrit original. Bibliotheca Buddhica Vol. XII.

13. *Madhyamāgama-sūtra.*

14. *Altun önglük yaruq yaltrïglïq qopda kötrülmüš nom bitiq.* Suvarṇaprabhāsa-uttama-sūtra-indra-rāja. Bibliotheca Buddhica vol. XVII.

15. *Dašakramapuda avtanamal.* Daśakarmapatha avadānamālā. Published SPAW 1918 vol. I p. 583, *Uigurica* vol. IV p. 6.

16. *Kalyāṇaṃkara and Pāpaṃkara.* Pelliot, *La version ouigure de l'histoire des princes Kalyāṇaṃkara et Pāpaṃkara* (In French: The Uigur version of the history of Kalyāṇaṃkara and Pāpaṃkara) *TP.* 1914 XV pp. 225-72.

17. *Fragment from a Buddha legend.* Radloff, *Alttürkischen Studien* Vol. III p. 2.

18. *Buddhacarita* fragment Published: *U. Spr.* 198 sk. (105 sz.).

19. *Kšanti qilmag nom bitiq.* Confession prayer. *Uig.* Vol. II pp. 76-81 no. 7, *Uig.* Vol. II pp. 84-89 no. 8.

20. *Alqu ančulayu kälmiš-lär-ning usnir lakšan-lar intin Örmiš adï kötrülmiš sita-tapatra atlï utsuqma-siz darnï.* Ārya (sarva)-tathāgata-uṣṇīṣa-sitātapatra-nāma. *Uig.* II pp. 50-75 no.6; Malov, *Sitātapatrādhāraṇī,* Doklady Akademii Nauk SSSR 1930, pp. 5, 88-94.

21. *Confession Prayer.* Bang & Gabain, in the Appendix of *Uigurische Studien* 1930, pp. 208-10.

22. *Alqu ani yaviz yol-lari artuqraq uz artidaci ušnisa vičai atlidarni.* Sarva-durgati-pariśodhana-uṣṇīṣavijayā-dhāraṇī.

23. *Abhidharmakośa-śāstra.* Nanjio1269.

24. *Yogācārabhūmi-śāstra.* Nanjio 1170.

25. *Udānavarga.* Nanjio 1439, 1321, 1365, Tohoku 326, 4099.

26. *Ming közlüg ming iliglig iduq yarluqančuči köngül atlï darnï nom.* The author is Singqu Sali tutung, the translator of the Suvarṇaprabhāsa-sūtra.

27. A translation of the work by Kumārajīva into Uigur. Georg Hazai, Peter Zieme, *Fragments der uigurischen Version des 'Jin' gangjing mit den Gāthās des Meister Fu* (in German: Fragments of the Uigur version of Jing gangjing with master Fu's Gāthās).

28. Pañcatantra fragments. F. Geissler and P. Zieme, *Uigurische Pañcatantra-Fragmente* (In German: Uigur Pañcatantra fragments). *Revue d'études Turques* Vol. II, Paris 1970.

29. *Bde-mchog Mandala abhisamayā.* Georg Kara, Peter Zieme: *Fragments tantrischer Werke in Uigurischer Übersetzung* (in German: Fragments of Tantric works in Uigur translation). Berliner Turfantexte *VII,* Berlin 1976, pp. 31-68.

30. *Kāyacakra-sādhana.*. A translation from Tibetan. Georg Kara, Peter Zieme, *Fragments tantrischer Werke in uigurischer Übersetzung* (In German: Fragment of Tantric works in Uigur translation). Berliner Turfantexte VII, Berlin 1976, pp. 68-79.

31. *Utmislar-nïng visay-i Budd avatansaka.* Buddha Avataṃsaka. A translation by Prajñāśrī. Reşid Rahmeti Arat, *Eski Türk Şiiri* (in Turkish: Old Turkish poetry). Ankara 1965, pp. 134-137.

32. *Yükünür-men bilge bilig paramit qutinga.* Prajñāpāramitā-stotra. A translation by Prajñāśrī. Reşid Rahmeti Arat, *Eski Türk Şiiri,* Ankara 1965, pp. 154-161.

33. *Samantabhadra bodhisatva.* A translation by Prajñāśrī. Reşid Rahmeti Arat, *Eski Türk Şiiri,* Ankara 1965, pp. 162-171.

34. *Maitreya Hymn.* A translation by Prajñāśrī. Reşid Rahmeti Arat, *Eski Turk Şiiri,* Ankara 1965, pp. 173-175.

7. THE SUVARṆAPRABHĀSA-SŪTRA AND ITS PLACE IN TURKISH BUDDHIST LITERATURE

Among the Mahāyāna texts which were preferred as sources for translations into Chinese, Tibetan, and different Central Asian languages — the sūtras were specially favoured material for renderings into Uigur. Manuscripts of the Saddharmapuṇḍarīka-sūtra are kept in Berlin and St. Petersburg. This sūtra contains many manuscripts of the 25th chapter on Avalokiteśvara. Parts of the Uigur version correspond to the translation of Kumārajīva made between 384 and 417 AD[1]. The manuscript from St. Petersburg contains a note according to which the translation was made on the order of a layman called Damoğuč Säli. On the basis of insertions in the text it can be asserted that this text was widely used by traveling merchants and caravan leaders of Central Asia. The text of the 25th chapter called *Kuan-ši-im Pusar*[2] (the title originates from the Chinese name of Avalokiteśvara) published by Radloff holds a fragment of a small Prajñāpāramitā-sūtra about the 'seven objects of senses'[3]. Such works on the teachings of consciousness were probably translated more or less faithfully from other texts[4].

In many texts a so-called *Maitri-sudur* or Maitreya-sūtra is mentioned. However the text itself has not yet been found. About the Maitreya cult of the Uigurs information is given by the Avadānas on Maitreya's life[5], and a drama written on Maitreya[6]. Many of the prayers end with the name of Maitreya.

Chronologically the Maitreya cult is followed by the Amitābha cult. There is a book called *Abitaki* (from Chinese *A-mi-to king*=Amita book=Amitābha-sūtra) written on pothi pages. It has many unpublished pages partly in Peking, partly in London and a few pages in Ankara. According to A. Gabain it is a translation and a further development from Chinese[7].

Another Amitābha text called *Amitāyur-vyūha* published by Radloff and Malov, *Uigurische Sprachdenkmäle*[8] (in German: Uigur documents) has many Sanskrit notes, which according to the opinion of the authors are not directly related to the Uigur text of the manuscript.

Some apocryphal sūtras originate from a relatively late period. They are in several copies and block-prints. The *Säkiz yükmak* is a translation of the Chinese *Fo-shou-pa-yang-shên-ch'ou-king*.

[1]A. von Gabain, *Die Alttürkische Literatur* (in German: The Old Turkish literature), Fnd.II, p.225.

[2]W. Radloff, *Kuan-ši-im Pusar*, Petersburg 1911.

[3]*Op. cit.* pp. 93-103.

[4]The source of this translation has not yet been cleared.

[5]W. Radloff & S.E. Malov, *Uigurische Sprachdenkmäler* (in German: Uigur documents), Leningrad 1928 p. 177.

[6]Dr. Ş. Tekin, *Maytrisimit* (*Burkancilarin mehdidi Maitreya ile bulusma uygurca iptidai bir dram*) (in Turkish: Maitreya, the Messiah of the Buddhists, a primitive drama), Ankara 1976.

[7]A. von Gabain *op.cit.* p. 226.

[8]W. Radloff & S.E. Malov, *Uigurische Sprachdenkmäler*, p. 148.

It was published in the *Türkische Turfantexte*[9]. It has a large number of copies and prints in Berlin, London, Tokyo and St. Petersburg, and also one in Brahmi script[10]. The text contains parts about the Buddhist teaching of Consciousness, parts connected with meditation, prescriptions on the planning of a new house, cosmologic speculations on the four quadrants of the macrocosmos and microcosmos with their colours and animals (zodiacs), and it also contains a magic formula.

The *Yitikänsudur*[11], the *Great Bear Sutra*, has been preserved in many copies and books. It was translated into Uigur in 1328, and some of the prints originate from 1328, and others from 1373. The Sūtra (or as it is called in Uigur *sudur*) incorporates a divination book and a magic part connected with the stars. On account of these latter parts the *Yitikänsudur* is held to be a Tantric text.

The St. Petersburg print of the Arya-rājāvavādaka-sūtra[12] is comparatively young. It is a fragment which contains a sermon of the Buddha to Prasenajit the king of Kośala. Here the initial and word-final *t/d*, *s/z* and *q/ğ* are confused. The colophon is: *enetkek ilindäki upadyayi činamitri šila intira bodi-li kelemeči inyana sin toyin üze evirtilip. yangï til üze yme sepilip orunga intürülmiš ärur. bodstv oğ ušuluğ χagan χan yrligi üzä goludï sangga širi töpüt tilintin yangïrtï uygur tilingä...* "In the Indian Land preaching Upādhyāyas named Jinamitra and Śīlendrabodhi made the translator monk Jñānasena to translate it into the new language, to correct and confirm it. On the order of the rulers of Quludi sangha, it was again translated from the Tibetan language into Uigur language......". Jinamitra and Śīlendrabodhi were the translators of the second Tibetan version of the Suvarṇaprabhāsa-sūtra from Sanskrit and they worked during the reign of king Ral-pa-can (804-816). However the text seems to be relatively young, probably the new translation was done much later.

A fragment of the Mahāmāyūrī-sūtra can be found in Radloff and S. Malov, *Uigurische Sprachdenkmäle* (in German: Uigur monuments)[13].

From the 10th century onwards the manuscripts in Uigur language and script bear witness to how important it was for the Uigurs to keep the exact Sanskrit terms, names and dhāraṇīs. In the manuscripts, but mainly in the blockprints, the Sanskrit equivalents of the names and terms which were considered to be very important were given between the lines.

The Suvarṇaprabhāsa-sūtra, the *Altun yaruq,* is the most extensive Uigur Buddhist text. The Prussian Expedition under the leadership of A. von Le Coq found and took to Berlin fragments of six copies of the Uigur text of the Suvarṇaprabhāsa-sūtra. This text was published by F.W.K. Mueller in 1908 in the first volume of the *Uigurica.* In this volume besides publishing a Christian text on pages 10-35[14], F.W.K. Mueller published some fragments of the

[9]TT VI.
[10]TT VIII.
[11]TT VII pp. 23-55, 48-52, 65-68.
[12]W. Radloff, *Kuan-ši-im Pusar* pp. 69-90.
[13]W. Radloff & S.E. Malov, *Uigurische Sprachdenkmäler.*
[14]F.W.K. Mueller, *Uigurica,* 1908 pp. 20-35.

Suvarṇaprabhāsa-sūtra side by side with Dharmakṣema's translation, correlating it with the Chinese text of I-tsing. He also published the colophon of the manuscript[15]: *Yme qutlug öngtüg uluğ tvğač ilinte taišing šivsing alqua šastrlayiğ qamağ nomlariv qatïsiz ötgürü + topulu bilmiš bošğ unmiš bodistv kiči samčo atli ačarï ++ enetkek tïlïntïn tavğ ač tilinča avïrmïš yana bu kelyük bulğ-anyuq bis čöbik yavlaq ödteki kinki bošyutluğ bišbalïg-lïg sïnggu salï tutung tvg-ač tïlïntïn ïkileyü türk tilinča aqtarmïš ++ altun önglug yruq yaltriq li qop-da kötrülmiš.... nom iligi atlï nom bitiq tükädi.* "So in the majestic Chinese Empire, all the Mahāyāna and Hīnayāna śāstras and all the teachings were studied tirelessly, understood and learnt. The Bodhisattva Kitsi Samtso (the Indo-Scythian Tripiṭaka scholar) ācārya translated it into the Chinese language from the Indian (*änätkäk*) language. Later from the Chinese language in the Kaliyuga [supposedly aeon of the evils] living, wise Sinqu Säli Tutung of Bešbaliq translated it from Chinese language into the Turkish language, completed the translation with the name "King of the Sūtras, the excellent Sūtra of golden light"".

The name of the translator of the text from "Indian" is Kitsi Csamtso can be understood as Gst-si sam-tsong with his title of Indo-Scythian Tripiṭaka-scholar Dharmarakṣa, who understood thirtysix languages and dialects and worked from 266-313/317 AD. He translated other works into Chinese like the *Sarva-puṇya-samuccaya-samādhi-sūtra*. The first Chinese translation of the Suvarṇaprabhāsa-sūtra was done by another person, Tripiṭaka scholar who translated it between 414-421 AD. However, W. Radloff interpreted the name as referring to I-tsing. There was a tradition among the Uigur scribes and may be even in Chinese literature which mixed up the two persons Dharmarakṣa and Dharmakṣema because in the Canon the two works, the Suvarṇaprabhāsa-sūtra and the Sarva-puṇya-samuccaya-samādhi-sūtra, followed one after the other[16].

The translator of the Chinese text into Uigur is Sinqu Säli Tutung. He lived in the 10th century during the brightest period of the Uigur Empire. P. Zieme has established the following translations as the works of Sinqu Säli Tutung[17]:

1. The Sūtra of Golden Light (Suvarṇaprabhāsottama-sūtra).
2. A. Hsüan-tsang biography written on pothi pages and kept in Peking and Paris. The first two parts of the text were published by A. Gabain[18].
3. *Ät özüg kongül-üg körmäk atli nom bitig* "Contemplation on the bodies and the senses"[19].
4. *Ming közlüg ming iliglig ïduq yarlïqančuči köngül atlï darni nom.* The full title cannot be found in any fragment, but as P. Zieme established, the Sanskrit title of the work might have been:

---

[15]*Op.cit.* pp. 14-15.

[16]*Op.cit.* p. 15.

[17]P. Zieme, *Singqu Seli Tutung — Übersetzer Buddhistischer Schriften ins Uigurische* (in German: Singqu Seli Tutung—translator of Buddhist works into Uigur), Tractata Altaica, Wiesbaden 1976.

[18]A. v. Gabain, *Die Uigurische Übersetzung der Biographie Hüen-tsangs. Bruchstücke 5. Kapitels* (in German: The Uigur translation of the Biography of Hsüan-tsang. Fragments of the chapter V), SPAW 1935.

[19]G. Hazai, *Fragments eines uigurischen Blockdruck Faltbuches* (in German: Fragments of an Uigur Blockprint Folding Book), Berlin 1975, pp. 91-108.

Sahasrākṣa-sahasrabāhv-avalokiteśvara-bodhisattva-dhāraṇī ṛddhi-mantra-sūtra[20] (Compare B. Nanjio, *A Catalogue of the Chinese Translation of the Buddhist Tripiṭaka*, Oxford 1882 no. 318; in the Taisho Tripiṭaka, vol. 20 no. 1057). In the Uigur title *ïduq yarliqančuči* 'holy compassion' means Avalokiteśvara. The translator of the Indian text into Chinese was Zhitong.

The name of the scholar and translator Sinqu Sali Tutung originates from the Chinese word Sheng-guang meaning "the master of Dharma"[21].

The Chinese part reproduced in the *Uigurica* agrees with Dharmakṣema's and I-tsing's translations. The Uigurica contains — after the above-cited colophon — an enumeration of the Bodhisattvas, and part of a chapter on Goddess Śrī. This manuscript is kept in Berlin and has many unpublished parts.

Another manuscript of the Uigur Suvarṇaprabhāsa-sūtra was found by S. Malov in 1910 in Kansu near Su-chou in a Chinese village called Wunshigu (the name is transcribed from Russian)[22]. S. Malov went on a scientific mission to East Turkistan and Kansu in 1909-1911 with the aim of collecting linguistic data of the area. Turki people came for worship to the Buddhist temples of Wunshigu. Their other name is the Yellow (Salï) Uigurs, and they lived 2-3 days traveling distance from the temples. On such an occasion S. Malov also paid a visit to the Buddhist temple of the place called Wunshigu, or as it is called in Uigur Inǰan. According to his account "there are plenty of new temples on the hills in Wunshigu, but they are not as popular among the Buddhists as the old cave-temples. In these old cave-temples there are frescoes on the walls with Tibetan, Chinese and Uigur inscriptions. S. Malov found Uigur manuscripts in one of the new temples behind a large image of Buddha "neglected as a sort of holy junk"[23] in his words. Apart from this he got another bulk of manuscripts from the headman of the village Wunshigu, and further from the Governor of Su-chou Tin-dun[24] (the name is transcribed from Russian). The discovery of the other text of the Uigur Suvarṇaprabhāsa-sūtra was especially important because till then all the scholars concerned presumed that Uigur literature lasted till the 14th or maximum till the 15th century in the offices of the Timurs. The discovery of this text and its colophons made it clear that literary activities in Uigur language went on till the beginning of the 18th century[25].

The manuscript was written on strong, durable yellow paper. One page (60x 23cms) consists of 22-25 lines written in large Uigur letters. On the first pages of the fourth, fifth and eighth books are printed miniature pictures of the Buddha. Something is written on the pictures according to Radloff and Malov in Uigur, Chinese and Tibetan, but these are not readable. These pictures represent the Dhyāni-Buddhas. One of them keeps his hand in bhūmisparśa attitude. Some words, the names of

---

[20]P. Zieme, *op.cit.* p. 768.
[21]*Op.cit.* p. 768.
[22]PDTP pp. 140-141.
[23]PDTP pp. 142.
[24]The name is transcribed from Russian, *op.cit.* p. 142.
[25]W. Radloff & S.E. Malov, *Suvarṇaprabhāsa-sūtra Tekst uygurskoy redakcii* (in Russian: Suvarṇaprabhāsa-sūtra Text of the Uigur version), Petrograd 1917, p. XVII.

chapters, proper names, the names of Buddha are written in red, in the edited books these words are underlined.

The text contains more colophons:

1. *I.16b p. 30*

line 5 *yaratmïš-iğ tanavasin ačarï*
6 *qumğan tutung + ög ötüki*
7 *on-a tavïškan yil bisinč ay-ya*
8 *töpüt til-inti uygur til-inke*
9 *evirtim*

"On the wish of Tanavasin ācārya I Qumğan tutung in the fifth month of the year of the Hare translated it from the Tibetan language into the Uigur language".

2. *I.18b p. 34*

line 17 *tay-čing küü kang-ši yigirmi altinč otčuq tagi cot*
18 *qutlug tavïškan yil kü-yi ku-ya vihar qa tayiğlïg*
19 *bilgä taluy šabi + ratna včir-ying otükinka tug*
20 *kwan süsäg yeti onunč ay yigirmi tört-ya qutluy güu*
21 *ösa-e bitijü tolu boltï + kreki tus + ötüg bolsuš satu*

"During the reign of the famous Mahāyāna Kanghsi in the year of the Hare, which belongs to the fire element, it was written by Bilgä taluy šabi in the Ku-yi-ku-ya vihāra at the request of Ratna Včir from the place of Tun-huang and was finished in the tenth month twentyfourth day. Sādhu".

3. *III.37a*

line 15 *tay čing kang-hi +*
16 *altï. tus jil öse + erinč ratna včir šabi*
17 *ertmiš og kang-larin ösku kutrulmu üčün*
18 *bu üčünč kün ay os iligin öz-e örkentüg*
19 *onunč ay eng igirmi sekiz-ya ačilmiš qutluğ kün*
20 *öz-e bitijü tĕkintim + tolu tükäl boltï*

"During the reign of the Mahāyāna Kanghsi, in the thirty-sixth year, I, poor Ratna Včir sabi myself wrote it down for the delivery and salvation of my father and mother, on the lucky day of the twentyeighth day of the tenth month; now it is finished".

4. *IV.74a*

line 2 *ymä qutluğongtïn oluğ tavğ-ač ilintä*
3 *taysing savsïng alqu šastir-lariğ om-*
4 *-larïğ qalisï ötgürmiš bodisatv*
5 *kivü samčo atlïğ ačarï enetkek*
6 *til-intin tavğ-ač tilinča evrilmiš-*

7 *-ti yana bu+ biš čobitig*
8 *kelyüg bulganyug yavïs ötte*
9 *qolu ta kenki bošğ utluğ*
10 *biš-balïg-liğ sinkku säli tutung*
11 *tavgač til*
12 *türk uygur tilinče likileyü evrilmiš*
13 *altun önglüg yaruq yaltrïğ-*
14 *liğ qopta kötrülmiš nom yeliki*
15 *atlig nom bi+ tig bitiyeyü*
16 *ögiyeyu yatiltiyu + satu edgu*
17 *jeme qutluğ bolsun +++*
18 *bu törtünč tegsinč nom erdinig erinč čy-sapt*
19 *manggal toyin evkinig ismin ratna včir igeyü*
20 *onug ötügünke + sin tağiğu kun tolu bolti +*
21 *kang-si igirmi altinč yïl altinč ki inig*
22 *sekiz-inkisi či ti taki tutmiš köye sim sičkan*

"After the Bodhisattva named Kitsi Samtso (who knows the Tripiṭaka) in the holy eastern Chinese empire had studied through all the books of Mahāyāna and Hīnayāna, he translated it from Indian language into Chinese language in the Kaliyuga (wicked times) of five obstacles of sufferings and then Sinku Säli Tutung who lived in the times of Kaliyuga (wickedness) and five obstacles translated it from the Chinese language into Turkish Uigur language. This Sūtra, which shines with golden light was read and written down. *Sādhu*, good, you might bring luck again. This fourth roll of the Sūtra at the wish of Mangal Toğin, Evkin Ismin and Ratna Včir I started on the day of the Sim-Hahn, in the twenty-sixth year of the reign of Kanghsi in the sixth month. It was written and finished on the full moon of the first month on the sim mouse-day".

5. *V.30a*

21 *yma bušï itig-i süsüg köngülüg ratna včir ikyang ismän*
22 *ikeyü ög kirtkünč yeke*
23 *altun önglüg yaruqlug nom erdinig öz-e*
24 *erinč čğ-šapt mangal toyin bisinč aying igirmi iki-*
25 *si ++ ki tikuz či tiken a tutmiš kün gamiğ*
26 *binsum tïnlïğ-lar asïč yeke yağiqa*
26 *iner kün öz-e*
27 *tung-kuan belik-te ratna včir ev-inti*

IV.*74b*

line 23 *kün öz-e bašliga bitiyü sekizinč ay inig*
24 *ay tolun-biš igirmi-sintä bitiyü tolu qïltïm*
25 *kinki-larda olamïš-i bolsan satu edgü.*

"At the wish of the generous Ratna včir, Ikyang and Isman started to write on the twentysecond day of the fifth month on the pig-day which is also called *či*, in the place of Tung-huang in the house of Ratna včir this text was copied for the salvation of all the living beings by Istavri toyïn, Svasti toyïn and Bilge taluy toyïn and was finished by Istavri toyïn in the seventh month, on the seventh day of the *šim*-mouse which is also called *či*. Good is that. *Sādhu*".

From the above-cited colophons it is evident that the colophon of the Suvarṇaprabhāsa-sūtra text discovered in Turfan coincides with the colophon at the end of the fourth chapter of the Kansu manuscript: Kitsu sa-mtso (in F.W.K. Mueller's translation Dharmarakṣa meaning Dharmakṣema, in Malov's interpretation I-tsing) translated it into Chinese and Sinkku Säli Tutung rendered it into Uigur. Only the colophon of the first book cited on p.9 contradicts this, which proves that the text was translated from Tibetan by Qumgan Tutung.

The copies of the manuscript or of the different chapters were made by order. The notes of the copiers contain valuable information about the date of copying and the function of the Sūtra. Here we may cite another note:

VI.30b p.458
line 16 *kang-si igirmi altunč jil altunč*
17 *ay-ong igirmi ikisi kun öz-r*
18 *altïnč bölükün bitiyü tolu boltï*
19 *erinč*
20 *suvasti*
21 *toyïn + ötüg bola on +edgü*
22 *toyin-lar-qa +satu liğsa +*

"The sixth chapter was copied in the twenty-sixth year of Kanghsi's reign, in the sixth month on the twenty-second day. Pious Suvasti toyïn. It should be for the salvation of the good monks".

The same twenty-sixth year of the reign of Kanghsi occurs on page I.18b. The reign of Kanghsi lasted from 1662-1722. It means that the twenty-sixth year of his reign and the date of one of the last copies was 1687.

The orthographical features of the text are very similar to those of other Uigur texts. The sounds *p* and *b*, *š* and *s*, *ž* and *z*, *g*, *q* and *χ*, have one letter each. The letter denoting *y*, *i* and *ï* may sometimes replace the letter denoting *v*. For example:

viXar "temple"

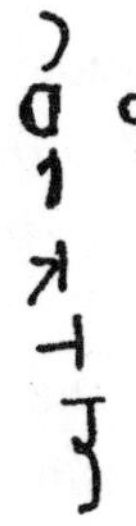
quvraq "assembly"

In the text the sound *a* is sometimes denoted by the letter usually denoting *k* and *g*. This occurs when *a* is at the end of the word or when it is written separately, 2. usually after *k* and g : sometimes also after *r*. For example: *ara* "between, among" *bilgä* "wise". In exceptional cases dots are put on the letters, in most of the cases on *n*, if it is followed or preceded by the same letter. However the practice of using dots was not regular in the text under consideration and this makes its reading difficult.

Unfortunately, S. Malov could not get possession of the full manuscript, some chapters were incomplete, some pages were missing and some were fragmentary. However, the text consists of more or less 700 pages which gives a comparatively large body of material for philological, philosophical, and linguistic research.

The contents of *Altun yaruq* Sūtra consist of different *tegsinč*-s. The *tegsinč* (word originates from the word *tegsin*- DTSl. p. 549) "to roll, to turn, to whirl" (the same in EUT), and then these are divided into different *bölük*-s (DTSl. *bölük* p. 117-118 "chapter of a book", EUT p.50 "chapter, part").

The first page starts with *om a hung* (meaning *oṃ āḥ hūṃ*). On the second page I.lb starts the introduction and foreword. In this first tegsinč are two legends which do not occur in other versions of Suvarṇaprabhāsa-sūtra in other languages. On pages AI.2b-A9a is told the first legend about the magical deliverance of the head-man of Indǰou, Ku-tag from awful punishments for killing many animals and the rebirth of these animals in human form. All this was achieved through the desire of Kū-tag to get the text of this sūtra copied.

On pages AI.9a-AI.l0b comes the next legend. It is told how after reading this sūtra, the wife of a headman Künčing was delivered from suffering and how the animals killed by her also became human beings.

Next follows the *torma* "sacrifice" to the four Mahārājas. This is a very fragmentary part. At the end of this is written Tanvasin Ācārya's note.

On page AI.18a are told the circumstances in which the reading of this book should be started. First of all one has to withdraw into meditation, then to pray, kneel down and bend low. Thus one has to offer sacrifice (*turma*) and one has to cite the title of the book in Indian or in Uigur language.

The second tegsinč is not complete: it has 48 pages. AII-AII.29a contains a philosophical tract on the three bodies (trikāya) on pages 37-93.

AII.29b-AIII pp. 92-130 is: The fourth chapter (bölük) of the second tegsinč is called *altun kuvruk körüg kšanti qïlmïš törtünč bölüg ol ötüa somakitu bodhisatv* "This is the part where Somaketu Bodhisattva saw a golden drum in his dream".

AIII. Two pages are missing. According to the last lines the fifth boluk (chapter) of the third tegsinč is entitled: *qilinč atartmiš-in öčürmäk atlïg* "Defeating the limits of the deeds" (pp. 130-199).

AIV-AIV.74a (p.201-343). This is the sixth bölük (chapter) of the fourth tegsinč. From this tegsinč two pages p.51 and p.52 are missing. It is entitled *arïgyir orunlar sayu-qï tray darnï tutrug nom-lariğ ögitmiš atlïg* "The teaching of the dhāraṇī, which belongs to all the pure places".

AV.6a, p.345-355. This is the fifth tegsinč seventh bölük. The title of the part is: *čečeg yolasurki öz-e* "praise to the vision of the lotus flower".

AV.6a-AV.10 on p.355-363. This is the fifth tegsinč eighth bölük. The title of this bölük: *altun daranig ogitmiš* "which teaches the golden dhāraṇī".

AV.9b-AV.A4a (p. 363, 371). This is the ninth bölük of the fifth tegsinč. The title of this part in Uigur is: *yog korïg töz-i ögitmiš* "the root of śūnyatā".

AV.14a-AV.28a *yog qoruğ tözigi tayini közimiš kösüš ügköntürmäk altïg* on p.371-399. This is from the fifth tegsinič, tenth bölük entitled: "the elimination of craving on the basis of śūnyatā".

AV.28a-AV.30b on p.399-404. This is the fifth tegsinč eleventh bölük, entitled: *tört mχaranč tengri-ler tengri yalangig quvragi körmüš* "the assembly of the four Mahārājas, of Gods and humans".

AVI.2a-30b on p. 405-458. This is already the sixth tegsinč twelfth bölük. *tört mχaranča tengriler jirtinčüg kösetmig* "the observance of the world by the four Mahārājas". Three pages are missing from this part: 1, 20,21.

AVII.1a-4a on p.459-465. This is the seventh tegsinč thirteenth bölük. The first page is lost, but the title is probably "the teaching of the immaculate dhāraṇī".

AVII.4a-7b on p.465-472. This is the seventh tegsinč fourteenth bölük entitled: *čintamani atliy drani nomug agitmiš atlï* "the teaching of the dhāraṇī formula called Cintāmaṇi".

AVII.8a-20a on p.473-489. This is the seventh tegsinč fifteenth bölük, entitled: *sarasvati atlïg tengrike ötüg ötünmek atli* "worship of Goddess Sarasvatī".

AVIII.8b is the second part of the Sarasvatī bölük going on till p.512.

AVIII.8b-11b on p.512-518. This is the eighth tegsinč, sixteenth bölük entitled: *sirigini atli tengri-ke-si ötüg ötünmäk atli* "worship of Goddess Śrī".

AVIII.11b-16a on p. 518-527. This is the eighth tegsinč seventeenth bölük, entitled: *sirigini qut tengri qatunï etüg tavarïğ üstemäk atlï* "praise of Śrī the Goddess of Luck".

AVIII.16a-21b on p.527-538. This is the eighth tegsinč eighteenth bölük, entitled: *vasuntarï atlïg yir qatuni ötüg ötümesi atli* "worship of Vasundharā (Dṛḍhā), the Goddess of the Earth".

AVIII.21b-25b on p.538-546. Eighth tegsinč, bölük nineteenth, entitled: *Sancanačavï atlïg tengriler orungati ötüg ötümek atlï* "worship of the leader of the Gods Saṃjñāya".

AVIII.25b-AIX on p. 546-580. This is the eighth tegsinč, twentieth bölük, entitled: *iligler qanlar iyig koyay törü siz aymïš/ rača šastïr tarma begler törüsin ögitmiš atli* "teaching the right ruling the rāja-śāstra for rulers and khans".

AIX.1a-6b on p.570-580. It is in the ninth book (tegsinč), twentyfirst bölük, entitled: *sučati atlïg ilig qan iyig tiltigyi ögitmiš atlï* "teaching about the Great King Sujāta"[26].

---

[26]His name in the Chinese version of I-tsing and in the Sanskrit text is Susambhava.

AIX.6b-18 on p.580-598. Ninth tegsinč, twentysecond bölük, entitled: *tengri-ler yek-ler köšetmek atlï* "the preservation of the Gods and demons"[27].

AIX.18-27. Twentythird and twentyfourth bölük are missing on these pages.

AIX.27b-AX on p.598-606. This is the twentyfifth bölük, of the tenth tegsinč, entitled: *yotaki vasanti orinïng isiz kötükï-inig ögitmiš atlï* "teaching about the deeds of Yotaki Vasanti"[28].

AX.4-23 on p.606-643. From the tenth tegsinč the first four pages are missing. Chapter twenty-sixth, the page containing the title is missing. This is the chapter on the hungry tigress, which is one of the most popular jātakas of Uigur Buddhist literature[29]. It is supposed to be a late insertion.

AX.23b-25b on p.644-648. This is the twentyseventh bölük of the tenth tegsinč entitled: *ontin singir-ke bodisatv-lar tengri tengrisi burganig ukligi atlï* "praise of God of Gods the Buddha".

AX.26b-28a on p.649-652. This is the twentyeighth chapter in the tenth tegsinč entitled: *Somakit-i bodisatv tengri tengrisi burqan-ig ukligi atlï* "The praise of Buddha by the Bodhisattva Somaketu". This bölük is very fragmentry.

AX.28a-30a on p.653-656. It is in the tenth tegsinč, the twentyninth bölük, entitled: *bodi sögüt-üg tengri-si tengri burqan-ig ukligi atlï* "the praise of the God (Buddha) by the God of the trees, Bodhi".

AX.30a-32a on p.657-661. It is in the tenth tegsinč, thirtieth bölük, entitled: *sarasvati tengri tengri tengrisi burqanïg üglüg etlig ötün* "the God Sarasvatī pays her respect to the God of Gods Buddha".

AX.32a on p. 661. In the tenth tegsinč the last or thirtyfirst bölük is entitled: *erdini tutušmig* "Releasing the Sūtra".

At the end of the Suvarṇaprabhāsa-sūtra manuscript the last five pages of the book contain another manuscript entitled *pujan evirmek* "to do puṇya". This manuscript was written in the twentyseventh year of the reign of K'anghsi in 1688. It is interesting that on the fourth page the manuscript mentions Su-chou as: *süǰcï balïk.*

The Suvarṇaprabhāsa-sūtra gained wide popularity among the Buddhists which is evident from the number of translations into Tibetan, Chinese, Khotanese, Uigur, and Mongolian. The Suvarṇaprabhāsa-sūtra was translated into Mongolian and Tangut from the Uigur version.

---

27 DTSl. p.253 *yek* 'demon' from the Middle-Persian *jakkhā.*

28 His name in Chinese is Jalavāhana.

29 J.R. Hamilton, Le cont bouddhique du Bon et du Mauvais Prince en version ouigoure (in French: A Buddhist story of the Good and Bad Princes in the Uigur version), Paris 1971. P. Zieme: Ein uigurisches Turfan-fragment der Erzahlung vom Guten und vom Bosen Prinzen (in German: An Uigur Turfan fragment of the Good and Bad Princes), AOH 1974 pp. 263-268.

8. COMPARISON OF THE CONTENTS OF THE TURKISH SUVARṆAPRABHĀSA-SŪTRA WITH THE SANSKRIT, CHINESE AND TIBETAN VERSIONS

The Pāli Tripiṭaka contains three piṭakas (baskets): namely the Vinaya-piṭaka, the Sutta-piṭaka and the Abidhamma-piṭaka. The order of enumeration also indicates their chronological evolution, first the Vinaya-piṭaka was created, then the Sutta-piṭaka and finally at the time of the schism the Abhidhamma-piṭaka[1]. The earliest that we know of the existence of these scriptures according to J. Thomas was at the time of the Third Council held in 247 BC[2].

According to H. Kern the Pāli word *sutta* originally meant 'short rule' but later short or long explanations in the form of prose sermons or dialogues were called sūtras. These sūtras are supposed to be the narratives of Ānanda, who was present when Buddha uttered them originally[3].

The Mahāvastu—as Winternitz asserts in his *History of Indian Literature*—is a work of Hīnayāna, but has many features of Mahāyāna[4]. H. Kern holds the opinion that judging from the language and composition, the Mahāvastu is intermediate between the Pāli Canon and the Vaipulya Sūtras[5]. The "Nine Dharmas", which are also called Vaipulya Sūtras—Aṣṭasāhasrikā Prajñāpāramitā, Saddharmapuṇḍarīka, Lalitavistara, Laṅkāvatāra, Suvarṇaprabhāsa, Gaṇḍavyūha, Tathāgataguhyaka, Samādhirāja, Daśabhūmīśvara—were very popular in the Northern Buddhist countries[6]. The Vaipulya Sūtras provided much material for the Tibetan Canon, which had a different division from the Pāli Canon. It has two basically different parts: the sūtras and the tantras, taking the Vinaya (in Tibetan *Dul-va*) under the sūtra division and arranging the sūtras into five parts. The last division of the five levels of the sūtras in the Kangyur are the *mDo* or *mo-sde*. Most of the works come under this division: the Lalitavistara, Saddharma-puṇḍarīka, Mahāparinirvāṇa and Udānavarga[7]. The Suvarṇaprabhāsa-sūtra is not placed among the sūtras, but under the tantras.

Tsoṅ-kha-pa's disciple Mkhas-grub-rje also classified the Suvarṇaprabhāsa-sūtra under the tantras. "Some claim that the Suvarṇaprabhāsa-sūtra belongs to the mantra category, and belongs among the tantras of the Tathāgata family. Others claim that it belongs to the sūtra category.

---

[1]H. Kern, *Manual of Indian Buddhism*, Delhi 1974, p.1.

[2]E.J. Thomas, *The Life of Buddha as Legend and History*, London 1975, p.254.

[3]H. Kern, *op.cit.* p.2.

[4]M. Winternitz, *A History of Indian Literarure*, Delhi 1972, vol. II pp. 239-247.

[5]H. Kern, *op.cit.* p.4.

[6]M. Winternitz, *op.cit.* p.295.

[7]L.A. Waddel, *The Buddhism of Tibet or Lamaism*, Cambridge 1971, pp. 159-164.

According to our school, it belongs to the mantra category, and many Indian pandits also place it among the mantras (i.e. in the Tantra literature)"[8].

Situ paṇ-chen places this Sūtra among the Tantras because of the number of dhāraṇīs[9].

G. Tucci says in referring to the Suvarṇaprabhāsa-sūtra, the Laṅkāvatāra-sūtra and to the dhāraṇīs included in them: "The dhāraṇī is the first kernel from which the tantras developed.... The prevalence of magical thought breaks the law of the karma when the Mahāyāna Sūtras declare that their recitation helps to annul the greatest sins a breach has been opened: the process from now on, will develop uninterruptedly.... no doubt that the dhāraṇī were the first codification of the ideas underlying it: the Tantras begin with them.

"Some Mahāyāna Sūtras or parts of them may be considered as Tantras, Kriyā-tantras. For instance: the Suvarṇaprabhāsa-sūtra and the chapters on the dhāraṇī of the Laṅkāvatāra, by the Vajrayāna masters among the Kriyātantra"[10].

The Kriyātantras are much simpler than the Tantras of the remaining three classes. According to A. Wayman in Bu-ston's system of the Tantras the Suvarṇaprabhāsa belongs to the Tathāgata family, to the Tantras of the Mother (yum) together with certain Prajñāpāramitā texts and the work Pañcarakṣā of the five protecting goddesses[11].

The Suvarṇaprabhāsa-sūtra was liked and admired in the Northern Buddhist countries. It was translated for the first time as early as the fifth century into Chinese[12], and it was translated into Tibetan for the first time in the first half of the eighth century[13]. The Sutra has also Kalmuck[14], Mongolian[15], and Manchurian translations. Besides the Central Asian fragments of the Sūtra in Sanskrit, translations in Tibetan, Uigur, Sogdian, Tangut and Khotanese are important because they reflect different stages of development of the Sūtra.

As the colophons of the Uigur version of the Suvarṇaprabhāsa-sūtra show, the text was translated either from the Tibetan or from I-tsing's Chinese translation of the Sūtra. The opportunity for a comparative study of the relationships of the Uigur Suvarṇaprabhāsa-sūtra with those in other languages are provided by the editions of the text in Sanskrit, Chinese, Tibetan, and Uigur.

A portion of the Sanskrit text was first published by Sarat Chandra Das and Pandit Sarat Chandra Shastri in 1898[16]. H. Idzumi was the first to edit the complete Sanskrit text of the

---

[8]F.D. Lessing and W. Wayman, *Introduction to the Buddhist Tantric Systems*, Delhi 1978, pp. 109-111.

[9]G. Bethlenfalvy, *A Catalogue of the Urga Kanjur*.

[10]G. Tucci, *Tibetan Painted Scrolls*, Roma 1949, pp. 223-224.

[11]A. Wayman, *The Buddhist Tantras*, New York 1973, p. 237.

[12]B. Nanjio, *A Catalogue of the Buddhist Tripiṭaka*, Oxford 1883.

[13]J. Nobel, *Suvarṇaprabhāsottama-sūtra. Das Goldglanz-Sutra Ein Sanskrittext des Mahāyāna-Buddhismus. Die Tibetische Übersetzungen mit einem Wörterbuch* (in German: Suvarṇaprabhāsottama-sūtra. The Sutra of Golden Light. A. Sanskrit text of Mahāyāna Buddhism. The Tibetan translations with a Dictionary), Leiden 1944.

[14]E. Haeinsch, *Altan Gerel, Die westmongolische Fassung des Goldglanzsūtra* (in German: Altan Gerel. The Kalmuck or West Mongolian version of the Sūtra of Golden Light), Leipzig 1929.

[15]G. Kara, *Aranyfeny Sutra* (in Hungarian: The Sutra of Golden Light), Budapest 1975.

[16]Sarat Chandra Das and Pandit Sarat Chandra Shastri, *Suvarṇa Prabhā*, Calcutta 1898.

Suvarṇaprabhāsa-sūtra[17]. The text edited by him was first copied by B. Nanjio in 1881, when B. Nanjio was studying at Oxford. He copied a manuscript at the Bibliothèque Nationale in Paris, and another manuscript at the Royal Asiatic Society in London. He collated these manuscripts with one kept in Cambridge University and further with the manuscripts in the Tokyo and the Kyoto Imperial University. H. Idzumi completed the work of collating the above-mentioned manuscripts and edited the text in 1931.

J. Nobel published the Sanskrit text of the Suvarṇaprabhāsa-sūtra[18] based on manuscripts, which he marked A, B, C, D, E, F and G. He used the same Tibetan texts which he had used later in the Tibetan edition of the Suvarṇaprabhāsa-sūtra. The manuscripts which were marked A, B and G belong to the University Library of Cambridge. The manuscript marked C belongs to the Academy in Leningrad, D and E to manuscripts in the Bibliothèque Nationale in Paris and F to the Royal Asiatic Society in London. This manuscript contains some minor deviations marked whenever mentioned. Nobel's description of these seven manuscripts is as follows:

A is a paper manuscript, which consists of 79 pages in Nepali script.

B consists of 90 pages and is written in gold on black paper. The script is Nepali and it was written in 1794 AD.

C consists of 133 pages but has only four lines on a page. The manuscript is full of mistakes. There are also a number of corrections and notes in another hand. The first page has a miniature of the Buddha. The script is Nepali.

D has 120 pages in Nagari script. The mistakes show that it was copied from another manuscript in Nepali script.

E consists of 120 pages in Nepali script. The manuscripts D and E are paper manuscripts from the 19th century.

F consists of 87 pages. On the first page there is a miniature. The script is Nepali and it is full of mistakes.

G deviates from the ones mentioned till now. It is written on 76 palm leaves. Every page contains six lines in Nepali script. This manuscript is fragmentary. Pages 1-7, 12-13, 16, 22, 27-34, 37, 41-43, 46-47, 49-50 and 52 are missing. Pages 15, 18, 19, 23 and 60 were rubbed out probably for writing exercises. All the texts have the same numbering of chapters except manuscript G. The most reliable of the texts is G, belonging to the Cambridge University Library. This manuscript does not hold those corrections which are to be found in most of the manuscripts. The corrigenda are of the same kind, and their main aim is to replace the expressions which were written in the dialects with Sanskrit translations. On the basis for a comparison of the Sanskrit texts with the Tibetan it becomes clear that the most archaic text is G. The corrections of the other texts probably originate from a lost text.

---

[17] H. Idzumi, *The Suvarṇaprabhāsa-sūtra. A Mahāyāna text called The Golden Splendour,* Kyoto 1931.

[18] J. Nobel, *Suvarṇabhāsottamasūtra. Das Goldglanz-sutra* (in German: Suvarṇabhasottamasūtra. The Sūtra of Golden Light), Leipzig 1937.

This fact divides the texts of Suvarṇaprabhāsa into two main groups: one group consisting of all the texts except G, which by itself forms a separate group of the Sūtra.

S. Bagchi prepared his edition of the Suvarṇaprabhāsa-sūtra[19] on the basis of the text edited by H. Idzumi in 1931. He used one manuscript from the Cambridge University Library which he marked C, and another manuscript which belongs to the Royal Asiatic Society in London which he marked A. He also used manuscripts belonging to the Bibliothèque Nationale in Paris. He has not made it clear whether he used one or more manuscripts from St. Petersburg, but used some other manuscripts in addition to those which were used by J. Nobel. These are the manuscripts marked: K(manuscript belonging to the Kyoto University), T(manuscript belonging to the Tokyo University), Ms.(copybook prepared by Bunyiu Nanjio), and I(incomplete edition by Sarat Chandra Das and Satish Chandra Acharya Vidyabhusana published in 1900 from Darjeeling). S. Bagchi used a Tibetan text which belongs to the Otani University Library in Kyoto.

The Central Asian fragments of the Sanskrit manuscripts deserve special interest. They were discovered during an expedition in the years 1906-1908. A fragment published by J.N Reuter[20] contains the end of the XIII and the beginning of the XIV chapters. The beginning of the XIV chapter agrees with Dharmakṣema's and I-tsing's translations while in the other Sanskrit texts the introductory words are missing. Another fragment was revised by F.W. Thomas and published by A.F.R. Hoernle[21]. It is a broken up piece from the fifth chapter, and also another part from the Sūtra which does not occur in any of the Sanskrit chapters, but it occurs in the Chinese version of I-tsing in the eighth chapter. This fragment contains a part from the end of the XIII chapter. There is also a part of the beginning of the XIV chapter in the fragment. The second group of fragments partly covers the ones which were published by J.N. Hoernle. They belong to the text groups marked R and H in Nobel's edition of the Sanskrit text. While the above-mentioned documents are probably extended revisions of the discussed Sanskrit text the numbering of the chapters usually covers the numbering of the Sanskrit texts. Besides this group there is another group of Central Asian Sanskrit manuscripts which belongs to another tradition. The first fragment belongs to chapter III, the second and the third to chapter VI, and the fourth to chapters VII and VIII. These according to our knowledge have not yet been published. All this information about the unpublished fragments was given by N.D. Mironov to J. Nobel[22]. Another small fragment in Sanskrit was found in Iduqutshahr and published by H. Stonner[23]. This is a part from the third chapter.

The oldest Sanskrit manuscripts with their dialectical pecularities give especially precious material for research. The manuscripts H, M and R show peculiarities common to manuscript G and

[19]S. Bagchi, *Suvarṇaprabhāsa-sūtra*, Darbhanga 1967.

[20]J. N. Reuter, *Some Buddhist Fragments from Chinese Turkestan in Sanskrit and Khotanese*, JSFOu 30 pp. 7-10. H.W. Bailey, *Khotanese Texts*, Cambridge 1963.

[21]A.F.R. Hoernle, *Manuscript Remains of Buddhist Texts Found in East Turkestan*, Vol. I, Oxford 1916.

[22]J. Nobel, *op.cit.* p. XII.

[23]H. Stomer, *SBAW* 904 pp. 1310-1313.

this fact increases their value. These fragments have not got the title Suvarṇaprabhāsottama but they are entitled Suvarṇabhāsottama. There is also a Khotanese text which is entitled Suvarṇabhāsottama. In this aspect the palm leaf manuscript shows similarity with the Central Asian group of Sanskrit texts which carries the title Suvarṇaprabhā. The poetic parts have great importance in the reconstruction of the original title. In the metric parts the title does not fit the metre used in the rest of the text. Only if the title is pronounced as *Suvarṇabhāso*, can it be made to fit the rest. Thus J. Nobel holds the opinion that the Sūtra was originally entitled Suvarṇabhāsottama. The new title originated in the third chapter which is about the golden drum, where it is named as *suvarṇaprabhāsottamadundubhena*. The change in the title of the Sūtra came about comparatively early. So the name of the Sūtra was transcribed in Tibetan from the longer title and the Sūtra carried this name in the Mahāvyutpatti (1339 AD). But in the Śikṣāsamuccaya the title occurs as: *imāś ca Suvarṇabhāsoktā maitrīkaruṇāgarbhā gāthāḥ*[24].

The Chinese translations have a great importance for the Uigur Sūtra as well as for the Sanskrit text. The first Chinese translation is the work of Dharmakṣema who went to China in 414 AD. and by 421 had translated a large amount of Buddhist Sanskrit texts. As it has already been mentioned in the previous chapter, the names Dharmakṣema and Dharmarakṣa have been confused. The two names Dharmarakṣa and Dharmakṣema occur in literature as the author of the first Chinese translation. The first name is suggested by B. Nanjio and followed by H. Idzumi and S. Bagchi F.W.K. Mueller read the name as Dharmakṣema and J. Nobel also holds the opinion that the author of the first Chinese translation was Dharmakṣema[25]. Dharmarakṣa went to Loyang in 266 AD and the Chinese translated his name *Fa-hu*. The author of the first Chinese translation is Dharmakṣema who went to China in 414 AD and till 421 he translated a great number of Sanskrit Buddhist texts into Chinese. His name was translated into Chinese *Fa-fêng*. The Sūtra in his translation carries a title which correlates with Suvarṇabhāsa-sūtra. The translation has 18 chapters in four chüan.

In time followed the versions of Paramārtha and Yaśogupta. Both the translations have been lost, but information is given about them in the Chinese catalogues. An even better source of information about Paramārtha's and Yaśogupta's work is the text compiled by Pao-kuei in 597 AD which is based on the earlier translations, and is provided with critical remarks and a foreword.

Paramārtha originated from Ujjayinī and died in 569 AD. His translation of the Suvarṇabhāsa-sūtra consisted of 22 chapters in 7 chüan. As Pao-kuei says four new chapters were added in Paramārtha's translation as compared with that of Dharmakṣema. The titles of these four chapters were: *San chên fên pieh p'in, Yeh chang mieh p'in, T'o-lo-ni tsui ching ti p'in, I k'ung man yüan p'in.* In Pao-kuei's "synthetic version" these chapters are numbered III, V, VI and IX. The best known among them is the III chapter about the trikāya. Paramārtha's version is more of an independent work than a translation.

---

[24] J. Nobel, *op.cit.* pp. XII-XIII.

[25] *Op. cit.* p. XIII.

Similar is the case of the other translation partly ascribed to Yaśogupta, and partly to Jñānagupta. The two monks worked together and thus shared work on the Suvarṇaprabhāsa-sūtra. Jñānagupta originated from Gandhara and died in 605 AD at the age of 77. Their version incorporated two chapters more than the translation of Dharmakṣema. Yaśogupta added the seventh chapter, and the second chapter of Dharmakṣema's work. The texts of Paramārtha, Yaśogupta and Jñānagupta are looked upon not as completed versions of Dharmakṣema but as new translations.

All the existing works were used by the monk Pao-kuei who started his translation around 600 AD. To the core of his compilation (which carried the name "The synthetic version of the Sutra of Golden Light") he added new chapters and made other additions. It contains altogether 24 chapters in 8 chüan. Because of the additions, the Sūtra became longer and the dhāraṇī part gave it a new significance.

An absolutely new translation was made by the famous I-tsing, who traveled in India during 675-695 AD. He visited the famous Buddhist places Gṛdhrakūṭa, Rājagṛha, Vaiśālī, Kuśīnagara, Mṛgadāva, Buddhagayā and collected a large number of Buddhist texts. He traveled back to China by ship to Canton. He lived at a time when Buddhism was flourishing in China. When he died in 713 AD he had to his credit 56 works in 230 chüan translated into Chinese.

His translation of the Suvarṇaprabhāsa-sūtra was published in 703 AD[26]. In the caves of Tun-huang a manuscript was found which was written during the lifetime of I-tsing. The text in the translation of L. Giles reads: "Newly translated at the Hsi-ming Temple in Ch'ang-an, in obedience to imperial command, by the san-tsang and master of the law I-tsing, who also gave unity to the composition and corrected the characters, on the 4th day, jên-hsü of the tenth moon, the first day of which was chi-wei, of the year kuei-mao, the third of Ch'ang-an in the Great Chow dynasty" This date according to L. Giles is 17th November, 703. The remainder of the colophon gives the information that Pao-ssŭ-wei an Indian monk verified the meaning of the Sanskrit, another Indian Shih-li-mo-to whose name appears in two other Stein manuscripts "read the Sanskrit texts", eleven scholars "verified the meaning", two wrote down from dictation and two "examined the final result". These monks belonged to no fewer than eleven different monasteries, four of which are known to us only from this manuscript, whereas the Hsi-ming and the Lung-hsing occur very frequently. The Fo-shou-chi and the T'ien-kung are mentioned in S. 2278"[27].

I'tsing's translation is the last and the longest Chinese translation of the Suvarṇaprabhāsa-sūtra.

A large number of Chinese Suvarṇaprabhāsa-sūtra texts were discovered in Tun-huang. Among these fragments the ones that occur most frequently are from I-tsing's translation of the 15th chapter (Sarasvatī) which has 35 copies, then follows manuscript of the 5th chapter ("Elimination of the hindrances of deeds") which has 31 copies. The 6th chapter ("The Dhāraṇī of the Fully Pure

---

[26]J. Nobel, *Suvarṇaprabhāsottamasūtra, Das Goldglanz-Sutra, ein Sanskrittext des Mahāyāna-Buddhismus. I-tsing's chinesische Version und ihre Übersetzung* (in German: The Sūtra of Golden Light, A Sanskrit Text of Mahāyāna Buddhism. I-tsing's Chinese version and its translation), Leiden 1958.

[27]L. Giles, Dated Chinese Manuscripts in the Stein Collection, *BSOS* vol. 9 pp. 2-3.

country") and 12th chapter (the four Mahārājas) have 22 copies each. Chapter 26 (the hungry tigress) has 21 copies.

The texts were copied by monks for different purposes. Their introductions give interesting information. By copying a part or the whole text, laymen hoped for the realization of their wishes, like restoration of health, rebirth in the Pure Land, annulment of sins and so on.

The three versions in the Tibetan Canon are three partly different translations of the Suvarṇaprabhāsa-sūtra. The first in the Canon is the latest of the three Tibetan versions, the version by Chos-grub, who followed the Chinese version of I-tsing. Chos-grub also translated the Laṅkāvatāra-sūtra and Guṇabhadra. Three other smaller works in the Kanjur give the name of Chos-grub as translator. The Chinese fragment from Tun-huang calls him Fa-ch'eng. He worked in the monasteries Hsiu-to in Kan-chou and Yung-t'ang in Sha-chou[28]. Chos-grub's translation is marked as Tib. III in accordance with J. Nobel[29]. It is based mainly on the manuscript Kanjur found in Berlin. It consists of 169 pages and is the most extensive text of the Suvarṇaprabhāsa-sūtra. Only a little shorter is the translation which immediately follows Chos-grub's. This text is marked as Tib. II and consists of 148 pages. It was translated by Jinamitra, Śīlendrabodhi and Ye-śes-sde, during the reign of King Ral-pa-can (804-816). The Indian original of this translation is not to be found. It has about twice as much material as the Sanskrit text available to us. Tib. II covers the third Tibetan translation. Tib. I has 91 pages, and it corresponds to the Sanskrit text which has reached us. This translation is not to be found in some blockprints of the Kanjur. Some editors of the Kanjur might have found it superfluous. The translators of the oldest version Tib. I are not named anywhere. However, according to Bu-ston's history of Buddhism (Bu-ston lived 1290-1364[30] under the king Khri-lde-btsug-brtan who reigned from 705-755) Mūlakośa from Blan-ka and Jñānakumāra from Gnags translated the Karmaśataka and Suvarṇaprabhāsa into Tibetan. Both these scholars are not mentioned in the Kanjur. As J. Nobel sets it forth there were certainly other translations of the Suvarṇaprabhāsa-sūtra, as is evident from some Central Asian fragments which are not identical with any of the above-mentioned versions.

The translation by Chos-grub, which follows I-tsing's translation (Tib. III) is identical mostly with the red blockprint of the Bibliothèque Nationale in Paris. A similar text is the handwritten Kanjur in the Berlin Library. There is also a xylograph in the Library of Cambridge, which will be marked henceforth with C. According to J. Nobel the print in Cambridge is the best from the point of view of language. As J. Nobel points out the interesting part of the Tibetan text is[31] the corrections made at such places which the author felt were not perfectly done in the Sanskrit original lost to us.

---

[28]P. Pelliot, *J A* 1914.

[29]J. Nobel, *Suvarṇaprabhāsottamasūtra. Das Goldglanz-Sutra. Ein Sanskrittext des Mahāyāna-Buddhismus. Die Tibetischen Übersetzungen mit eine Wörterbuch* (in German: Suvarṇaprabhāsottamasūtra. The Sutra of Golden Light. A Sanskrit Text of Mahāyāna Buddhism. Tibetan translations with a dictionary), Leiden 1944.

[30]*Op.cit.* p. XIII.

[31]*Op.cit.* p. XVIII.

On page 40 line 5 the expression *byaṅ-chub yon-tan rin-chen rdzogs* is changed to *byaṅ-chub yon-tan rdzogs gyur-cig* because the Sanskrit original seemed to be meaningless to the author. In this regard the red blockprint from Paris agrees very much with that in Cambridge. The mistakes of the Paris block-print and of the Berlin manuscript do not occur in the Cambridge xylograph.

The text of Chos-grub's translation (Tib. III) in the red Kanjur of the Bibliothèque Nationale Paris, and the manuscript in the Library of Berlin represent an earlier stage in comparison with the manuscript in Cambridge. This Kanjur manuscript (which will be marked henceforth as Hs.) consists of 108 volumes. The original is from the temple of Yung Ho Kung in Peking. It is in a beautiful hand but as J. Nobel puts it[32] it appears that the copyists were Chinese who did not know Tibetan probably.

The red blockprint in the Bibliothèque Nationale in Paris consists altogether of 107 volumes and was originally printed in Peking. It is very readable and has only a few mistakes. The page numberings are on the edge of the page to the left in Tibetan, and to the right in Chinese. A comparison of the blockprint in Paris and the manuscript in Berlin, makes it clear that the two works are related to each other despite differences. The arrangement of the different groups of the texts in the Berlin Kanjur is different from that of the print in Paris. The red Kanjur in Paris begins with the Tantra section (the volume starts with *oṃ*) which in Beck's catalogue describing the Peking Kanjur is numbered 106. Afterwards in the Kanjur in Paris follow the numbers from *ka* to *ya* (1-24) which carry the numbers 85-108 in Beck's description. The difference is that one volume of the Paris print (volume *za* 22) is not in the manuscript from Berlin. This work is the Bhagavaty-āryā-tārā-mūla-kalpa (*phags-ma sgrol-mai rtsa-bai rtog-pa*). The volumes *ra-tsi* in P. contain Prajñāpāramitā texts, which correspond to the volumes *ra-tsi* (25-47) in Beck's description. In this group there is a deviation in the arrangement, as volume 35 in Beck's volume *mi* (46). To the Prajñāpāramitā group of texts is added the group Ratnakūṭa with the volumes *ts'i* to *'i* (48-53) which in Beck's description are between 47-52. Afterwards follow the Avataṃsaka, volumes *yi* to *hi* (54-59) which in Beck's catalogue are 44-46. Then comes the Sūtra section volumes from *i* to *ke* (60-91) which in Beck's catalogue are 53-84. Afterwards comes the Vinaya group, volumes from *khe* to *phe* (92-104) which are in the beginning in the Berlin Kanjur and correlate with Beck's 1-16. This section includes volume 13 of the Paris print which agrees with volume 16 of the Berlin manuscript. The difference in the numbers of the volumes disappears, when the volume *tse* in *P* correlates to two volumes in Beck's system: volumes 4 and 5 in Beck's description correlate with the volumes from *ṅe* (101) to *phe* in the blockprint, arranged into volumes 11-16 of the manuscript. At the end of the Paris Kanjur in red block-print is a Chinese-Mongolian-Tibetan index, which does not exist in the manuscript.

The different text groups agree except for the above-mentioned exceptions. In the Tantra group and in the Prajñāpāramitā group the red Paris Kanjur and the Berlin manuscript seem to have no

---

[32] *Op.cit.* p. XVII.

basic difference. Occasionally the same mistakes occur in both the Kanjurs. Thus there is no doubt that the red Paris blockprint and the Berlin manuscript are very similar. However it cannot be said that they are identical. There are many differences in writing: in the manuscript the word *śin-du* usually occurs as *śin-tu* in the blockprint as a rule. In many places the text is corrected in such a way that the correction has the same number of syllables. The changes are not noticeable on the prints because they have been introduced in the blocks. It seems that the Paris blockprint is a corrected form of the original of the Berlin manuscript. The red Paris block-print has a different arrangement of the text than the Berlin manuscript. The blockprint holds more texts in its first part than the Berlin manuscript. According to Nobel's opinion, the original of the Berlin manuscript was older than the Paris blockprint. For this reason in the search for original forms the changed forms of the Paris blockprint should not be taken into account.

Two of the Tibetan translations (Tib. I and Tib. II) are based directly on Sanskrit originals. The second translation must be about 80 years later than the first. The Indian original has not reached us. By extending the old chapters and by adding some new ones the size of the old text became twice the size of the original. Smaller fragments of the Sanskrit text and the Tibetan versions from Central Asia show that many versions of the Sūtra existed. The later chapters III, V and VI are on the trikāya, karman and the different conditions of Bodhisatvas. In these chapters the central problems of the philosophy of Mahāyāna are discussed thoroughly. These chapters contributed much to the fact, that the Suvarṇaprabhāsa-sūtra was widespread all over Central and East Asia. Besides the philosophic and dogmatic additions, the dhāraṇīs were added to the text. The dhāraṇīs gave a multiplicity and popularity to the Suvarṇaprabhāsa-sūtra.

It has been mentioned that Tib. II agrees with the text marked Tib. I in the common parts. However the authors of Tib. II did not follow the oldest translation (Tib. I) blindly. While examining the Suvarṇaprabhāsa-sūtra, one can frequently come across minor changes. For example:

Skr. *jāti,* Tib. I *skye-ba,* Tib. II *ts'e-rabs* 'the time of an existence'

Skr. *śatasahasra,* Tib. I. *brgya-stoṅ (phrag)*, Tib. II. *'bum-/-phrag/*

These changes also show that the Berlin manuscript represents a more archaic stage. While checking the other texts, J. Nobel sets forth the theory that the Berlin manuscript represents the oldest model, the red Paris blockprint is based on the same model, but it has many corrections which follow another print[33]. The black Narthang print is an even later revised composition. The red blockprint in Cambridge is probably even later than that.

The remains of the Central Asian manuscripts of the Tibetan translations of the Suvarṇaprabhāsa-sūtra were discovered largely by the French Central Asian Expeditions in Tun-huang. These manuscripts from Tun-huang are numbers 499-516 in M. Lalou's catalogue. The Central Asian fragments have great importance because of their antiquity. Among them are

[33] *Op.cit.* p. XXII.

some more fragments which belong to Tib. I. The larger number of pages belong to Tib. III i.e. the Tibetan translation of I-tsing's Chinese version. Among the Central Asian remains fragments of Tib. II are not represented.

As concerns the size and the contents, Tib. II is not very different from Tib. III. After the compilation of Tib. II the old Tibetan translation (Tib. I) was supposed to be out of date, for the new Tibetan translation was not only much more modern from the point of view of translation, but it was also much more acceptable because it incorporated detailed discourses on new philosophical problems, like the teaching about the trikāya, the teaching about the Nirvāṇa and the teaching about the ten conditions of Bodhisattvas (*daśabhūmi*). The authors of the Narthang blockprint held the text of Tib. I. to be superfluous, so they did not incorporate it in the Canon. The reason for not finding any fragment among Central Asian manuscripts which could be identified with Tib. II could be that it was not extant. These texts were written down by the translators Jinamitra, Śīlendrabodhi and Ye-śes-sde who were active during the reign of King Ral-pa-can (804-816). It seems that the Tun-huang fragments of Suvarṇaprabhāsa-sūtra originated in the second and third part of the 8th century.

Among the Central Asian texts can be found the remains of other unknown texts. Such a text is number 507[34] in Lalou's catalogue. From the existing colophons it is clear that these fragments belong to the 19th and 22nd chapters. This 19th chapter correlates to Tib. II and Tib. III with the 18th, in Tib. I it correlates with chapter 10th. The titles of the chapters also prove this fact, the title of the chapter in fragment 507 is *sa lha-mo brtan-pai leu* which is in Tib. I, II and III *sai lha-mo brtan-mai leu*. The 22nd chapter of the fragment correlates with chapter 21 in Tib. II and III, chapter 13 in Tib. I. The title of the chapter in the fragment is: *dbaṅ-poi bzaṅ-poi 'byuṅ-bai leu*, while in Tib. II it agress with Tib. I. *legs-par-byuṅ-bai leu* in Tib. III is: *rgyal-po legs-skyes-kyi leu*. The Sūtra as a whole carries the name in fragment 507: *gser-'od dam-pa mdo-sdei rgyal-po*. This name is not shorter than that which is written in Tib. I: *gser-'od dam-pa mdo-sdei dbaṅ-po rgyal-po*. In other manuscripts the title is: Suvarṇaprabhāsasūtrendrarāja. The form of the title in Tib. II and Tib. I agrees, Tib. III has a longer title: *gser-'od dam-pa mchog-tu rnam-par rgyal-ba mdo-sde*.

In this connection it must be mentioned that J. Nobel, while checking the text of Tib. III, realized the existence of another text which will be marked with Tib. IV. However the text Tib. IV has nothing to do with the text of fragment 507 and the title agrees with Tib. III.

The fragments of Central Asian manuscripts which correlate with Tib. I are under the numbers 504, 505, 506 and 512 in Lalou's catalogue. Nobel marked these fragments in his edition of the text with P_1, P_4, P_2, and P_3. P_1 consists of two pages and it represents the last part of the seventh chapter. P_2 is a fragment which consists of three pages. The third page is torn. The first two pages give the text of the last line of the 12th stanza of the second *parivarta*. The torn page belongs to the tenth *parivarta*. A photocopy of this page is included at the end of J. Nobel's work. P_3 is also a torn page

[34] M. Lalou, *Inventaire des manuscripts tibêtains de Touenhouang (Fonds Pelliot tibêtain) Nos. 1-49* (in French: A catalogue of the Tun-huang manuscripts of the Pelliot Collection), Paris 1939.

from the seventeenth chapter. The page P_4 consists of a larger part of the nineteenth chapter from the last line of the stanza 4 to the stanza 17 of the twentieth chapter.

In some cases the text of the blockprints and the fragments differs. For example the name of Buddha's wife Gopa is transcribed in the fragments while the prints translate it as *sa-'ts'e-ma*. Instead of *bskyed-pa* is given *bskrund-pa*, and for the Sanskrit *avarupta* is given the correlating form: *avaruptakuśalamala*. In three places in the original translation was *bskruopa* which was replaced afterwards with the more general *bskyed-pa*.

Our transcription of the Tibetan script is slightly different from that of Nobel. In our transliteration of the dhāraṇīs in chapter 8 the following system has been used:

ཀ	ka	ཁ	kha	ག	ga	ང	ṅa
ཅ	ča	ཆ	čha	ཇ	ǰa	ཉ	ña
ཏ	ta	ཐ	tha	ད	da	ན	na
པ	pa	ཕ	pha	བ	ba	མ	ma
ཙ	ca	ཚ	cha	ཛ	ja		
ཝ	wa	ཞ	ža	ཟ	za	འ	'a
ཡ	ya	ར	ra	ལ	la		
ཤ	śa	ས	sa	ཧ	ha	ཨ	a

The manuscripts are marked by the following abbreviations:

P the red blockprint in the Bibliothèque Nationale in Paris.

P_1, P_2, P_3, P_4 the Central Asian fragments from Tun-huang in the Bibliothèque Nationale of Paris

Hs. The manuscript Kanjur in the Berlin Library.

C The red blockprint in the Cambridge University Library.

II Hs. The second Tibetan text in the Berlin manuscript Kanjur.

II Bl. The second Tibetan text in the Narthang blockprint. It will be marked later as Bl.

II P The second Tibetan text in the red blockprint in the Bibliothèque Nationale, Paris. Later it will be marked as P.

III The Tibetan translation of I-tsing's Chinese version.

A chart showing the correlation of the Uigur, the Tibetan, the Chinese and the Sanskrit texts is given at the end of this chapter. The chart shows that Tib. I and Dharmakṣema's text are the closest to the original Sanskrit text. A significant deviation in the numbering is in the third chapter on the golden drum, which is the core of the Sutra. In the Sanskrit manuscripts ABCDF and in Tib. I this chapter is split up into two chapters: the first is a small introduction in prose, the second is a metrical part consisting of 102 stanzas. In the palm-leaf manuscript, and also in Dharmaksema's text the third chapter is not split up. In I-tsing's version, in Tib. II, Tib. III and in the Uigur version it is the fourth chapter.

Another less significant deviation is between the texts ABCDEF and G in the last chapter of the Sanskrit text. In this case Dharmakṣema's text agrees with the ABCDEF group of Sanskrit texts.

There are some significant differences between Dharmakṣema's Chinese version and the Sanskrit inspite of the agreeing titles of chapters. Dharmakṣema handled the Sanskrit text with the freedom the Chinese authors excercised in translating Indian texts.

The contents of chapters are as follows. The first chapter of the Sanskrit version is a sort of introduction to the core of the Sūtra of the third chapter. The second paragraph of the text according to J. Nobel is a later insertion and opposed to this the text of Dharmakṣema represents the original form. The first chapter in the Uigur text has two legends and the torma sacrifice for the Four Mahārājas.

There is a more significant difference in the second chapter between the B version of the Sanskrit text and the version of Dharmakṣema which is about the span of the life of Buddha. In this part Ruciraketu reflects upon the question how could it be that Buddha's life was limited to eighty years. There is also a long discourse between the Brahmin Kauṇḍinya and the Litsavi prince Sarvaloka-priyadarśana. The Brahmin asks for a relic of Lord Buddha. The prince teaches Kauṇḍinya thirteen stanzas about how one should not desire relics of the Buddha. In Dharmakṣema's text the part about Kauṇḍinya is missing. In fact I-tsing's version has an even longer addition where the four Tathāgatas, Yakṣas and Nāgas tell the truth about Buddha's age. This part was added first to the Chinese text by Jñānagupta. Tib. II also contains this added part (p. 191). This chapter is missing from the Uigur text.

In the third chapter, the Bodhisattva Ākāśagarbha (in other texts he is called Ruciraketu) asks the Buddha to explain the secret of the Tathāgatas. Buddha in his answer unfolds the teaching of the three kāya-s. The three kāya-s (bodies) of the Buddha are:

1. Nirmāṇakāya (the assumed body, which the Buddhas assume in order to carry out their work of releasing beings),
2. Sambhogakāya (the superhuman body with which the Buddhas enjoy their glory, virtue and wisdom),
3. Dharmakāya (the absolute body).

Their features are related in the following part. The nirmāṇakāya changes its place, time and conditions. The sambhogakāya has 32 prominent signs and 80 minor signs, the so-called lakṣaṇa-s. The first two kāya-s are only fictive names, only the dharmakāya is absolute which gives a basis for the existence of the first two kāya-s. In the nirmāṇakāya and sambhogakāya the Buddhas show different signs, but the dharmakāya has no signs. The first two kāya-s also hold the nirvāṇa with the rest-base (*sopadhiśeṣa nirvāṇa*). The dharmakāya holds the nirvāṇa without the rest-base (*nirupadhiśeṣa nirvāṇa*). On all the three kāya-s rests the *apratiṣṭhita nirvāṇa*. It is discussed further why ordinary persons cannot realize the three kāya-s. The nirmāṇakāya and the sambhogakāya can be studied through their activity and development as stable and unstable. The dharmakāya is only unstable. The third chapter explains the dharmakāya as Mahāyāna itself. Discussion follows about the way Dharmas bring the Buddhas into existence. In the dharmakāya one cannot find any difference nor can it be ended. Then follows the teaching of the middle way.

The ten conditions of Bodhisattvahood and the condition of the Tathāgata are discussed. The absolute pureness of the condition of the Tathāgata is also discussed. Ākāśagarbha and the gods explain the four merits the land has in which the Sūtra of Golden Light is preached. In the existing Sanskrit text the above part is missing. It is included in I-tsing's version and also in the Uigur text. I-tsing's translation of this chapter is basically identical with the translation of Paramārtha (who died in 569 AD). Paramārtha's version was incorporated into Pao-kuei's "synthetic edition". I-tsing made only stylistic changes, and inserted expressions or words. In general the chapter became longer. The text of this chapter is present in Tib. II. It was translated into Tibetan probably around 810 AD. In Tib. III the chapter was translated from I-tsing's text. The other Tibetan translation (Tib. II) goes back to the translation of Paramārtha, which must have been very close to the original Sanskrit text. Tib. II explains, in some places, the philosophical notions of Mahāyāna on its own, and this gives a special value to the translation.

The fourth chapter, which is third in the Sanskrit version, starts with prose. According to J. Nobel this is the oldest chapter of the Sūtra, and the rest of the Sūtra was constructed around this. The Chinese version starts with prose, the Sanskrit text with gāthās. In Chinese this part is followed by prose. The Uigur text also begins with the prose part and is followed by the gāthās. The subject of this chapter is how Bodhisattva Ruciraketu dreams about the golden drum. The sounds of the drum reveal the gāthās of the repentant consciousness. The beings who listen to the gāthās get freed. Then follows a part about repenting one's evil deeds and sins (*deśanā*). The happiness resulting from the good deeds of other beings, called *anumodanā,* is unfolded. Then follows a part of the desirability of living in the *daśabhūmi*. Afterwards follows a teaching of the repentant consciousness. The praise (*vandana)* of the Buddhas follows. The next part teaches the removal of the sufferings of other beings and the happiness resulting from fulfilling their wishes. After the praise of Buddha there is a reference to the seventh chapter. This reference is not to be found in the Sanskrit text. At the end of the Uigur text there are two dhāraṇīs entitled Cintāmaṇi (precious stone) dhāraṇīs, which are repeated in the sixth chapter of the Uigur text.

The seventh chapter in the Chinese text is the one immedialtely following the fourth chapter in the Sanskrit text.

The insertion of dhāraṇīs in the Uigur text takes place in the twelfth chapter of Tib. II, Tib. III, and the Chinese text.

The fifth chapter which is missing in Sanskrit but is present in Tib. II, Tib. III and the Uigur text is entitled "The Elimination of the hindrances to good deeds". This chapter unfolds the ideas of the previous fourth Chinese and third Sanskrit chapter. I-tsing's translation is based on the translation of Paramārtha which was incorporated in Pao-kuei's translation. While the Buddha dwelt on meditation, immeasurable light poured from his hair which filled the Buddhist lands with light. Through this light in the worlds beings got freed from their sufferings and sinful deeds. Indra (in the Chinese text Śakra, in Tib. II Śāriputra, in the Uigur text Hormuzda: this is Indra's Uigur name, of Sogdian origin) is surprised and asks in what way can one eliminate bad deeds which stand in the way of one's repentance. Buddha explains in detail how the repenting (*deśanā*) consciousness can be expressed. Even those born in a rich house or among the gods must repent their bad deeds if they want to enjoy the fruits of the stream of knowledge. Buddha explains the different types of hindrances to deeds and the means of their removal. The removal is based on the recognition of the essence of all the dharmas. Śakra (Tib. Śāriputra, Uig. Hormuzda) asks Buddha to explain how to attain *anumodanā*. There is also a discussion on the dharmakāya-s. Afterwards Śakra asks Buddha about the pariṇāmanā, and Buddha answers to enlighten the details. In the end Buddha tells a story from the past and the Tathāgata of that time (Ratnarājamahāprabhāsāloka) appears. Buddha speaks about the merits which are attained by a king, a minister, Śramaṇa-s and Brāhmaṇas, as well as all the subjects in whose country the Sūtra is preached. (It is interesting that when the Chinese and Tibetan texts generally speak about sins the Uigur text specifies five sins).

The sixth chapter is entitled "The Dhāraṇī of the absolutely pure lands". Similar is the title in the Uigur text, but the Tibetan version III(b) has the title "The absolutely pure Dhāraṇī". After the introductory part about the bodhi-thoughts and about the essence of the bodhi, the main part of the chapter follows which is about the ten pāramitās (namely: generosity, virtue, renunciation of the world, wisdom, energy, patience, truthfulness, determination, friendliness towards all creatures, and equanimity). There is a long explanation of the ten conditions of Bodhisattvahood. In the description of the fifth condition the Uigur text and Tib. III agree. The dhāraṇī-s of the different conditions (pāramitās) follow. This is the first time that the dhāraṇīs are mentioned in the Chinese and Tibetan versions. The Chinese translation in Pao-kuei's synthetic version originates from Paramārtha.

The seventh chapter "Praise to the vision of the lotus flower" correlates with the seventh in the Uigur text, the fourth in the Sanskrit and the seventh in the Tibetan text. Thus the chapter starts (quoted from Emmerick's English translation): "Then indeed the Lord spoke thus to the noble goddess Bodhisattvasamuccayā". The opening sentence in the Chinese, Tibetan and Uigur texts refer to the fourth chapter in the Chinese and Uigur, and the third chapter in the Sanskrit text. Bodhisattvasamuccayā is called the goddess of the Bodhi tree. She recalls an earlier event which gives a suggestion for Ruciraketu's dream of the golden drum in the fourth chapter. In olden times lived a king Suvarṇabhujamgendra. The name is translated into Tibetan as *rab gnag-ciṅ* 'absolutely black'. The Uigur version translates the name as: *coğ-luğ Yalir-miš qutlug oluglug ir ilikbeš bir erti* "there was a king who was full of the light of energy, a fortunate king". The king praises in gāthās all the past, present and future Buddhas. The following gāthās praise Buddha.

The eighth chapter is missing in the Sanskrit version, but it is to be found in Tib. II and Tib. III. The title of the chapter in the Chinese translation is: "The golden victory dhāraṇī", which agrees with the Tibetan title. The title of the Uigur is "Teaches the golden dhāraṇī". Buddha teaches in this chapter the use of the above-mentioned dhāraṇī to the Bodhisattva Supratiṣṭhita and the merits which one can attain through this dhāraṇī. The Uigur names might have been based on the lost Sanskrit version, or any version which was close to it. (See the names on p.V.7a, 7b: Dundubesvari, Vaipuli, Kunuprabāsi, Ratnakusi, Smanta prabi, Btmavičavi, Samantadharsani and so on).

The ninth chapter is about Śunyatā in the Chinese, Tib.II, III and also in the Uigur version. It agrees with the fifth chapter of the Sanskrit text. Buddha unfolds the gāthās about Śūnyatā before a large assembly. He also explains the essence of Saṃsāra. The Chinese, Uigur and Tibetan texts describe the effect of his speech on the listeners.

Chapter ten is not included in the Sanskrit text. The Chinese translation in Pao-kuei's synthetic version is based on Paramārtha, and is strongly dependent on it. In this chapter the Buddha teaches the goddess Ālokacintāmaṇi about the five skandhas and the dharmadhātu. In this part there is a common mistake in the Uigur and Tib. III text. I-tsing's text reads "when on the other hand it is told that they are different, then one begins to think that the different Buddhas and Bodhisattvas have different shapes and signs….." Tib. III has at the same place: *'du-byed-kyi mthsan-ñid*. In the Uigur text, which is similar to Tib. III reads: *birök öngi irkü ča erser + galtï qamag burganlaring bodisatvalaring yorïg-lari belkuleri bolar ög yana atkanmïš japsïnmiš bulug* "And when the Buddha's and Bodhisattva's movement and signs are understood….."

In another place I-tsing's text and the Tib. III deviate from each other, but at that place Tib. III agrees with the Uigur text: "but if and when they would get to know that this Sūtra does not exist they would altogether disappear and sink away….." *ötrü atïn nomlug erdini-ler jeme barča orun orun sayu yitlingiyu yoget gajular* "If and when they would get to know that this Sūtra does not exist they would disappear from everywhere……" The Tibetan text has in this context: *gnas de-ñid-du* "from everywhere".

The eleventh chapter, together with the following twelfth chapter, is the sixth chapter in the Sanskrit text. Pao-kuei's version incorporates the translation of Dharmakṣema. As regards the Tibetan, Tib. II originates from Tib. I. In Uigur it carries the same title as the Chinese chapter: "The Assembly of the Four Mahārājas, of Gods and Humans". The Four Mahārājas Vaiśravaṇa, Dhṛtarāṣṭra, Virūḍhaka and Virūpākṣa praised the Sūtra and the merits which one attains from this Sūtra. They want, as protectors of the world, to protect the kings from enemies and diseases.

The twelfth chapter is entitled in Uigur, I-tsing, Tib. II, and Tib. III: "The observance of the world by the Four Mahārājas. Buddha asks them to protect the kings who respect and support the Sūtra. In a long discussion he unfolds the merits which one can attain by spreading and popularizing the Sūtra. At the end of the Sanskrit Sūtra, it is said that Suvarṇaprabhāsa-sūtra is the best among the śāstras. The Sanskrit text finishes here, but the Chinese, Tib. II, III and the Uigur texts continue. The great king Vaiśravaṇa reveals the Cintāmaṇi-dhāraṇī. The Four Great Kings praise the qualities of Buddhas, and the merits of the Sūtra. The Four Great Kings take a vow to respect the Sūtra and the teacher of the Dharma.

The thirteenth chapter is not included in the Sanskrit text. In Pao-kuei's synthetic version it is the eleventh chapter. The translation originates from Jñānagupta. In Tib. II and in Uigur it is the thirteenth chapter, as in I-tsing. I-tsing's translation is independent of Jñānagupta's translation. The title of the chapter is: "The immaculate dhāraṇī". In this chapter Buddha reveals the immaculate dhāraṇī to Śāriputra.

The fourteenth chapter is not to be found in the Sanskrit text, but it is also not incorporated in the "synthetic version" of Pao-kuei. In Tib. II and in the Uigur translation this chapter is entitled "The teaching of the immaculate Cintāmaṇi Dhāraṇī". In this part the Buddha speaks to Ānanda in the great assembly. The Bodhisattva Avalokiteśvara reveals the dhāraṇī called Cintāmaṇi. The Bodhisattva Vajrapāṇi Guhyādhipati, Brahmā Sahāṃpati, Śakra (Uig. Hormuzda), the Four Mahārājas and the Nāga-kings reveal their dhāraṇīs.

The fifteenth chapter "Worship of Goddess Sarasvatī" correlates with the seventh chapter in the Sanskrit text. The Central Asian Sanskrit fragments and the Chinese translation by Dharmakṣema show that this chapter devoted to the goddess Sarasvatī was originally much shorter. Dharmakṣema's text has altogether 184 Chinese characters. In his "synthetic version" Pao-kuei added a translation from Jñānagupta after Dharmakṣema's translation. This part has about the same contents as the Sanskrit text. Tib. II agrees with the text of Tib. I and the Uigur version agrees with the chapter of I-tsing. Goddess Sarasvatī greets Buddha and relates the wonderful abilities of the Sūtra and asks everyone to support and protect it. Afterwards she reveals the secret of the ritual bath with the thirtytwo drugs. (Here the Tibetan texts as well as the Uigur text enumerate the Sanskrit names of the drugs). She reveals the dhāraṇī in all details of the ritual. In this chapter Sarasvatī proclaims three dhāraṇīs. Again she unfolds the power of the Sūtra. The Brahman Kauṇḍinya praises Sarasvatī in three stanzas. The Chinese text has another longer dhāraṇī which is not in the Sanskrit, but is incorporated in the Uigur and the Tibetan texts. Sarasvatī relates the wishes that this dhāraṇī can fulfill. Kauṇḍinya praises Sarasvatī under the name Nārāyaṇī. The Brahman Kauṇḍinya gives the details of the Assembly of Gods of different heavens, the names of the disciples of Buddha Maudgalyāyana and Śāriputra, the Brahman kings, the Śuddhāvāsa devas and so on and how Sarasvatī should be addressed. This part of the chapter is missing from the Sanskrit version.

The sixteenth and seventeenth chapters entitled: "Worship of Goddess Śrī" and "Praise of Śrī the Goddess of Luck and Fortune" in the Chinese text of I-tsing correlate with the eighth chapter of the Sanskrit text. The ninth chapter of the Sanskrit text, however, is not an independent chapter in I-tsing's text, but is a part of the seventeenth chapter. Tib. II and Tib. I nearly agree. The Uigur text is close to the Chinese as well as to the Tib. III. Śrī, the Goddess of Fortune, greets Buddha, and promises to support and spread the Sūtra with all her capabilities. She tells about the Tathāgata Ratna-kusuma-guṇa-sāgara-vaiḍūrya-kanaka-giri-suvarṇa-kāncaña-prabhāsa-śrī under whom she herself collected many merits. The beings who read and recite the Sūtra should pay homage. She would see to it that the people gain the fruits of their work, and that the gods are happy.

In the seventeenth chapter, which corresponds to the eighth and ninth chapters in the Sanskrit text, Goddess Śrī speaks to the Buddha. She gives directions about the rituals conducive to a rich harvest. Here, the Tathāgata named above again plays an important role. She gives a dhāraṇī and exclaims that after reciting the dhāraṇī Buddhas and Bodhisattvas should be called by name. The names of the Bodhisattvas and Buddhas are enumerated in another context in the Sanskrit text. The recitation of the dhāraṇī will also secure a long life for the believers.

Chapter eighteen entitled "Worship of Dṛḍhā the Goddess of the Earth"correlates with the tenth chapter of the Sanskrit text. In the Uigur text Dṛḍhā is called Vasuntari. Tib. I and the first part of Tib. II agree. Dṛḍhā greets the Buddha and promises that to whatever land this Sūtra goes she will accompany it. Her presence will make the earth rich and this will support the Sūtra. Buddha says that he is happy when anybody pays homage to the Sūtra. Dṛḍhā recites a dhāraṇī (it consists of three parts) and gives instructions for its use.

The ninteenth chapter correlates with the eleventh chapter of the Sanskrit text. It is entitled "Worship of the leader of the gods Saṃjñāya". Saṃjñāya, like the other gods, greets Buddha and pays homage to the Sūtra. He explains as to why he is called Saṃjñāya. He presents a dhāraṇī and describes the circumstances under which the dhāraṇī should be performed. The dhāraṇī is not in the Sanskrit text.

The twentieth chapter correlates with the twelfth chapter in the Sanskrit and is entitled "Instructions concerning divine kings". The Uigur title is slightly different: "Teaching the right ruling (rāja-śāstra) for the rulers and Khans". This is a short rāja-śāstra which is also translated into Uigur. This chapter is also to be found in the Tibetan texts. Dṛḍhā asks Buddha how the kings should reign. Buddha tells the story of the king Bālendraketu and the teachings he gave to his son. (The Sanskrit text starts with an invocation). The Four Mahārājas ask the Brahman why the kings of men are called Devas and Devaputras. Brahman also unfolds the rules by which to reign rightly.

Chapter twentyone is about king Susaṃbhava. It agrees basically with the thirteenth chapter of the Sanskrit text. In Uigur the king Susaṃbhava is called Sučari. The chapter is found in all the Tibetan versions. The beginning and the end of the chapter is written in prose. The other parts are in verse (about 32 stanzas). Speaking in front of an assembly of people Buddha narrates the following story: After the nirvāṇa of the Tathāgata Ratnaśikhin, there lived a king named Susaṃbhava, who saw in his dream the dharma-teacher Ratnoccaya. In the morning he went to ask him for an explanation of the essence of the Sūtra. Susaṃbhava was the Buddha Śākyamuni and the preacher was the Buddha of the East, Akṣobhya.

The twentysecond chapter correlates with the fourteenth chapter of the Sanskrit version. In Uigur this chapter is also the twentysecond and is entitled "The preservation of the gods and demons". In this chapter Buddha speaks to Goddess Śrī about the merits of the Sūtra and the consequences of getting acquainted with the Sūtra. All the gods, goddesses, Yakṣas, Nāgas, Asuras and so on listen to the Sūtra and recite it together.

The twentythird chapter correlates with the fifteenth chapter of the Uigur version and the Sanskrit text. The following two chapters (on the following pages IX.18-27) are missing. The two chapters partly agree. Buddha tells the Bodhisattva Ruciraketu and both his sons that they will be enlightened. The gods come to listen as Buddha teaches the Dharma. The Sanskrit text starts with the dialogue of the Bodhisattvasamuccayā and Buddha.

The twentyfourth chapter is entitled: "On healing illnesses". This is the sixteenth chapter in the Sanskrit text. This chapter is much shorter in the Uigur translation. It starts with the dialogue of the

Buddha and Bodhisattvasamuccayā (in Chinese: the Goddess of the Bodhi Tree) about the ten thousand devaputras. This chapter is important because it gives some information about medicine. First, Buddha tells the story of Jalavāhana, and Jaṭiṃdhara. When he speaks about the knowledge of Jaṭiṃdhara it becomes clear that medicine in the age of the Sūtra was a scholastic system (with eight branches of medical science, based on the six elements). This system of medicine is probably based on the Ayurvedic system. It also explains what food and drinks are to be consumed during the different seasons of the year. It has a part on diagnosing diseases, and how the food a person eats influences him.

The twentyfifth chapter is again about Jalavāhana. He is called Yotaki vasanti in the Uigur text. It is the seventeenth chapter in the Sanskrit text. Jalavāhana, taking pity on the fishes who had died from thirst, used his influence to get twenty elephants from the king and change the direction of the stream. He explained to the animals the causes of suffering. At the end of the chapter Buddha identifies the persons: Jalavāhana was Buddha himself, Jālāmbugarbhā was Gopā (Buddha's wife), and Jalavāhana's son was Rāhula. Jalavāhana's other son was Ānanda (the favourite pupil of Buddha). At the end of the Chinese chapter are two dhāraṇīs recited by Jalavāhana. The chapters are not present in Tib. III and in the Uigur text.

The twentysixth chapter in the Chinese, Uigur, Tib. III translations correlates with the eighteenth chapter in the Sanskrit version. The first part is missing in the Sanskrit version, where there is a dialogue of the Buddha and Ānanda. The core of the chapter is the story of the hungry tigress, which was incorporated in the Uigur translation and which was a favourite story with Buddhists. This tale illustrates how body is submitted for merit. In the story the prince Mahāsattva gives his own body to the tigress to eat, instead of her own cubs. At the end of the chapter Buddha reveals that he was the Bodhisattva Śākyamuni, and formally he was also the prince Mahāsattva.

Chapter twentyseven is entitled "The praise of the Bodhisattvas of the ten directions". The title of the chapter in the Uigur version is: "Praise of the Buddha by the Gods". This is the nineteenth chapter in the Sanskrit text. The innumerable Bodhisattvas of the ten directions praise the Bodhisattva Śākyamuni. In the Sanskrit text they praise the Tathāgata Suvarṇa-ratnākara-cchatra-kūṭa. After this follows the praise of the Buddha.

Chapter twentyeight is entitled: "The praise of the Bodhisattva Ruciraketu". In the Uigur text he is called the Bodhisattva Somaketu. The Bodhisattva Ruciraketu greets and praises the Buddha.

Chapter twentynine is the "Praise of the Goddess of the Bodhi Tree". The title of the corresponding Uigur chapter is the same. The Goddess praises Buddha, the wisdom of the Buddhas, and also the announcement of the Sūtra.

In chapter thirty, the Goddess Sarasvatī praises the Buddha, his exterior, his words which are without confusion, and his efforts to set off the wheel of Dharma. The Uigur text also contains this chapter.

Chapter thirtyone is entitled: "Releasing the Sūtra". Buddha exhorts those who are present to protect and spread the right Dharma-ways, so that the Dharma can live longer. Then all step forward one by one and praise the Dharma.

It was generally accepted till now that the text of the Uigur Suvarṇaprabhāsa-sūtra had been translated from the Chinese version of I-tsing. The overall impression given by the colophons was that probably the different chapters had been translated at different times but certainly copied down at different times. This originates from the fact that the Sūtra was used as a sort of offering. To attain certain aims parts of it were copied or recopied. So it could happen that the first book (*tegsinč*) was translated from Tibetan, while the others from Chinese.

The comparison with the Chinese and Tibetan texts has modified this picture. It has turned out that the Chinese text of I-tsing and the Uigur text though close to each other and though the chapters agree etc., the Tibetan texts and the Uigur text show a number of special similarities, common misunderstandings and mistakes even in such chapters which were supposed to be translated from Chinese. Such minor differences are to be found in the seventh chapter.

It seems that however closely connected the I-tsing translation and the Uigur text are, the Uigur text is also related to the Tibetan text in some way, especially to Tib. III which was translated from I-tsing's Chinese version.

CHART OF CHAPTERS IN THE DIFFERENT VERSION

Uig.	I-tsing Tib.III	Dharma-kṣema (Dh)	Pao-kuei (P)	Sanskrit ABCDEF	Sanskrit G	Tib.I	Tib.II
I		I	I (Dh)	I	I	I	I
missing	II	II	II (Dh)	II	II	II	II
III	III		III (P)				
IV	IV	III	IV (Dh)	III, IV	III	III, IV	IV
V	V		V (P)				V
VI	VI		VI (P)				VI
VII	VII	IV	VII (Dh)	V	IV	V	VII
VIII	VIII						VIII
IX	IX	V	VIII (Dh)	VI	V	VI	IX
X	X		IX (P)				X
XI	XI	VI	X (Dh)	VII	VI	VII	XI
XII	XII	VI	X (Dh)	VII	VI	VII	XII
XIII	XIII		XI (Jñ)				XIII
XIV	XIV						XIV
XV	XV.1	VII	XII (Dh, Jñ)	VIII	VII	VIII	XV
XV	XV.2	VII	XII (Dh, Jñ)	VIII	VII	VIII	XV
XVI	XVI	VIII	XIII (Dh)	$IX_1 X_2$	VIII, IX	IX	XVI
XVII	XVII	VIII	XIII (Dh)	$IX_1 X$	$VIII_1 IX$	IX	XVII
XVIII	XVIII	IX	XIV (Dh)	XI	X	X	XVIII
XIX	XIX	X	XV (Dh)	XII	XI	XI	XIX
XX	XX	XI	XVI (Dh)	XIII	XII	XII	XX
XXI	XXI	XII	XVII (Dh)	XIV	XIII	XIII	XXI
XXII	XXII	XIII	XVIII (Dh)	XV	XIV	XIV	XXII
missing	XXIII	XIV	XIX (Dh)	XVI	XV	XV	XXIII
	XXIV	XV	XX (Dh)	XVII	XVI	XVI	XXIV
XXV	XXV	XVI	XXI (Dh)	XVIII	XVII	XVII	XXV
XXVI	XXVI	XVII	XXII (Dh)	XIX	XVIII	XVIII	XXVI
XXVII	XXVII	XVIII	XXIII (Dh)	XX	XIX	XIX	XXVII
XXVIII	XXVIII	XXIII	XXIII (Dh)	XX	XIX	XX	XXVIII
XXIX	XXIX	XVIII	XXIII (Dh)	XIX	XIX	XXI	XXIX
XXX	XXX						
XXXI	XXXI		XXIV (Jñ)				

9. SIGNIFICANCE OF THE DHĀRAṆĪS IN BUDDHIST LITERATURE

"It happened that this poet, the least primitive of poets, could, through the combination of words, strangely enchanting and, through the musical splendour of verses and their unique plenitude, produce the impression of the most powerful quality of poetry; that of magical formulas" (T.I. about Mallarmé)

Murmuring words in a situation of emotional tension and stress is a part of our everyday life and belongs to the earliest layer of human culture. However in different cultural complexes magical formulas have received different emphasis. Instant repetition of the name of God, *dhikr* is a highly esteemed practice among the sufis[1].

The meaning of the words dhāraṇī and mantra is sometimes synonymous, while the word dhāraṇī is mostly used in Mahāyāna texts. The importance of dhāraṇīs increased enormously and in fact by the 8th century the dhāraṇīs occupied such an important role that the main stream of Mahāyāna Buddhism of those times was called Mantrayāna. The term mantra was used as early as the Vedic texts, and is an integral part of the present day Hindu and Buddhist ritual as well.

In the times of the Vedas magic spells must have been very widely used and some of them were also incorporated in the canon of the Rigveda and Yajurveda. In contrast to the Brāhmaṇas, which were supposed to be the utterances of Brahman, expositions of religious teachings, the hymns and formulas, which were incantated during the sacrifices were called mantras. As J.N. Farquhar states "The word mantra means originally religious thought, prayer, sacred utterance, but from an early date it also implied that the text was a weapon of supernatural power"[2].

V.S. Agrawala, in his *India as Known to Pāṇini*, presents Pāṇini's system of sūtra's as follows: "Pāṇini has used in his sūtras the following terms associated with certain texts: (1) *chandas*, (2) *mantra*, (3) *ṛc* (*chandas* denoted sacred literature, as distinguished from *bhāṣā* the spoken language). The term mantra had a more restricted scope being applied to a sacred formula whether in verse (*ṛc*) or in prose (*yajuṣ*), as opposed to brāhmaṇa. Thus the particular linguistic forms noted for mantras do not occur in the Brāhmaṇas ... Brāhmaṇa stands for the Brāhmaṇa works, and *a-mantra* also points to non-mantra literature, or the Brāhmaṇas"[3].

Though Buddha himself opposed ritualistic religion, mantras appeared early in Buddhist texts. In the Majjhima Nikāya — as it is quoted by Agehananda Bharati — Buddha himself instructs Aṅgulimāla to cure a woman by pronouncing a healing mantra. In other Pali texts, in the Aṅguttara Nikāya and in the Dīgha Nikāya mantras are written for warding off different dangers[4].

---

[1]M. Eliade, *Yoga, Immortality and Freedom*, New Jersey 1973, p. 408.

[2]J.N. Farquhar, *An Outline of the Religious Literature of India*, Delhi-Patna-Varanasi 1967, p. 25.

[3]V.S. Agrawala, *India as Known to Pāṇini*, Lucknow 1953, p. 318.

[4]Agehananda Bharati, *The Tantric Tradition*, New York 1975, p. 104.

In Vasubandhu's Bodhisattva-bhūmi the dhāraṇīs of the Bodhisattva are of four kinds — as quoted by S. Dasgupta: "Dharma dhāraṇī, Artha dhāraṇī, Mantra dhāraṇī and the dhāraṇī for the attainment of the transcendental merit of forbearance belonging to the Bodhisattvas (*Bodhisattva-kṣānti-lābhāya ca dhāraṇī*). The Dharma-dhāraṇī is composed of that kind of mantras through the hearing of which (even though they are not explained by any Śāstra or by any preacher) the follower attains memory (*smṛti*), perfect knowledge (*prajñā*) and spiritual strength (*bala*). Artha-dhāraṇī is that type of mantras through the mystic power of which the correct significance (*artha*) of the Dharmas (which significance is never explained in any Śāstra or by any preacher) is revealed to the follower in a spontaneous way. The mantra-dhāraṇī enables man to attain perfection. The dhāraṇī for the attainment of forbearance (*kṣānti*) is the mantra through which the ultimate nature of the dharmas is revealed to the reciter; through the realization of the ultimate immutable nature of the dharmas the follower attains generosity of heart which produces in him the merit of forbearance"[5].

Edgerton's *Buddhist Hybrid Sanskrit Dictionary* classifies dhāraṇī's in the same way, as Vasubandhu did. This dictionary agrees with Vasubandhu when it says: dhāraṇī's "often consisting of meaningless combinations of syllables"[6].

Asaṅga wrote about the mantras in the Yogācāra-bhūmi-śāstra: "the reciting of which should be accompanied by music and certain distortion of the fingers (mudrā), a state of mental fixity (samādhi) might be reached, characterized by nor thought or annihilation of thoughts, and consisting of sixfold bodily and mental happiness (yogi), whence would result endowment with supernatural miracle-working power"[7].

According to Hsuen Tsang the old canon of the Mahāsāṅghikas included the Sūtra-, Vinaya-, Abhidharma-, Saṁyukta-, and Dhāraṇī- (or Vidyādhara-) piṭaka. This last Piṭaka can also be interpreted as the basket or collection of magical knowledge[8].

In the countries of Northern Buddhism mantras gained great popularity.

The Hevajra Tantra has a chapter on mantras, which gives a list of mantras for different purposes. In the chapter on 'Reality' it says[9]: "There is neither mediator, nor whatsoever to meditate, there is neither God nor mantra. It is as (aspects of) the undifferentiated unity that God and mantra have their existence".

Kloṅ-chen rab-'byams-pa of the Nyingma School gives the etymological explanation of the term mantra[10]: "*man* means 'mind as an ego-act (*yid*) taking this as a self' and *tra* means to protect, that is to protect 'quickly' and to protect 'easily'. 'Quickly' means that in a single moment it

---

[5]S. Dasgupta, *Obscure Religious Cults*, Calcutta 1962, p. 21.

[6]F. Edgerton, *Buddhist Hybrid Sanskrit Grammar And Dictonary* Vol. II: Dictonary, Delhi-Varanasi-Patna 1977, p. 284.

[7]L.A. Waddel, *The Buddhism in Tibet or Lamaism*, Cambridge 1971, p. 141.

[8]H. Kern, *Manual of Indian Buddhism*: Delhi 1974, p. 4.

[9]D.L. Snellgrove, *The Hevajra Tantra: A Critical Study*, London 1959, Part I p. 61.

[10]Klong-chen rab-'byams-pa, *Kindly Bent To Ease Us*, translated from the Tibetan and annotated by Herbert V. Guenther, Emeryville 1975, p. 282.

conquers what opposes the transmutation of the emotions into pristine cognitions and 'easily' means that the sensuous objects become friends without there being any such frustrating exercises as mortifications and so on".

In chapter 9 entitled "The Existential Approach" Klong-chen rab-'byams-pa stresses the unity aspect of mantra: "....your mind has been since the very beginning a deity, its body is a maṇḍala and speech a mantra"[11].

'Jigs-med gliṅ-pa gives a slightly different explanation[12]: "*man* is cognitive capacity, the appreciative discrimination that is cognizant of the thisness of being; *traya* is to protect the world, or, protection is absolute compassion. The indivisibility of these two (appreciative of the openness of Being and compassion as its dynamic aspect) is *gsang-sngags* (*'amtra*)". This definition probably goes back to an earlier rNying-ma definition: "The nature of gsaṅg-snags is Openness and Compassion"[13].

Nāropa defined mantras as follows[14]: "Birth is purified when the deities (male and female) have put on their respective apparel". As H.V. Guenther explains: These are certain mantras, syllables in specific colours which transform themselves into deities during meditation "and when in a general way the adept feels graced by authentic being".

Tsoṅ-kha-pa the founder of the Ge-lugs-pa sect put it thus: "The word 'mantra' means mind-protection. It protects the mind from ordinary appearances and conceptions". "Mind here refers to all six consciousnesses—eye, ear, nose, tongue, body and mental consciousness—which are to be freed or protected from the ordinary appearances. Whatever appears to the senses is viewed as the emanations of a deity and whatever are heard are viewed as the mantras of a deity. One is thereby protected from ordinary appearances, and through this transformation of attitude, the pride of being a deity emerges. Such protection of mind together with its attendant pledges and vows is called the practice of mantra"[15].

Tsoṅ-kha-pa gives another definition of mantra, which recalls the one of Kloṅ-chen rab-'byams-pa[16]. "In another way, the syllable *man* in mantra is said to be 'knowledge of suchness', and *tra* is etymologised as *traya*, meaning 'compassion, protecting migrators'".

It seems that Agehananda Bharati and H.V. Guenther etymologize the word mantra under the influence of Tibetan definitions: "The word mantra is defined in many ways. The original elements of the word are: *man*- 'to think' with the element *tra* indicating instrumentality. The parts of mantras are the 'sacred syllables', or bījas". Agehananda Bharati stresses also another aspect of mantras that they have to be imparted from teacher to pupil in the course of initiation[17].

---

[11]Again in the translation of Guether *op.cit.* p. 165.

[12]*Op.cit.* p.282.

[13]*Op.cit.* p. 282.

[14]H.V. Guenther, *The Life and Teaching of Nāropa*, Oxford 1963, p. 45, 45n2.

[15]Tsong-kha-pa, *Tantra in Tibet*, transl. and ed. by J. Hopkins, Boston 1977, p. 48.

[16]*Op.cit.* p. 48.

[17]Agehananda Bharati, *op.cit.* p. 121-128.

H.V. Guenther summarises the importance of mantras as a necessary part of entering the world of the extra-ordinary, where words have their 'absolute' meaning: "The importance of a mantra, be it a single syllable or a longer formula, lies in the fact that it attempts to recapture the source from which language has sprung. The mantra (*gsang-sngags* 'hidden language'), on one hand, prevents the person's mind from sallying forth into the categorical and deadening schemata of representational thought and his language from becoming mere words that pass from hand to hand like a coin of little value; on the other hand, it is a first utterance, the first act of a form-giving process that asserts nothing and yet initiates everything, thus enabling us to speak at all. It is as if a hidden reality has only just crystallized in it"[18].

S. Dasgupta defines: "These mantras are to be chanted in the rites, ceremonies, meditations and also in connection with various yogic practices". Later quoting Vasubandhu he sets forth: "this absolute meaningness of the mantras will gradually lead to the realization of the void nature of dharmas"[19].

B. Bhattacharya summarises in his book on Buddhist Esoterism[20]: "The mantras or mystic syllables constitute the backbone of tantric esoterism and of Vajrayāna. They are of innumerable variety, such as bīja (seed) ... these mantras are mostly a string of unmeaning words but they sometimes disclose distinctly the influence of a language unknown".

Research on mantras and dhāraṇīs during the last decades has stressed the point that dhāraṇīs and mantras are intelligible exclamations and their linguistic background, details and origin should be investigated. The presence of South Indian words in dhāranīs was stressed by F. Bernhard[21] and Lokesh Chandra[22].

In Tibetan the notion mantra is defined by the word *sṅags*. The Tibetan *gzuṅs* corresponds to dhāraṇī denoting a full sequence of mantras and the genre, a passage of a sūtra or another independent work, in which instructions of the use of the mantra are also given. Sometimes for the latter meaning the term *gzuṅs-snags* is also used.

In Uigur however the word *darni* is used in both meanings, denoting the mantras and also the genre, works which hold dhāraṇīs, are often called by this name. Besides the word standing by itself there are combinations of this word with others, *darni arviš*, *darni nom*, *darni söz* all the three of them in the meaning of magical formulas[23]. The term *mantrar darni* is also met with[24].

Thus, summing up the different definitions of the mantra, it seems to be evident that in different ages it had different connotations. However one aspect of the mantra remained the same. It was a symbol of a god or goddess and it came to be identified with the god or goddess. In Tantric

[18]Klong-chen rab-'byams-pa, *op.cit.* p. 289.

[19]S. Dasgupta, *op.cit.* pp. 21-22.

[20]B. Bhattacharya, *An Introduction to Buddhist Esoterism*, London 1932, p. 55.

[21]F. Bernhard, Zur Entstehung einer Dhāraṇī (in German: On the genesis of a dhāraṇī), *ZDMG* 1969 pp. 148-168.

[22]Lokesh Chandra, *Nīlakaṇṭha Lokeśvara as the Buddhist Apotheosis of Hari and Hara*, New Delhi 1979. Lokesh Chandra, *Oḍḍiyāna: a new interpretation*, New Delhi 1979.

[23]PDTP p. 159.

[24]PDTP p. 336.

Buddhism, mantra was supposed to represent a god, and it was strongly believed that if it was correctly recited according to the prescriptions of a text or guru a person might enter into unity with the god or goddess the mantras represented.

It is not possible for this study to follow the development of the theory and usage of mantras step by step from the times of the Vedas upto their evolvement under the Śākta systems and the flourishing period of Mantrayāna.

The main subject of interest for the study is, that all the authors repectively stress the point, that the mantra is an original exclamation, which is not to be changed, which has to be passed on in exactly the same original condition, including the pronunciation.

The phonetic values were very important, and when a dhāraṇī was transmitted from one language to another, the translator went to great lengths to find the exact phonetic correspondences[25]. Just as in China, following the track of Hsüen Tsang the translators started tendering the exact Sanskrit equivalents, in a later Uigur tradition, especially in the case of blockprints, the habit was introduced that between the lines the Sanskrit equivalents of certain words (names of Gods, personal names, words of dhāraṇīs) were given[26].

The obligation of conveying exact phonetic values provides vast material for the philological comparison of the Uigur, Tibetan, Sanskrit and Chinese dhāraṇīs of the Suvarṇaprabhāsa-sūtra.

---

[25] Lokesh Chandra, *Sanskrit Texts from the Imperial Palace at Peking*, New Delhi 1966, p. vii.

[26] A. von Gabain, Fnd. II pp. 236-237.

10. DHĀRANĪS OF THE UIGUR VERSION ALONGWITH THE CORRESPONDING DHĀRAṆĪS IN THE SANSKRIT, CHINESE AND TIBETAN SŪTRAS

One of the significant changes in the development of the Suvarṇaprabhāsa-sūtra text is the increase in the number of dhāraṇīs. The earlier text of the Suvarṇaprabhāsa-sūtra, when it was translated into Chinese in the 5th century, had dhāraṇīs only in one chapter (chapter eighth, devoted to Goddess Śrī). The group of Sanskrit words starting with *tadyathā* and finishing with *svahā* were transcribed in Chinese characters by Dharmakṣema. The extant Sanskrit text is younger than Dharmakṣema's translation and it has dhāraṇīs not only in the eighth chapter, but also in the seventh chapter devoted to Sarasvatī. In course of time a number of chapters were added which had more dhāraṇīs (chapters 6, 8, 13, 14 and 18). Some of the other chapters, which originally had no dhāraṇīs (like chapters 12, 19 and in the Chinese text 25) grew bigger as dhāraṇīs were added to them, and so the character of the whole work changed. This change in the original text reflects a change in the development of Buddhism as well. Dhāraṇīs and mantras assumed a greater role and became an essential part of Buddhism.

Uigur, Sanskrit, Tibetan and Chinese versions of the text available in print afford an opportunity to make a comparison among them. The Uigur version from Kansu was edited by W. Radloff and S. Malov in 1911[1] and a fragment from the Śrī chapter discovered by the Second Prussian Expedition in Turfan was published by F.W.K. Mueller in 1908[2]. A part of the Sanskrit text was edited by Sarat Chandra Das and Sarat Chandra Shastri in 1898[3], the first complete editions of the Sanskrit text were made by Hokei Idzumi in 1931[4], later by J. Nobel in 1937[5] and S. Bagchi in 1967[6]. For the comparison of the Uigur dhāraṇīs with the Sanskrit, J. Nobel's and S. Bagchi's editions were used. For the comparison with the Chinese and Tibetan editions the edition of the main Tibetan versions[7] by J. Nobel and his translation of the Chinese version of I-tsing are

---

[1]W. Radloff & S.E. Malov, *Suvarṇaprabhāsa (Sutra zolotogo bleska). Tekst ujgurskoj redakcii* (in Russian: The Sutra of Golden Light. The text of the Uigur version). St. Petersburg 1917 (Bibliotheca Buddhica 17).

[2]F.W.K. Mueller, *Uigurica* (Abhandlungen der Preussischen Akademie der Wissenschaften. Philologische-historische Klasse). Berlin 1908 pp. 15-25.

[3]Sarat Chandra Das & Sarat Chandra Shastri, *Suvarna Prabha*, Fasc. I (Buddhist texts…. publ. by the Buddhist Text Society of India). Calcutta 1898.

[4]Hokei Idzumi, The *Suvarṇaprabhāsa-sūtra*. Kyoto 1931.

[5]J. Nobel, *Suvarṇaprabhāsottamasūtra. Das Goldglanz-Sutra: ein Sankrit text des Mahāyāna-Buddhismus.* (in German: The Sutra of Golden Light: A Sanskrit text of Mahāyāna Buddhism). Leipzig 1937.

[6]S. Bagchi, *Suvarṇaprabhāsasūtra*. Darbhanga 1967.

[7]J. Nobel, *Die tibetischen Übersetzungen Suvarṇaprabhāsottamasūtra. Das Goldglanz-Sutra. Die tibetischen Übersetzungen mit einem Worterbuch hrsg.* (in German: The Tibetan translations. The Sutra of Golden Light. Published with a Dictionary), Vol. 1-2. Leiden 1944-50.

available[8]. In this work, J. Nobel transcribed the Chinese dhāraṇīs and in his notes to the dhāraṇīs and also in the introduction to the Sanskrit text drew the reader's attention to the need for a comparative study of the dhāraṇīs[9]. The transcription of the dhāraṇīs from the Suvarṇaprabhāsa-sūtra of the Ming Tripiṭaka was done under the supervision of Lčaṅ-skya Qutuγtu Rol-paḥi-rdo-rje in the eighteenth century. The quadrilingual transcription of these dhāraṇīs was published in the Śatapiṭaka series by Lokesh Chandra[10]. The Tibetan transcription of the dhāraṇīs was used for this comparison. To refer to the different manuscripts and blockprints Nobel's or Bagchi's abbreviations have been used[11]. First the Uigur version has been given, in the case of the Śrī chapter two Uigur versions have been given, wherever available the Sanskrit versions, as they are the two poles of development. Then the Tibetan versions of dhāraṇīs have been given and finally the Chinese version.

The first place in the Uigur Suvarṇaprabhāsa where we find dhāraṇīs is probably the consequence of a mistake. This group of three dhāraṇīs is devoted to Vairocana and they belong probably to the twelfth chapter (bölük) in the twelfth book where there is a note saying that two pages are missing. The twelfth chapter of the Uigur version includes also the fourth dhāraṇī of this group, and the corresponding Chinese and Tibetan dhāraṇīs are incorporated in the twelfth chapter of the Chinese and Tibetan works. These three dhāraṇīs seem to be misplaced also because the chapter in which they occur, which is the third in the Sanskrit version is the Confession chapter, the oldest part of the Sanskrit version. According to J. Nobel this chapter is the core of the whole Sūtra. After the gāthās of the Sanskrit text which are translated in poetical form, the closing part follows. The misplaced dhāraṇīs occur after the closing part.

---

[8]J. Nobel, *Suvarṇaprabhāsottama-Sūtra. Das Goldglanz-Sutra, ein Sanskrit-Text des Mahāyāna-Buddhismus. I-tsing's chinesische version und ihre Übersetzung*. (Suvarṇaprabhāsottama-sūtra, a Sankrit text of Mahāyāna Buddhism. I-tsing's Chinese version and its translation). Leiden 1958.

[9]J. Nobel, *Suvarṇaprabhāsottamasūtra*. Ein Sankrit text pp. XLVII.

[10]Lokesh Chandra, *Sanskrit Texts from the Imperial Palace at Peking*, New Delhi 1966.

[11]Nobel's transcription of the Tibetan script has not been followed fully. The chart of our transcription is on p. The marking of different manuscripts and blockprints follows Nobel and Bagchi. The transcription of the Sanskrit text follows the general scientific transcription. As regards the transcription of the Chinese dhāraṇīs Nobel says in a note on p. 147 in his edition of I-tsing's text, that he followed Wade's transcription. He stresses the point, that it was very difficult setting forth the radicals and many times instead of *r, l* should be read.

The correlation of the dhāraṇīs in different versions is presented in the following chart:

Dhāraṇī	Uigur	Sanskrit	Tibetan I	Tibetan II	Ming Tripiṭaka	I-tsing
1	IV.65a p.325	—	—	VI leu p.250	B.IV No.1	Chüan IV Chapt.VI p.148 420B
2	IV.65 & p.326	—	—	VI leu p.251	B.IV No.2	Chüan IV Chapt.VI p.148 420B
3	IV.66a p.327	—	—	VI leu p.251	B.IV No.3	Chüan IV Chapt.VI p.148 420B
4	IV.66a p.327	—	—	VI leu p.252	B.IV No.4	Chüan IV Chapt.VI p.149 420C
5	IV.66b p.328	—	—	VI leu p.252	B.IV No.5	Chüan IV Chapt.VI p.149 420C
6	IV.66b p.328	—	—	VI leu p.252	B.IV No.6	Chüan IV Chapt.VI p.150 421A
7	IV.67a p.329	—	—	VI leu p.253	B.IV No.7	Chüan IV Chapt.VI p.150 421A
8	IV.67b p.330	—	—	VI leu p.253	B.IV No.8	Chüan IV Chapt.VI p.150 421A
9	IV.67b p.330	—	—	VI leu p.254	B.IV No.9	Chüan IV Chapt.VI p.151 421B
10	IV.68a p.331	—	—	VI leu p.254	B.IV No.10	Chüan IV Chapt.VI p.151
11	V.8b p.360	—	—	VIII leu p.261	B.V No.1	Chüan V Chapt.VIII p.165 423C
12	II.47b p.128	—	—	XII leu p.276	B.VI No.1	Chüan VI Chapt.XII p.150 421A
13	II.48a p.129	—	—	XII leu p.276-277	B.VI No.2	Chüan VI Chapt.XII p.210 430B
14	II.48b p.130	—	—	XII leu p.277	B.VI No.3	Chüan VI Chapt.VI p.210 431A

15	VI.24a p.445	—	—	XII leu p.279	B.VI No.4	Chüan VI Chapt.XII p.213 431BC
16	VII.3a p.463	—	—	XIII leu p.283	B.VII No.1	Chüan VII Chapt.XIII 433
17	VII.5a p.467	—	—	XIV leu p.285	B.VII No.2	Chüan VII Chapt.XIV p.223 433B
18	VII.5a p.468	—	—	XIV leu p.285-286	B.VII No.3	Chüan VII Chapt.XIV p.233 433C
19	VII.5b p.468	—	—	XIV leu p.286	B.VII No.4	Chüan VII Chapt.XIV p.224 433C
20	VII.6a p.469	—	—	XIV leu p.286	B.VII No.5	Chüan VII Chapt.XIV p.225 434A
21	VII.6b p.470	—	—	XIV leu p.287	B.VII No.6	Chüan VII Chapt.XIV p.225 434A
22	VII.7a p.471	—	—	XIV leu p.287	B.VII No.7	Chüan VII Chapt.XIV p.226 434A
23	VII.7b p.472	—	—	XIV leu p.288	B.VII No.8	Chüan VII Chapt.XIV p.227 434B
24	VII.9b p.476	VII parivarta p.105 B.VIII p.56	VIII leu p.81	—	B.VII No.9	Chüan VII Chapt.XV/1 p.235 435A
25	VII.10a p.477	VII parivarta p.106 B.VIII p.56	VIII leu p.82	—	B.VII No.10	Chüan VII Chapt.XV/1 p.239 435B
26	VII.10b p.478	VII parivarta p.106 B.VIII p.56	VIII leu p.82	—	B.VII No.11	Chüan VII Chapt.XV/1 p.240 435B
27	VII.11a p.479	VII parivarta p.106-107 B.VIII p.56	VIII leu p.82-83	—	B.VII No.12	Chüan VII Chapt.XV/1 p.241 435BC
28	VII.12b,13a p.482-483	VII parivarta p.108-109 B.VIII p.57	VIII leu p.84-85	—	B.VII No.13	Chüan VII Chapt.XV/1 p.243 435C/436B
29	VIII.13b,14a p.522-523	VIII parivarta p.117 B.VIII p.61	IX leu p.89-90	—	B.VIII No.1	Chüan VIII Chapt.XVII p.270 439C
30	VIII.20a p.535	—	—	XVIII leu p.304	B.VIII No.2	Chüan VIII Chapt.XVIII p.278 441A

31	VIII.20b p.536	—	—	XVIII leu p.304	B.VIII No.3	Chüan VIII Chapt.XVIII p.278 441A
32	VIII.20b p.536	—	—	Chapt.XVIII p.304	B.VIII No.4	Chüan VIII Chapt.XVIII p.278 441A
33	VIII.24a p.543	—	—	Chapt.XIX p.306	B.VIII No.5	Chüan VIII Chapt.XIX p.282 441C

As can be seen from the chart the first bigger group of dhāraṇīs are incorporated in chapter 6, in the fourth tegsinč or chüan respectively in the Uigur and Chinese versions. On the front page of the Uigur version one of the Dhyāni-Buddhas can be seen. He is seated on a lotus and his legs are crossed: the right foot over the left. A garment covers his legs above the ankles and both his shoulders, but the right arm and the chest can be seen. Unfortunately it can not be seen whether he holds something in his hand. The titles of chapter 6 vary in the versions in different languages. In the I-tsing version, in the third Tibetan version and in the Uigur version the chapter carries the title: "The dhāraṇī of the absolutely pure country". In Tib. II the title of the chapter is: "The absolutely pure country". The Sanskrit version does not contain this chapter. In this chapter Bodhisattva Siṃha-dhvaja-pratīta-prabhaṃkara (in the Tib. II he carries the name Akṣayamati, in the Uigur text his name is Sinma-nimita-prabankari) asks the Buddha about the essence of dharmas. The Buddha unfolds the theory of the ten pāramitās, as the results of bodhi thoughts. In certain places the Uigur version deviates from the Chinese, for example in the explanation of the different stages of Bodhisattvahood. As distinct from the Chinese version the Uigur text gives the attributes of the different stages (IV.58b, 59a): (1) Vasanabhāk, (2) Mokṣanabhāk, (3) Ādikarmika, (4) Avaivartaka, (5) Anatanasamprasthiti, (6) Asaṃkhyavipākabhūmi, (7) Rājabhūmi, (8) Karuṇāavakramantikā, (9) Caramabhavika, (10) Vairāgyabhūmi. Some works are missing in Tib. III (the work based on I-tsing's translation).

After the discussion of pāramitās, the Buddha discloses ten dhāraṇīs which brush aside the obstacles in reaching the different stages of Bodhisattvahood.

Dhāraṇī 1

The title of the first dhāraṇī is "Supported by the good merits". It agrees in the title in all the versions.

For the first dhāraṇī no instruction is given. The advantage of the dhāraṇī is detailed. It is stated that this dhāraṇī belongs to the Buddhas who are more numerous than the grains of sand of the Ganges. They (the Buddhas) proclaim it for the Bodhisattvas to defend them. It defends those who recite it, who memorize it, and they will be free from all kinds of horrors: namely from tigers, wolves, lions, other fierce animals, wicked ghosts, human beings and non-human beings, foes and robbers, from calamities and miseries. They will overcome the five obstacles, and if they do not forget it they will attain the first stage.

Uig.	tadyata	purana	manorati
Tib. Nob. II	tadya-thā	pu-rṇā	ma-no-ra-thē
P.	—	—	—
Hs.	—	—	—
Bl.	—	—	ma-nor-the
IPP.	ta-dya-thā	pū-rna	ma-no-ra-the
Chin.	tan-chih-t'a	pu-ru-ni	man-nu-ra-t'i

Uig.	duhu duhu duhu	yav-a	suriyu
Tib. Nob. II	du-hu du-hu du-hu	yā-bad	sūrya
P.	—	ya-	—
Hs.	—	ya-	—
Bl.	—	—	—
IPP.	do-ho do-ho do-ho	yā-bad	sū-rya
Chin.	tu-hu tu-hu tu-hu	ya-po	su-li-yu

Uig.	braban-a tanti	yav-a	čantir-a
Tib. Nob. II	a-ba-bhā-sa-te	yā-bad	can-dra
P.	a-pa-bha-sa-ta	ya-	—
Hs.	a-ba-bhas-ta	ya-	—
Bl.	—	—	—
IPP.	a-bhā-ba-sad-dha	ye-ban	can-dha-ra
Chin.	a-p'o-p'o-sa-ti	ya-po	chan-ta-ro

Dhāraṇī 1 (continued)

Uig.	atiyu tanti	tapati	oruksan-a	
Tib. Nob. II	dau-dān-tē	dā-bad	ra-kṣa	mān
P.	dan-tē	da-bad	—	man
Hs.	daṅ-tē	da-ba-da	—	man
Bl.	—	daba-da	rka	man
IPP.	dhau-taṁ-te	tā-pdad	tra-ro-sa	man
Chin.	t'iao-tan-ti	to-po-ta	ro-ch'a	man

Uig.	danun	pare sarana	kuru
Tib. Nob. II	daṇ-ḍa	pa-ri-hā-ram	kuru
P.	dan-ṭa	pa-ri-ha-ra-ma	—
Hs.	dan-ḍa	pa-ri-ha-ra-ma	—
Bl.	daṇ-ṭa	pa-ri-ha-raṃ	—
IPP.	dan-te	ba-re-ram	ku-ru
Chin.	tan-ch'a	po-ri-ho-ran	chü-ru

Uig.	svaha
Tib. Nob. II	svāhā
P.	—
Hs.	—
Bl.	—
IPP.	svā-hā
Chin.	so-ho

तद्यथा पूर्णमनोरथे दुहु[3]। यावत् सूर्य अवभासते यावच् चन्द्र ☐ तावद् रक्ष मां, दण्ड-परिहारं कुरु। स्वाहा।

Dhāraṇī 2

In the second stage the Bodhisattva Mahāsattvas reach the dhāraṇī which is called "The place of good health and happiness". It is again proclaimed by the Buddhas who are more in number than the grains of sand of the two Ganges. It is announced that the Bodhisattva Mahāsattvas who recite it and keep it in their minds will be protected from different horrors, fierce animals, wicked ghosts, humans and non-humans etc., foes and robbers, bad calamities and miseries. They will be freed, they will overcome the five obstacles, and if they do not forget the (dhāraṇī) they will attain the second stage.

Uig.	tadyata	urusu	urusu	arï arï
Tib. Nob. II	tadya-thā	ud-to-li	—	—
P.	—	ud-	—	—
Hs.	—	ud-	—	—
Bl.	—	utto-li	—	—
IPP.	ta-dya-thā	u-tto-li	—	—
Chin.	tan-chih-t'a	wu-ch'ui-ri	—	—

Uig.	cili cili	urusur a soranan	santu santu
Tib. Nob. II	ci-ri ci-ri	ud-to-rā-to-rā-nam	san-to sān-to
P.	—	—	san-to san-to
Hs.	—	—	san-to san-to
Bl.	—	utto-ra-rā-na-ma	—
IPP.	cir-ī ci-rī	u-don-ra-do-ra-nam	san-to san-to
Chin.	chih-ri chih-ri	wu-ch'ui-le ch'ui-lo-nan	shan-tu shan-tu

Uig.	orusu	ari	huru huru	svaha
Tib. Nob. II	ad-to-li		hu-lu hu-lu	svāhā
P.	—	—	—	—
Hs.	—	—	—	—
Bl.	atto-li	—	—	—
IPP.	u-tton-li	—	hu-lu hu-lu	svā-hā
Chin.	wu-ch'ui-ri	—	hu-ru hu-ru	so-ho

Dhāraṇī 3

In the third stage the Bodhisattva Mahāsattvas reach the dhāraṇī called "The power which is difficult to defeat". Remembering and reciting this dhāraṇī has the same advantages as the preceeding dhāraṇī. They will be defended from different horrors, fierce animals, wicked ghosts, humans and non-humans, foes and robbers, from bad calamities and will attain the third stage.

Uig.	tadyata	dantaki	pantaki
Tib. Nob. II	tadya-thā	dan-thi-ke	pan-thi-ke
P.	—	—	pan-thi-ka
Hs.	—	—	pan-thi-ka
Bl.	—	daṇ-ṭhi-ke	baṇṭhi-ke
IPP.	ta-dya-thā	dan-bha-ce-ka	ba-nce-ke
Chin.	tan-chih-t'a	tan-chai-chih	ran-chai-chih

Uig.	karati	kavrati	kiyurti
Tib. Nob. II	ka-ra-thi	kau-ra-ṭhi	ke-yu-re
P.	ka-ra-thā	—	kai-yu-re
Hs.	ka-ra-thā	—	kai-yu-re
Bl.	—	kau-ra-thi	—
IPP.	ga-ra-ce	kai-rai-ce	ke-yu-re-ke
Chin.	chieh-ra-chih	kao-ra-chih	chi-yu-ri

Uig.	tantari	svaha
Tib. Nob. II	dan-ti-li	svāhā
P.	—	—
Hs.	—	—
Bl.	—	—
IPP.	dan-dhī-ri	svā-hā
Chin.	tan-chih-ri	so-ho

Dhāraṇī 4

The Bodhisattva Mahāsattvas reach in the fourth stage the dhāraṇī called "The great furtherance". This dhāraṇī ensures safety from the same horrors and calamities as the previous one. Those who do not forget it will attain the fourth stage.

Uig.	tadyata	siri siri	dar o mini darmini
Tib. Nob. II	tadya-thā	si-ri si-ri	da-mi da-mi-ni
P.	—	si-ri si-ri-ni	di-ma di-ma-ni
Hs.	—	—	di-ma di-ma-ni
Bl.	—	—	—
IPP.	ta-dya-thā	si-ri si-ri	dha-mi-ni dha-mi-ni
Chin.	tan-chih-t'a	shih-ri shih-ri	t'o-mi-ni t'o-mi-ni

Uig.	dari darini	siri sirini	basi a basi a
Tib. Nob. II	da-ri da-ri-ni	si-ri si-ri-ni	bi-sā-la bi-sā-la
P.	—	—	bi-sa-lā bi-sa-lā
Hs.	—	—	pi-sa-lā pi-sa-la
Bl.	—	—	—
IPP.	dha-ri dha-ri-ṇi	si-ri si-ri-ni	bai-sa-ra
Chin.	t'o-ri t'o-ri-ni	shih-ri shih-ri-ni	p'i-she-lo

Uig.	basavini	vantamini	svaha
Tib. Nob. II	pa-sā-pa-sa-ni	ban-dha-nī-ye	svāhā
P.	pa-sa-pa-sa-ni	ban-dha-ni-ye	—
Hs.	pa-sa-pa-sa-ni	ban-dha-ni-ye	—
Bl.	—	—	—
IPP.	bā-sa-bā-sa-ni	ban-dha-mi-te	svā-hā
Chin.	po-shih-po-shih-no	p'an-t'o-mi-ti	so-ho

Dhāraṇī 5

The Bodhisattva Mahāsattvas reach in the fifth stage the dhāraṇī called "With manifold merits decorated". This dhāraṇī defends from the same miseries as the preceding ones. Those who recite it, and do not forget it, will attain the fifth stage.

Uig.	tadyata	hari harini	čiri čirini	karamini
Tib. Nob. II	tadya-thā	ha-ri ha-ri-ni	ci-ri ci-ri-ni	ka-ri-mā-ni
P.	—	—	—	ka-ri-mā-ni
Hs.	—	—	—	ka-ri-mā-ni
Bl.	—	ha-ri hā-ri-ni	ca-ri cā-ri-ni	—
IPP.	ta-dya-thā	ha-ri ha-ri-ni	ci-ri ci-ri-ni	ka-ri-ma-ni
Chin.	tan-chin-t'a	ho-ri ho-ri-ni	che-ri che-ri-ni	chieh-ra-mo-ni

Uig.	sankka pramani	sama santi	čamtari
Tib. Nob. II	saṅ-ka-ri-mā-ni	saṃ-bhā-sāni	jam-ba-ni
P.	saṅ-ka-ri-mā-ni	sā-ma-bā-sa-ni	—
Hs.	saṅ-ka-ri-mā-ri	sā-ma-bā-sa-ni	—
Bl.	saṃ-ka-ri-mā-ni	—	jam-bha-ni
IPP.	saṃ-ka-ri-ma-ni	sa-mbha-san-ni	jam-bha-ni
Chin.	seng-chieh-ra-mo-ni	san-p'o-shạn-ni	chan-po-ni

Uig.	...mtiri	mon ...i	sovayambuyi	svaha
Tib. Nob. II	si-tam-bha-ni	mo-ha-ni	sva-yam-bu-ke	svāhā
P.	—	ma-hā-ni	sva-ya-ma-bu-ke	—
Hs.	—	mahā-ni	—	—
Bl.	stam-bhā-ni	—	sva-yam-bu-ke	—
IPP.	stam-bha-ni	mo-ha-ni	sau-yam-bhu-ke	svā-hā
Chin.	hsi-tan-p'o-ni	mo-han-ni	sui-yen-pu-pi	so-ho

तद्यथा हारि-हारिणि चिरि-चिरिणि क्रमणि-संक्रमणि संभाषणि जम्भनि स्तम्भनि मोहनि स्वयम्भुवे स्वाहा।

Dhāraṇī 6

The Bodhisattva Mahāsattvas reach in the sixth stage the dhāraṇī called "Perfect knowledge". This dhāraṇī belongs to the Buddhas who are more numerous than the grains of the six Ganges, and they proclaim it for protecting the Bodhisattva-Mahāsattvas. Those who recite and memorize this dhāraṇī-formula will be freed from the same horrors as in the case of the previous dhāraṇī and will attain the sixth stage.

Uig.	tadyata	vituri vituri
Tib. Nob. II	tadya-thā	bi-to-ri bi-tor-i
P.	—	—
Hs.	—	—
Bl.	—	—
IPP.	ta-dya-thā	bi-di-ri bi-di-ri
Chin.	tan-chih-t'a	p'i-t'u-ri p'i-t'u-ri
Uig.	marin i kari kari	vitur a anti
Tib. Nob. II	ma-ri-ṇi-ka-li-ka-le	bi-dho-han-te
P.	—	bi-dho-ha-na-te
Hs.	ma-ri-ni-ka-li-ka-le	bi-dho-ha-na-te
Bl.	ma-ri-ṇi-ki-li-ki-li	po-to-hante
IPP.	ma-ri-ni-ka-ri-ka-le	bi-do-tan-te
Chin.	mo-ri-ni chia-ri-chia-ri	p'i-tu-han-ti
Uig.	oru oru oru oru	čuru čuru
Tib. Nob. II	lu-lu lu-lu	cu-lu cu-lu
P.	—	—
Hs.	—	—
Bl.	—	—
IPP.	ro-ro ro-ro	cu-ru cu-ru
Chin.	ru-ru ru-ru	chu-ru chu-ru
Uig.	turu turu	baysači a
Tib. Nob. II	to-lū-ba to-lū-ba	sa-sa-sad-cā
P.	—	—
Hs.	—	sa-sa-san-cā
Bl.	to-lu-ba to-lu-ba	sa-sa-sad-tsa
IPP.	du-ru-ba du-ru-ba-ga	sa-sa-sad-ca
Chin.	tu-ru-p'o tu-ru-p'o	she-she-she-che

Dhāraṇī 6 (continued)

Uig.	barisu	suvasti	sirin satvaranca
Tib. Nob. II	ba-ri-sa	sva-sti	sa-rba-satva-nān
P.	ba-ri-sa	svā-sti	sarba-satva-ṇā-na
Hs.	ba-ri-sa	svā-sti	sa-rba-satva-ṇā-na
Bl.	—		—
IPP.	pa-ri-sa	so miṅ-gzug si-ste	sa-rba-sa-tva-nām
Chin.	p'o-ri-sha/	so-his-ti	sa-p'o-sa-to-nam

Uig.	sidirantu	—
Tib. Nob. II	sid-dhyan-tu	ma-ma
P.	—	mā-ma
Hs.	sid-dhan-tu	mā-ma
Bl.	sid-ddhyan-tu	—
IPP.	si-dhyan-tu	—
Chin.	hsi-tien-tu	—

Uig.	mantr-a padan-i	svaha
Tib. Nob. II	man-tra-pa-dā-ni	svāhā
P.	man-tra-ba-di-ni	—
Hs.	man-dra-pa-di-ni	—
Bl.	—	—
IPP.	man-tra-pa-te	svā-hā
Chin.	man-tan-ro-po-t'o-ni	so-ho

Dhāraṇī 7

The Bodhisattva Mahāsattvas reach in the seventh stage the dhāraṇī called "The excellent transformation in the Dharma". This dhāraṇī belongs to the Buddhas who are more numerous than the grains of sand of seven Ganges. It is proclaimed for protecting the Bodhisattva-Mahāsattvas of the seventh stage. Those who keep it in their minds and recite it will be freed of all kinds of horrors, as in the preceding dhāraṇīs.

Uig.	tadyata	čahi čahi
Tib. Nob. II	tadza-tha	ja-ha ja-ha-ru
P.	—	—
Hs.	—	—
Bl.	—	—
IPP.	ta-dya-thā	ca-ha ca-ha-lo
Chin.	tan-chih-t'a	shao-ho shao-ho-ru

Uig.	čaha čaharu
Tib. Nob. II	ja-ha ja-ha ja-ha-ru
P.	—
Hs.	—
Bl.	ja-ha ja-ha-ru
IPP.	ca-ha ca-ha ca-ha-lo
Chin.	shao-shao-ho shao-ho shao-ho-ru

Uig.	vayruki vayruki	amrita ovani
Tib. Nob. II	bai-lu-ke bai-lu-ke	a-mri-ta-gha-ne
P.	bai-lu-kai bai-lu-ke	a-mri-ta-ga-ne
Hs.	bai-lu-kai bai-lu-ke	a-mri-ta-ga-ni
Bl.	bai-lu-ke/ bai-lu-ke	—
IPP.	be-ru-ke be-ru-ke	a-be-ru-ta-ka-ha-na
Chin.	pi-lu-chih pi-lu-chih	a-mi-ri-ch'e-ru/ han-ni

Uig.	bari sari	vinutaki	maruvati
Tib. Nob. II	pu-ru-sa-ne	be-ru-ti-ke	ba-ru-bhad-te
P.	—	—	—
Hs.	—	—	—
Bl.	pa-ru-sa-ne	bai-ru-ti-ke	ba-ru-bhatte
IPP.	bai-ri-sa-ne	bai-ru-dhi-ke	ba-lo-bad-ti
Chin.	p'o-ri-shan-ni	pi-ru-ch'ih-chih	p'o-ru-fa-ti

Dhāraṇī 7 (continued)

Uig.	vinitikike	binda vayrini	aṃirtaki
Tib. Nob. II	bi-dhi-hi-ke	bin-da-bi-li-ni	a-ma-mri-lu-ti-ke
P.	—	—	—
Hs.	bi-dhi-he-ke	—	—
Bl.	—	—	a-mri-li-ti
IPP.	be-de-hig-ke	bin-du-bi-le-ne	a-mri-te-ke
Chin.	pi-t'i-hsi-chih	p'in-t'o-pi-ri-ni	a-mi-ri-ti-chih

Uig.	mahučuyu	mah učuyu	svaha
Tib. Nob .II	bai-ju-yu	bhai-su-ju-yu	svāhā
P.	bi-ju-yu	—	—
Hs.	—	—	—
Bl.	—	—	—
IPP.	ba-hu-ju-yu	bha-hu-ju-yu	svā-hā
Chin.	po-hu-ju-yu	po-hu-chu-yu	so-ho

Dhāraṇī 8

The Bodhisattva Mahāsattvas reach in the eighth stage the dhāraṇī called "The abundant (inexhaustible) fortune". This dhāraṇī belongs to the Buddhas who are more numerous than the grains of sand of eight Ganges. They proclaimed it for the protection of the Bodhisattva-Mahāsattvas of the eighth stage. Those who recite this dhāraṇī and keep it in their minds will be freed from all kinds of horrors, from fierce animals, evil spirits, humans, non-humans etc., from foes and robbers, from calamities and miseries, and if they do not forget it they will attain the eighth stage.

Uig.	tadyata	siri siri sirani
Tib. Nob. II	tadya-thā	si-ri si-ri/ si-ri-ni
P.	—	—
Hs.	—	—
Bl.	—	sir-i si-ri/si-ni
IPP.	ta-dya-thā	si-ri si-ri-si-ri-ni
Chin.	tan-chih-t'a	shih-ri shih-ri shih-ri-ni

Uig.	viti	kiri kiri	huru huru
Tib. Nob. II	mi-te-mi-te	kā-ri-kā-ri	he-ru he-ru
P.	—	ka-ri-ka-ri	—
Hs.	—	ka-ri-ka-ri	—
Bl.	—	—	—
IPP.	bi-te-bi-te	ka-ri-ka-ri	he-ru he-ru
Chin.	mi-ti-mi-ti	chieh-ri-chieh-ri	hsi-ru hsi-ru

Uig.	čuru čuru vantamiti	svaha
Tib. Nob. II	cu-ru-cu-ru/ bhan-dha-ni	svāhā
P.	—	—
Hs.	—	—
Bl.	cu-ru-cu-ru/ ban-dha-ni	—
IPP.	cu-ra-cu-ra-ba-ti-mi	svā-hā
Chin.	chu-ru-chu-ru p'an-t'e-mi	so-ho

Dhāraṇī 9

The Bodhisattva Mahāsattvas reach in the ninth stage the dhāraṇī called "The immeasurable gate". This dhāraṇī belongs to the Buddhas who exceed in number the grains of sand of nine Ganges. They proclaim this dhāraṇī for the sake of the Bodhisattva-Mahāsattvas of the ninth stage to protect them from all the horrors enumerated in connection with the preceeding dhāraṇīs. Those who do not forget this dhāraṇī will attain the ninth stage.

Uig.	tadyata	hari čandaraki
Tib. Nob. II	tadya-thā	ha-ri-caṇ-da-li-ke
P.	—	ha-ri-can-dha-li-ke
Hs.	—	ha-ri-can-dha-li-ke
Bl.	—	—
IPP.	ta-dya-thā	ta-re-caṇ-da-li-ke
Chin.	tan-chih-t'a	ho-ri-chan-ch'a-ri-chih

Uig.	korimba rati	tura o si	pata pata si
Tib. Nob. II	ku-la-ma-bhad-tre	to-ra-si	pa-ta-pa-ta-si
P.	—	—	—
Hs.	ku-lam-bhad-tre	—	pa-ta-ma-ti-si
Bl.	ku-la-ma-bha-te	to-ra-si	pa-ta-pa-ta-si
IPP.	ru-gu-ram-bha-rad-te	to-ra-se	pad-ta-pad-ta-ba-se
Chin.	chu-lan-p'o-ra-t'i	tu-ra-ssu	po-ch'ih-po-ch'ih-ssu

Uig.	siri siri	kosiri kosiri karpa siri
Tib. Nob. II	si-ri-si-ri	ga-si-ri/ gā-bi-si-ri
P.	—	—
Hs.	—	—
Bl.	—	ga-si-ri/ga-bi-si-ri
IPP.	ri-si-ri-si-ri	ka-si-ri-ka-bi-si-ri
Chin.	shih-ri-shih-ri	chia-shih-ri/ chia-pi-shih-ri

Uig.	suvasti	sirva satvananča	svaha
Tib. Nob. II	sva-sti	sarba-sa-tva-nān	svāhā
P.	—	—	—
Hs.	—	sarba-sa-tva-nā-na	—
Bl.	—	sarba-sa-tva-nam	—
IPP.	sva-sid-dhi	sa-rba-sa-tva-nan	svā-hā
Chin.	so-hsi-ti	sa-p'o-sa-to-nan	so-ho

Dhāraṇī 10

The Bodhisattva Mahāsattvas reach in the tenth stage the dhāraṇī called "The destroyer of the vajra hill". These blessed words of initiation belong to the Buddhas who exceed in number the grains of sand of ten Ganges. Those who recite and remember this dhāraṇī will be freed from all kinds of horrors, fierce animals, wicked ghosts, humans and non-humans etc., from foes and robbers, from calamities (from yakṣas and rākṣasas in the Uigur and from all harms from poison in the Chinese) and all such horrors will be fully destroyed by it, they will be freed from the five obstacles and if they do not forget it, they will attain the tenth stage.

Uig.	tadyata	siddi susiddi	mončani moqsani
Tib. Nob. II	tadya-thā	sid-dhe/ su-sid-dhe	mo-ca-ni mo-ksa-ni
P.	—	—	—
Hs.	ta-dya-thā	—	—
Bl.	—	sid-dhi/ su-sid-dhi	—
IPP.	ta-dya-thā	sid-dhi-su-sid-dhe	mu-ca-ne mo-ksa-ni
Chin.	tan-chih-t'a	hsi-t'i/ su-hsi-t'i	mo-che-ni mu-ch'a-ni

Uig.	vimukti	amali vimali dimili
Tib. Nob. II	bi-mug-te	a-ma-le/bi-ma-le/da-ma-le
P.	bi-mug-ti	a-ma-le/bi-ma-li
Hs.	—	dam-le
Bl.	pi-mug-ti	—
IPP.	pi-mog-ti	am-ba-re bi-ma-le da-ma-le
Chin.	pi-mu-ti	an-mo-li p'i-mo-li nieh-mo-li

Uig.	mankkali	hiranya-a garbi
Tib. Nob. II	māṅ-ga-le	bi-ra-nya-garbhe
P.	—	he-ra-na-ya-garbhe
Hs.	—	he-ra-na-ya-garbhe
Bl.	—	hi-re-nya-garbhe
IPP.	man-ga-le	hi-lan-ja-gar-bhe
Chin.	mang-chieh-li	hsi-ran-jo-chieh-pi

Dhāraṇī 10 (continued)

Uig.	ratna garbi		samantabadri
Tib. Nob. II	ratna-garbhe		sa-man-ta-bha-dre
P.	—		sa-man-ta-bha-tra
Hs.	—		sa-man-ta-bha-tre
Bl.	—		—
IPP.	ha-re-dan-ta-gar-bhe		sa-man-ta-bha-dre
Chin.	ho-ra-tan-no-chieh-pi		san-man-to-po-chih-ti
Uig.	sarva arti saktani		manasi maham i
Tib. Nob. II	sarba arṭha sā-dha-ne		ma-na-si mahā ma-na-si
P.	sarba arṭha sa-dha-tre		—
Hs.	sarba arṭha sa-dha-tre		man-si maha man-si
Bl.	sarba artha sa-dha-ni		mā-sa-ni
IPP.	sa-rba-a-rtha-sa-dha-ni		ma-na-si ma-hā-ma-na-si
Chin.	sa-p'o-o-t'a-p'o-tan-ni		mo-na-ssu mo-ho-mo-na-ssu
Uig.	butti isibutti		arasi virasi
Tib. Nob. II	aṅ-tya-bhū-te		a-ra-de bi-ra-je
P.	aṅ-tyad-bu-te		—
Hs.	a-ṅa-tya-da-bu-te		—
Bl.	a-tya-bhu-te		—
IPP.	a-dhbo-te an-dyar-bho-te		a-ra-ce bi-ra-ce
Chin.	o-pu-ti/ o-chih-pu-ti		a-rai-shih p'i-ra-shih
Uig.	arčiti	amirti	arasi virasi
Tib. Nob. II	an-tsyu-te	a-mri-te	a-ra-je bi-ra-je
P.	an-cu	a-mri-te	—
Hs.	—	—	—
Bl.	—	—	—
IPP.	u-cchu-te	a-mri-te	a-ra-ce bi-ra-ce
Chin.	o-chu-ti	an-mi-ri-ti	a-rai-shih p'i-ra-shih

Dhāraṇī 10 (continued)

Uig.	varampi varabma	svasi purani
Tib. Nob. II	bra-hma bra-hma	sva-re pū-ra-na
P.	pra-hma pra-hma	sa-re pū-ra-na
Hs.	pra-hma pra-hma	sa-re pū-ra-na
Bl.	—	sva-re-pū-ra-ni
IPP.	bra-hma-bha-hma	sa-re-pur-ṇi
Chin.	po-ran-mi/ po-ro-han-mo	so-ri/ pu-ra-ni

Uig.	pu yanaturati	svaha
Tib. Nob. II	pū-ra-ṇa ma-no-ra-the	svāhā
P.	—	—
Hs.	phu-ra-na ma-no-ra-the	—
Bl.	—	—
IPP.	pur-na ma-no-ra-the	svā-hā
Chin.	pu-ra-no man-nu-ra-t'i	so-ho

तद्यथा सिद्धे-सुसिद्धे मोचनि-मोक्षणि विमुक्ते अमले-विमले मांगल्ये हिरण्यगर्भे-रत्नगर्भे समन्तभद्रे सर्वार्थसाधने मनसि-महामनसि अत्यद्भुते अरजे-विरजे अच्युते अमृते अरजे-विरजे ब्राह्मि ब्रह्मस्वरूपे पूरणि पूर्ण-मनोरथे स्वाहा।

Dhāraṇī 11 .

The next group of dhāraṇīs is chapter XII of Tib.II, Tib.III, Uigur and the Chinese texts. This chapter, together with chapter eleven, constitutes the sixth chapter of the extant Sanskrit text. The extant Sanskrit text does not contain the dhāraṇī part, and the last sentences of the Chinese, Uigur, Tib.II and III texts are also missing there.

The next dhāraṇī 11 is in the fifth tegsinč, or chüan of the Uigur and the I-tsing texts. On the front page of the fifth book of the Uigur text a Dhyāni-Buddha can be seen. His right hand is in the bhūsparśa attitude, the left hand rests in his lap and probably holds a bowl. The print unfortunately is not clear. This dhāraṇī is placed in the eighth chapter and the corresponding Tibetan and Chinese dhāraṇīs are also in chapter eight. This chapter does not exist in the Pao-kuei version, therefore it seems to be a later addition. It is entitled in Uigur: "The chapter teaching the golden dhāraṇī", in Chinese it is called "The golden victory dhāraṇī", and in Tibetan it is called "The chapter containing the golden dhāraṇī".

In this chapter the Buddha imparts the golden dhāraṇī to the Bodhisattva Supratiṣṭhita (in the Uigur text his name is written Supratištiti). On page V.8a a number of names are given which are not easily readable in the Chinese and Tibetan versions. Such are the names of the Buddha Gantarasi, Samantadaršani, Vimalaprabi etc. After paying respect to all the Buddhas on p. V.8b follows the golden dhāraṇī. As the succeding part says, this dhāraṇī is the mother of all the Buddhas of the three times. The person who keeps this dhāraṇī can have according to his wishes clothes, drinks, jewels, intelligence, riddance from diseases, and long life. The following instructions are given for the usage of the dhāraṇī: he must recite the dhāraṇī 10008 times. Then he must pour water in a dark house , hang up nets and screens, where the Tay-ču was done. On the first day of a dark month, take some water, have a bath and clean oneself, put on new clean clothes, lit the incense, scatter flowers, and offering meals and drinks he should start the bodhimaṇḍa cermony. First he should call by name all the Buddhas and Bodhisattvas, pay his respect to each of them, one by one, should repent all the sins he committed. Then he should bend his right knee and recite the dhāraṇī 10008 times. If he has any wishes he should think of them. Before sunrise he should eat food of black colour. He should eat only once a day and on the fifteenth day he should go out of this house for the first time. After this he will become happy and all his wishes will be fulfilled. In case his wishes are not be satisfied, he should do again according to the order of directions. When his wish is satisfied he should not forget this dhāraṇī and should always remember it.

The dhāraṇī is written in red immediately after the enumeration of names of all the Buddhas who should be paid respect.

Dhāraṇī 11 (continued)

Uig.	namo ratna-tiray-a-y-a	tadyata
Tib. Nob. II	na-mo rad-na-tra-yā-ya	tadya-thā
P.	—	—
Hs.	na-mo ran-na-tra-yā-ya	—
Bl.	na-mo radna-tra-yā-ya	—
IPP.	na-mo rad-na-tra-yā-ya	ta-dya-thā
Chin.	nan-mo ho-ra-tan-no-tan-ra-yeh-yeh	tan-chih-t'a

Uig.	kuti kuti	kučari
Tib. Nob. II	ku-ti ku-ti-ni	ko-sa-ṇi
P.	—	—
Hs.	—	—
Bl.	—	—
IPP.	kun-te kun-te	ku-ca-le ku-ca-le
Chin.	chun-ti chun-ti	chu-che-ri chu-che-ri

Uig.	iriti	miriti	svaha
Tib. Nob. II	i-mi-ri	ne/i-rī	svāhā
P.	—	—	—
Hs.	—	—	—
Bl.	—	—	—
IPP.	i-dri	mi-dri	svā-hā
Chin.	i-chi-ri	mi-chih-ri	so-ho

Dhāraṇī 12

The title of the twelth chapter is: "The observance of the world by the Four Mahārājas". The title agrees in Uigur, Chinese and Tibetan versions. In this chapter the Buddha tells the Four Mahārājas as to how they can divert the miseries of beings and secure their happiness and luck by supporting this Sūtra. He also tells that the Suvarṇaprabhāsa-sūtra is the best among the Śastras.

Mahārāja Vaiśravaṇa tells the Cintāmaṇi dhāraṇī to the Buddha. "Lord, I have the Cintāmaṇi dhāraṇī which will give people peace and happiness". The following part is fragmentary in Uigur. Vaiśravaṇa announces that those who will recite this dhāraṇī called Cintāmaṇi, he will defend them and divert their sufferings.

Uig.	namo vaysiravanay-y a	maharañča
Tib. Nob. II	na-mo bai-sra-ba-ṇā-ya	ma-hā-rā-jā-ya
P.	na-mo bai-sa-ra-ma-nā-ya	—
Hs.	na-mo bai-sa-ra-ma-nā-ya	—
Bl.	—	—
IPP.	na-mo bai-sar-ma-ṇā-ya	ma-hā-rā-jā-ya
Chin.	nan-mo pi-shih-ro-mo-nu-yan	mo-ho-ho-ro-she-yan

Uig.	tadyata	a a a a	kur u kur u	
Tib. Nob. II	ta-dya-thā	ra-ra-ra-ra	ku-ṇo-ku-no	khu-no-khu-no
P.	—		—	
Hs.	—		—	
Bl.	—		—	
IPP.	ta-dya-thā	ra-ra-ra-ra	ku-ṇu-ku-ṇu	khu-nu-khu-nu
Chin.	tan-chih-ta	ro-ro-ro-ro	chü-nu-chü-nu	ch'ü-nu-ch'ü-nu

Uig.	or onu or onu	sarva	kara kara
Tib. Nob. II	ru-nu-ru-nu	sa-ba-sa-ba	ka-ra-ka-ra
P.	—	—	—
Hs.	—	—	—
Bl.	—	—	—
IPP.	ru-ṇu-ru-ṇu	sa-ba-sa-ba	ka-ra-ka-ra
Chin.	chü-nu-chö-nu	sa-fu-sa-fu	chieh-ro-chieh-ro

Dhāraṇī 12 (continued)

Uig.	—	maha vikarpa
Tib. Nob. II	ma-hā-bi-ka-ra	ma-ha-bi-ka-ram
P.	—	—
Hs.	—	—
Bl.	bi-kā-raṃ	ma-hā-bi-kā-raṃ
IPP.	—	ma-hā-bi-ka-ram
Chin.	—	mo-ho-p'i-chieh-ra-mo

Uig.	maha vikarpa	—
Tib. Nob. II	—	ma-hā-kā-la
P.	—	—
Hs.	—	—
Bl.	—	ma-hā-ka-la
IPP.	ma-hā-bi-ka-rma	ma-hā-kā-la
Chin.	mo-ho-p'i-chieh-ra-mo	—

Uig.	maharanča	rakšasaya	
Tib. Nob. II	ma-hā-rā-ja	rakṣa-raksa tu	mān
P.	—	rakṣa-ntu	mān
Hs.	—	rakṣa tu	mān
Bl.	—		tu māṃ
IPP.	ma-hā-rā-jā	ra-kṣa-ra-kṣa miṅ-bžug du-	man
Chin.	mo-ho-ho-ro-she	ho-ro-ch'a/ ho-ro-ch'a-tu	man

Uig.	sarva satvananča	svaha
Tib. Nob. II	sarba sat-vanān tsa	svaha
P.	sarba sat-vanan ca	svā-hā
Hs.	sarba sat-vanan ca	—
Bl.	—	—
IPP.	sa-rba sat-tva-nā-ca	svā-hā
Chin.	sa-p'o sa-to-nan che	so-ho

नमो वैश्रवणाय महाराजाय। तद्यथा रर-रर कुनु-कुनु खुनु-खुनु रुनु-रुनु सर्वाकार-कर महाविकार महाविकारं महाविकर्म महाकाल महाराज रक्ष-रक्ष मां सर्वसत्त्वान् च स्वाहा।

Ra (= *ra* of *rakṣa*), ku ru (= kṣa), khunu (-*kṣa* read as *kh*)

Dhāraṇī 13

It is a body-defending dhāraṇī, which should be recited according to the following rules. (The rules are given after Vaiśravaṇa has announced the dhāraṇī. In the Uigur text the page containing this part (11.48a) is rather fragmentary, so we made use of Nobel's translation of I-tsing's version of the Chinese text). The person who wants to recite this dhāraṇī should take a white thread, say the first dhāraṇī seven times, and then bind the thread above the elbow. Then what was wished will certainly happen. One has to take incense and also sandal, camphor, olibanum, Tabernae montana coronaria and incense. One should mix together all this, taking from each equal portions, take the bowl (which is kept for smoking), light the incense and pay homage. Then one should take bath, put on fresh and clean clothes, recite the formula in a quiet house, and call me Vaiśravaṇa Mahārāja. Then follows the next dhāraṇī.

Uig.	namo vaysiravani y a		namo danaday a (ta)
Tib. Nob. II	na-mo bai-sra-ba-nā-ya		mahā-dha-na-dā-ya
P.	namo bai-sa-ra-ba-nā-ye		mahā-dan-ta-ya
Hs.	namo bai-sa-ra-ba-nā-ye		—
Bl.	—		mahā-dha-na-dā-ya
IPP.	na-mo bai-sa-ra-ma-nā-ya		na-mo-dā-na-dā-ya
Chin.	nan-mo p'i-shih-ro-mo-nu-yeh		nan-mo-t'an-na-t'o-yeh

Uig.	isvaray a y a	akatča	aparamita
Tib. Nob. II	can-de-sva-rā-ya	a-kar-sa	a-pa-ra-mi-ta
P.	tsan-de-sva-rā-ya	a-kār-sa	—
Hs.	tsan-de-sva-rā-ya	a-kā-ra-sa	—
Bl.	can-de-sva-rva-ya	a-karsa	—
IPP.	dan-ji-sva-rā-ya	a-kar-sa	a-bā-ra-mi-tā
Chin.	t'an-ni-shu'o-ro-yeh	a-chieh-ch'e	a-po-rai-mi-ch'i

Uig.	danti isvar	...ram a	kartika
Tib. Nob. II	can-de-sva-ra	pa-ra-ma	ka-ru-ni-ka
P.	—	—	—
Hs.	can-de-sva-ra	—	ka-ru-ni-ka
Bl.	can-de-sva-rva	—	—
IPP.	dan-ti-sva-ra	bā-ra-ma	kā-ru-ni-ka
Chin.	t'an-ni-shuo-mo	po-ro-mo	chia-liu-ni-chia

नमो वैश्रवणाय। नमो धनदाय चण्डेश्वराय। आकर्ष अपरिमित-चण्डेश्वर परम-कारुणिक।

Dhāraṇī 14

After he has recited this dhāraṇī seven times, he has to recite the main dhāraṇī. He has to call by name the Three Gems and the Mahārāja, to spend all he has and to fulfil the wishes of those around him. After he has satisfied the happiness and health of other beings he should recite "The Essence of the gem Cintāmaṇi of the Mahārāja Vaiśramaṇa" so that he would secure the health and happiness of all beings. Mahārāja Vaiśramaṇa announced the "Essence of the gem Cintāmaṇi" in the presence of the Buddha.

Uig.	namo	ratna tiray a y a	namo
Tib. Nob. II	namo	rad-na-tra-zā-ya	na-mo
P.		—	—
Hs.	namo	ran-na-tra-yā-ya	—
Bl.	—		—
IPP.	na-mo	rad-na-tra-yā-ya	na-mo
Chin.	nan-mo ho	ra-tan-no-tan-ra-yeh-yeh	nan-mo

Uig.	ranay y a	maharančay a
Tib. Nob. II	bai-sra-ba-nā-ya	ma-hā-rā-jā-ya
P.	pe-sa-ra-ba-na-ye	—
Hs.	—	—
Bl.	—	—
IPP.	ba-sa-ra-ma-nā-ya	ma-hā-rā-jā-yā
Chin.	pi-shih-ro-mo-nu-yeh	mo-ho-ro-she-yeh

Uig.	tadyata	simi simi	sumu sumu
Tib. Nob. II	tadya-thā	si-mi-si-mi	su-mu su-mu
P.	—	—	—
Hs.	—	—	—
Bl.	—	—	—
IPP.	ta-dya-thā	si-mi si-mi	su-mu su-mu
Chin.	tan-chih-t'a	ssu-mi ssu-mi	su-mu su-mu

Dhāraṇī 14 (continued)

Uig.	čanda čanda	čara čara	sara …
Tib. Nob. II	can-da can-da	ca-ra ca-ra	sa-ra sa-ra
P.	—	—	—
Hs.	can-da can-da	—	—
Bl.	can-ta can-ta	—	—
IPP.	canda canda	ca-ra ca-ra	sa-ra sa-ra
Chin.	chan-ch'a chan-ch'a	che-ro che-ro	sa-ro sa-ro
Uig.	kara kara	kiri kiri	kur
Tib. Nob. II	ka-ra ka-ra	ki-li ki-li	kur-u ku-ru
P.	—	—	—
Hs.	—	—	—
Bl.	—	—	—
IPP.	ka-ra ka-ra	ki-li ki-li	ku-ru ku-ru
Chin.	chieh-ro chieh-ro	chih-ri chih-ri	chu-ru chu-ru
Uig.	muru muru		čuru čuru
Tib. Nob. II	mu-ru mu-ru		cu-ru cu-ru
P.	—		—
Hs.	—		—
Bl.	—		—
IPP.	mu-ru mu-ru		cu-ru cu-ru
Chin.	mu-ru mu-ru		chu-ru chu-ru
Uig.	sit …	musiknatu	nititi a
Tib. Nob. II	san-dā-ya	ād-ma-nam	ni-tya-na
P.	san-dā-yā	ād-ma-nam	nid-tya-na
Hs.	san-dha-ya	ā-da-ma-na-ma	nid-tya-na
Bl.	sam-da-ya	atma-nam	—
IPP.	sa-dha-ya	dha-ma-ni-dhyan	ni-dhyan
Chin.	sa-ta-yeh	o-t'an-mu-chia	ni-tien

Dhāraṇī 14 (continued)

Uig.	anta t…	dahu	svaha
Tib. Nob. II	an-dhar	dhā-tu	svāhā
P.	a-ndhar	—	
Hs.	a-ndhar	—	
Bl.	andhar	ddhā-tu	svāhā
IPP.	an-dha	dha-du	sva-ha
Chin.	o-t'a-ta	ta-tu	so-ho

Uig.	vaysira … ya	svaha
Tib. Nob. II	na-mo bai-sra-ba-nā-ya	svāhā
P.	namo be-sar-ba-nā-ye	svāhā
Hs.	namo bai-sa-ra-pa-nā-ye	svāhā
Bl.	namo bai-sra-ba-nā-ya	svāhā
IPP.	na-mo bai-sa-ra-ma-nā-ya	svā-hā
Chin.	nan-mo pi-shih-ro-mo-mu-yeh	so-ho

Uig.	dandayay a	svaha	maruta
Tib. Nob. II	dha-na-dā-ya	svāhā	ma-no-ra-tha
P.	dha-na-da-ye	svāhā	—
Hs.	dha-na-da-ye	svāhā	ma-nor-tha
Bl.	dhā-na-dā-ya	svāhā	na-mo-ra-tha
IPP.	dā-na-dā-ya	svāhā	na-mo-ra-tha
Chin.	t'an-na-t'o-yeh	so-ho	man-nu-ra-ta

Uig.	pari-puran-kay-a	svaha
Tib. Nob. II	pa-ri-pū-ra-ya	svāhā
P.	—	
Hs.	—	
Bl.	pa-ri-pūr-ya	svāhā
IPP.	pa-ri-pū-ra-ka-ya	svā-hā
Chin.	po-ri-fu-ra-chia-yeh	so-ho

नमो रत्नत्रयाय। नमो वैश्रवणाय महाराजाय। तद्यथा। सिमि२ सुमु२ छन्द२ चर२ सर२ कर२ किरि२ कुरु२ मुरु२ चुरु२।
सन्धाय आत्मनं नित्यं अन्तर्दधातु स्वाहा। नमो वैश्रवणाय स्वाहा। धनदाय स्वाहा।
मनोरथ-परिपूरकाय स्वाहा।

Dhāraṇī 15

After he has recited and memorized the dhāraṇī he should first recite it, according to the Uigur and Tibetan texts, a thousand and eight times (in Chinese a thousand times) and then smear his body with cowdung in a clean house and make a small maṇḍala. He should sacrifice food and drinks, and he should burn incense without a break. The person who recites this dhāraṇī should concentrate on it with all his mind, and then the son of Vaiśravaṇa will appear by name Canarsabi (Janarṣabha) and ask: "Why do you have to call my Father?" The person should answer him: "To pay homage to the three gems, I need wealth, I want him to secure it for me". Then Canarsabi goes to his father and tells him, that there is a man in Jambudvīpa, who pays homage with all his heart to the Gems, but as regards fortune he is poor. So he asks my father for it. Vaiśravaṇa answers him "go and give him every day a hundred kārṣāpaṇas (it is said in the Uigur text that one gold kārṣāpaṇa is equal to one thousand and six hundred yartmaq). Then he who recites the dhāraṇī knows that he will succeed in what ever he wants. He should go and live in a clean room, light incence, and hide a scented sack there. When the morning comes he will see that the sack is full of all kinds of things. He should give this away on the same day, he should pay tributes to the Three Gems, and give alms to the poor. He should not leave anything. He should not harbour hatred and injuries (of the soul). Where there is hatred, magic does not work. He should consider this seriously. He should pay his tributes to me, to my son and to my daughter. Then we, all of us, will protect those people who have this dhāraṇī. He will be free from other existences. If he wishes peace, happiness and respect he will find them easily. He will understand the language of the birds.

When people who have the dhāraṇī want to see me personally they may on the eighth day of a white half of a month or on the fifteenth day. A person who wants to see Vaiśravaṇa should ask a clever painter to paint the five colours on a piece of wood. He should paint the Lord in the middle, the Goddess Śrī on the left side and the picture of Vaiśravaṇa with his offspring on the right side. After this is finished he should carry on his tributes with flowers, lamps and incense day and night without a break, and make offerings with costly drinks and meals. But he should not be light-minded. Then he should call Vaiśravaṇa with the following dhāraṇī:

Uig.	namo siri kanta ya	namo	buday a
Tib. Nob. II	namo śrī-kaṇ-ṭhā-ya		bud-dhā-ya
P.	namo si-ri-kan-thā-yā		—
Hs	namo bai-sa-ran-ba-ya		—
Bl.	—		—
IPP.	na-mo si-ri-gan-dha-ya		bud-dhā-ya
Chin.	nan-mo shih-li-chien-na-yeh		p'o-t'o-yeh

Dhāraṇī 15 (continued)

Uig.	namo vaisiravani y a	yakš a rakš a saya
Tib. Nob. II	na-mo bai-sra-ba-nā-ya	yakṣa-rājā-ya
P.	namo be-sar-ba-na-ya	—
Hs.	namo bai-sa-ran-ba-ya —	
Bl.	—	—
IPP.	na-mo be-sa-ra-ma-nā-ya	ya-ksa-rā-jā-ya
Chin.	nan-mo pi-shih-ro-mo-nu-yeh	yao-ch'a-ro-she-yeh

Uig.	mharanča	ati-račay-a	namo sirini-y-a-ya
Tib. Nob. II	ma-hā-rā-jā-ya	a-ti-rā-jā-ya	namaḥ śrī-yē-ye
P.	ma-hā-rā-jā	—	nama sri-ye-ye
Hs.	—	—	nama sri-ye-ye
Bl.	—	—	srī-mahā-debyai
IPP.	ma-hā-rā-jā-ya	a-di-rā-jā-yā	na-mo srī-ya-ye
Chin.	mo-ho-ro-she(-yeh)	a-ti-ro-she-yeh	nan-mo shih-ri-ya-i

Uig.	mha divini-y-a-y-a	tadyata	tar-a tar-a
Tib. Nob. II	ma-hā-de-bi-ye	tadya-thā	ta-ra ta-ra
P.	—	—	—
Hs.	—	—	—
Bl.	—	—	—
IPP.	ma-hā-de-bi-ye	ta-dya-thā	ta-ra ta-ra
Chin.	mo-ho-t'i-pi-i	tan-chih-t'a	tan-ro tan-ro

Uig.	turu turu	ambar-a ambar-a
Tib. Nob. II	tu-ru tu-ru	ba-ra ba-ra
P.	—	—
Hs.	—	—
Bl.	—	—
IPP.	du-ru du-ru	ma-ra ma-ra
Chin.	tu-ru tu-ru	mo-ro mo-ro

Dhāraṇī 15 (continued)

Uig.	susitto su-sitto	har-a har-a
Tib. Nob. II	su-śud-dho su-śud-ho	ha-na ha-na
P.	—	—
Hs.	—	—
Bl.	su-sudha	—
IPP.	su-su-ddho su-su-ddho	ha-na ha-na
Chin.	su-shuai-t'u su-shuai-t'u	han-no han-no

Uig.	mani	kanaka	vačr-a vayturi-y-a
Tib. Nob. II	ma-ni	ka-na-ka	ba-jra bai-ḍū-rya
P.	—		ba-rja be-dū-rya
Hs.	—		bajra bai-dū-rya
Bl.	—		brjre bai-tū-rya
IPP.	ma-ni	ka-ne-ka	ba-jre be-du-rya
Chin.	mo-ni	chieh-no-chia	po-che-ro pi-liu-li-yeh

Uig.	mukti alankrata sarir-a-y-a
Tib. Nob. II	mug-ti-ka-a-lan-kri-ta-śa-rī-rā-ya
P.	mug-ti-ka-a-lan-kri-ta-sa-rī-rā-ya
Hs.	mu-gga-ti-ka-a-lan-kri-ta-sa-ri-re-ye
Bl.	mu-kti-ka-lam-kri-ta/ sa-rī-rā-ya
IPP.	mu-gti-ka-lan-kri-ta sa-rī-rā-ya
Chin.	mu-ti-chia-leng-chi-ri-ch'e/shou-ri-ro-i/

Uig.	ambo	sarva-satu-a
Tib. Nob. II	bho/	sarba-sa-tva
P.	bho/	sarba-sa-tvā-ni
Hs.	bho/	sarba-sa-tā
Bl.	—	
IPP.	bho	sa-rba-sa-tva-nām
Chin.	po	sa-p'o-sa-to

Dhāraṇī 15 (continued)

Uig.	hita-kam-a vaysiravana siridivi parikalpatar
Tib. Nob. II	ksa-ma
P.	—
Hs.	—
Bl.	srī-ya-de-bi-pra-bha-yā
IPP.	hid-kam-be-sra-ma-na srī-ya-de-bi-pra-bha-ya
Chin.	hsi-che'e-chia-mo pi-shih-ro-mo-nu/shih-ri-yeh-t'i-pi/po-ra-p'o-yeh

Uig.	i-hi i-hi	man	abilaba	gurina gurin
Tib. Nob. II	e-hi e-hi	mā	bi-lam-ba	ghū-rṇa ghū-rna
P.	—		—	ghu-ran ghu-rna
Hs.		ma	bi-la-ma-ba	ghu-rna ghu-rna
Bl.	—		bi-lbām	
IPP.	e-hi e-hi	ma	hi-lam-bha	ku-rṇa ku-rna
Chin.	i-hsi i-hsi	mo	p'i-lan-p'o	ch'u-ri-nu ch'u-ri-nu

Uig.	maris-a	ananajtiki	mam-a	amuka mu na
Tib. Nob. II	ba-ra-sya ba-ra-sya	da-dā-hi	ma-mā	—
P.	—	da-di-ha	ma-mā	—
Hs.	—	dadiha	ma-mā	—
Bl.	pa-ra-sya pa-ra-sya	—		—
IPP.	bha-ra-sa bha-ra-sa	dha-da-hi	ma-ma	a-mu-ka-na-ma-sya
Chin.	mo-ra-so mo-ra-so	ta-t'o-hsi/	mo-mo	a-mu-chia-na-mo-hsieh

Uig.	tarsana kamasi-a	mam-a	......im
Tib. Nob. II	dar-śa-na-kā-ma-sya	—	dar-śa-nam
P.	dar-sa-na-kam-sya	—	da-ri-sa-ṇa-ma
Hs.	dar-sa-na-kam-sya	—	da-ri-sa-na-ma
Bl.	dar-sa-na/ka-ma-sya	—	dar-sa-nam
IPP.	dha-ra-sa-na-kama-sya	—	dha-ri-sa-nā ma-ma
Chin.	ta-ti-shou-na/chia-mo-hsieh	—	ta-ri-shou-nan/mo-mo

Dhāraṇī 15 (continued)

Uig.	man	prahlatay-a	svaha
Tib. Nob. II	ma-ma-ma-na	pra-hlā-da-ya	svāhā
P.	—	pra-lba-da-ya	—
Hs.	—	pra-bha-da-ya	—
Bl.	—	pra-la-dā-ya	—
IPP.	ma-na	ba-ri-ha-ra-dha-ya	svā-hā
Chin.	mo-na	po-ra-ho-ro-ta-yeh	so-ho

नमः श्रीकण्ठाय बुद्धाय। नमो वैश्रवणाय यक्षराजाय महाराजाय अतिराजाय। नमो श्रियै महादेव्यै। तद्यथा।
तर[२] तुरु[२] मर[२] सुशुद्धो[२] हन[२] मणि-कनक-वज्र-वैडूर्य-मुक्तिकालंकृत-शरीराय। भो सर्व-सत्त्व-हित-काम वैश्रवण श्रीदेविप्रभ एहि[२], मा विलम्ब, घूर्ण[२] वरस्य[२] ददाहि मम अमुक-नामस्य दर्शन-कामस्य मम दर्शनम्। मां प्रह्लादय। स्वाहा।

Dhāraṇī 16

After this dhāraṇī Vaiśravaṇa will appear in the form of a child or an old man or a monk holding in his hand a golden holder the Cintāmaṇi gem. He will step into the Maṇḍala of the body of Vaiśravaṇa. He will ask them what they wish. The magic formula can satisfy whatever they want. If they want gold and silver etc. they can have that. If they want the ability to skip and fly they can have that. If they want people to like them and respect them, they can have it.

The 16th dhāraṇī is in chapter 13 in the seventh tegsinč of the Uigur and the seventh chüan of the Chinese text. The front page of the seventh book is missing. It is the thirteenth chapter of the Tibetan version as well. It is not included in the extant Sanskrit version. This part was probably first translated by Jñānagupta. In the thirteenth chapter Buddha announces to Śāriputra "the dhāraṇī called Immaculate". This dhāraṇī is "the mother of the Buddhas" and it protects from swords, sticks, poison, water, fire and wild animals. If there are two persons, one who is ready to spend any fortune, to give alms, and to pay tributes in all ways with offerings of meals, drinks and clothes, or another person who knows this dhāraṇī formula, can read it and recite it then his deed is in merits and more than that of the first person.

Uig.	tadyata	sardarani	udarani
Tib. Nob. II	tadya-thā	san-dhā-ra-ni	ud-dhā-ra-nā
P.	—	san-dha-ran-i	ud-tā-ra-ni
Hs.	—	san-dha-ran-i	ud-tā-ra-ni
Bl.	—	san-dha-ra-ni	ud-dhā-ra-ni
IPP.	ta-dya-thā	san-dhā-ra-ni	on-dhā-ra-ni
Chin.	tan-chih-t'a	shan-t'o-ra-ni	wu-to-ra-ni

Uig.	susan-burna-tisti-y-a	sutraba
Tib. Nob. II	su-sam-pra-ti-sthi-te	su-nā-mā
P.	—	—
Hs.	—	—
Bl.	su-sam-pra-ti-sthi-te	su-nā-ma
IPP.	su-sam-pra-ti-bi-sca-ta	so-nā-ma
Chin.	su-san-po-ro-ti-s/e/-chih-ch'e	su-na-mo

Dhāraṇī 16 (continued)

Uig.	supratištita	vani-a var-a
Tib. Nob. II	su-pra-ti-sthi-te	bi-ja-ya-ba-la
P.	su-pra-ti-stha	bi-ja-ya-ba-la
Hs.	su-pra-ti-stha	bi-ja-ya-ba-la
Bl.	—	—
IPP.	so-pra-ti-sthi-ta	bi-ja-ya-bha-dra
Chin.	so-pa-ra-ti-se-ch'ih-ch'epi-shih-yeh	

Uig.	sittay-a	brati-ite-čanča	su arohanča
Tib. Nob. II	sad-tya	pra-ti-jna	su-ā-ro-ha
P.	sad-tā	pra-	—
Hs.	sad-tā	pra-	—
Bl.	sattya	pra-ti-jnā	su-ā-ro-hā
IPP.	sā-dha-de-ya	pra-te-si-nca	so-a-ra-ha
Chin.	sa-ti-yeh	po-ra-ti-sheh-jo	su-a-ru-ho

Uig.	na nantamiti	—	rubatari
Tib. Nob. II	—	jnā-na-pa-ti	—
P.	—	—	—
Hs.	—	jna-na-pa-ti	—
Bl.	—	jnā-na-pra-ti	—
IPP.	si-nca-na-ma-te	—	om-pa-dā-ni
Chin.	shan-jo-na-mo-ti	—	wu-po-tan-ni

Uig.	itemari	apisatari	abibay-a-hari
Tib. Nob. II	—	—	—
P.	—	—	—
Hs.	—	—	—
Bl.	—	—	—
IPP.	a-ba-na ma-ni	a-bhi-si-sca-ni	a-bhi-bi-ya-har
Chin.	a-fa-na-mo-ti	a-p'i-shih-tan-ni	a-pi-p'i-ya-ho-ro

Dhāraṇī 16 (continued)

Uig.	suaviti	suvanirsta	mahu
Tib.Nob. II	su-bha-ba-sti	su-nis-sri-ta	ba-hu
P.	su-bha-ba-ti	su-dis-sri-ta	mahā
Hs.	su-bha-ha-ti	su-dis-sri-ta	pa-hu
Bl.	—	su-ni-srī-tā	—
IPP.	su-bha-ba-ti	su-ni-sī-dha	ba-to
Chin.	shu-p'o-fa-ti	su-ni-shih-ri-to	po-hu

Uig.	abītata	končaki	svaha
Tib.Nob. II	a-bhi-bā-da	gum-bha	svāhā
P.	—	gum-bha	—
Hs.	—	gu-ma-bha	—
Bl.	a-bhi-ba-dā	—	—
IPP.	a-bhi-pa-da	gun-bha	svā-hā
Chin.	a-p'i-p'o-to	chun-she	so-ho

Dhāraṇī 17

In the next fourteenth chapter a group of seven dhāraṇīs are incorporated. This chapter is missing from the extant Sanskrit version and also from the Chinese version of Pao-kuei. Chapter fourteen in the second and third Tibetan versions and in the Chinese version of I-tsing agrees with the fourteenth chapter of the Uigur version. The title of the chapter is: "The teaching of the dhāraṇī-formula called Cintāmaṇi".

The first dhāraṇī in this group of dhāraṇīs is proclaimed by the Buddha in front of Ānanda and of the assembly of gods. He announces the names of the Lords of Lightning: in the east he is Akati, in the south he is Čatura, in the west he is Čutapraba, and in the north he is Sudamara. Their names in Tibetan and Chinese are:

In Tib. III	a-ga-ta	in Chin.	a-chieh-to
In Tib. III	sa-te-ru	in Chin.	she-ti-ru
In Tib. III	cu-ta-kvan	in Chin.	chu-to-kuang
In Tib. III	su-ta-ma-ni	in Chin.	su-to-mo-ni

If a person knows their names he can divert horrors and accidents from afar. The dhāraṇī is announced by the Buddha:

Uig.	tadyata	nimi nimi nimi
Tib. Nob. II	'di-lta-ste	ni-mi ni-mi
P.	—	—
Hs.	—	—
Bl.	tadya-thā	—
IPP.	ta-dya-thā	ni-mi ni-mi ni-mi
Chin.	tan-chih-t'a	ni-mi ni-mi ni-mi

Uig.	nimintari	sairi-loka-lokani
Tib. Nob. II	ni-min-dha-re	saitra-lo-ka-lo-kani
P.	—	—
Hs.	—	—
Bl.	ni-min-dha-ri	—
IPP.	ni-min-dre	saitra-loka-lo-kani
Chin.	ni-min-ta-ri	chih-ri-lu-chia/lu-chieh-ni

Dhāraṇī 17 (continued)

Uig.	siri sirapati	rakš-a rakš-a
Tib. Nob. II	—	—
P.	—	—
Hs.	—	—
Bl.	—	—
IPP.	si-ri-so-la-ba-ti	ha-ra-ksa ha-ra-ksa
Chin.	chih-ri-shu-lo-po-ni	ho-ro-ch'a ho-ro-ch'a

Uig.	mam-a asi-a namuka namasi-a	svaha
Tib. Nob. II	—	svāhā
P.	—	—
Hs.	—	—
Bl.	—	—
IPP.	—	svā-hā
Chin.	—	—

In Chinese and Tibetan only the first part of the 17th dhāraṇī is transcribed, the second part is translated into Chinese or Tibetan. The translation of the second part of the dhāraṇī is: "....all the accidents of (the name of the person follows) should be diverted from him, svāhā".

तद्यथा निमि[३] निमिंधरे □ लोकालोकनि शीलि-शीलवति रक्ष[२] मामस्य अमुकनामस्य स्वाहा।

Dhāraṇī 18

After the 17th dhāraṇī, Bodhisattva Avalokiteśvara announces the Cintāmaṇi dhāraṇī. A part of this dhāraṇī is also translated in Chinese and Tibetan:

Uig.	tadyata	gati vigati	nikati
Tib. Nob. II	'di-lta-ste	ha-te bi-ha-te	ni-ha-te
P.	—	—	—
Hs.	—	—	—
Bl.	tady-athā	ka-te bi-ka-te	ni-ka-te
IPP.	ta-dya-thā	ka-te bi-ka-te	ni-ka-te
Chin.	tan-chih-t'a	ho-ti/p'i-ho-ti	ni-ho-ti

Uig.	parasi a tiki	prati mučiri	sutti	mukti
Tib. Nob. II	pra-tya-rthi-ke	pra-tya-nyi-tre	śud-dhe	mug-te
P.	—	—	—	
Hs.	bra-tya-rtha-ke	bra-tya-nye-tre	—	
Bl.	pra-tya-mi-tre	pra-tya-mi-tre	su-ddhe	mu-ket
IPP.	pra-tya-ke	pra-tya-nyi-te	sud-dhe	mug-de
Chin.	po-ra-chih-ti-chi	po/-ra-ti-mi-chih-ri	shu-t'i	mu-ti

Uig.	vimali	bari barasi		
Tib. Nob. II	bi-ma-le	pra-bha-sva-re	an-da-re	pan-da-re
P.	—	pra-ba-sva-re	an-da-re	
Hs.	—	pra-ba-sva-re	an-da-re	
Bl.	—	pra-bha-sa-re	an-da-re	
IPP.	bi-ma-le	ba-ri-bha-sva-re	a-nda-ri	ba-nta-ri
Chin.	p'i-mo-li	po-ra-p'o-so-ri/	an-ch'a-ri/	pan-ch'a-ri

Uig.	saviti	mantar-a vansini	hanari
Tib. Nob. II	śve-te	pan-da-ra-bā-si-ni	ha-ri
P.	—	pan-da-ra-bā-si-ni	ha-ri
Hs.	—	pan-da-ra-bā-si-ni	ha-ri
Bl.	—	pan-da-ra/bā-si-ni	—
IPP.	sud-dhe	pa-nta-ra-ba-si-ni	ha-re
Chin.	shui-ti	pan-ch'a-ro/p'o-ssu-ni	ho-ri

Dhāraṇī 18 (continued)

Uig.	kantari	kapili	kinkkali
Tib. Nob. II	kan-da-ri	ka-pi-li	pin-ga-lā-kse
P.	ka-rā-di	—	bin-ga-lā-kse
Hs.	ka-rā-di	—	pim-ga-la/a-ks
Bl.	—	—	pid-ka-le-a-kse
IPP.	ka-nta-ri	ka-bi-re	bid-ka-le-a-kse
Chin.	chieh-ch'a-ri	chieh-pi-li	ping-chieh-lo-o-ch'i

Uig.	rakša rakš-a	darimuki	rakša
Tib. Nob. II	—	da-dhi-mu-khi	—
P.	—	da-hī-mu-khi	—
Hs.	—	da-hī-mu-khi	—
Bl.	—	da-dhi-mu-khi	—
IPP.	—	dha-ti-mu-gi	ra-ksa ra-ksa
Chin.	—	ta-ti-mu-ch'i	ho-ro-ch'a ho-ro-ch'a

Uig.	mam-a asi-a (n)amuka(n)amasi-a	svaha
Tib. Nob. II	—	svāhā
P.	—	—
Hs.	—	—
Bl.	—	—
IPP.	—	svā-hā
Chin.	—	—

तद्यथा। हते विहते निहते प्रत्यर्थिके प्रत्यमित्रे शुद्धे मुक्ते विमले प्रभास्वरे ☐ पाण्डरे श्वेते पाण्डरवासिनि हरे गन्धारि कपिले पिंगलाक्षे रक्ष[२]। दधिमुखि रक्ष मामस्य अमुकनामस्य। स्वाहा।

Dhāraṇī 19

After this the Bodhisattva Vajrapāṇi announces the dhāraṇī called "Victorious". It gives protection against various accidents and also from sudden death.

Uig.	tadyata	muni muni muhali
Tib. Nob. II	'di-lta-ste	mu-ni mu-ni mu-ni-ri-re
P.	—	—
Hs.	—	—
Bl.	tadya-thā	mu-ni mu-ni/mu-nin-dha-re/
IPP.	ta-dya-thā	mu-ni mu-ni mu-ni-le
Chin.	tan-chih-t'a	mu-ni mu-ni-ri

Uig.	vati vati	suvati	mahavati
Tib. Nob. II	ma-ti ma-ti	su-ma-ti	ma-hā-ma-ti
P.	—		—
Hs.	—		—
Bl.	ma-ti ma-ti		—
IPP.	mu-ni-ma-ti ma-ti/	su-ma-ti	ma-hā-ma-ti
Chin.	mo-ti mo-ti	su-mo-ti	mo-ho-mo-ti

Uig.	haha	mavi ayi	sitinatu prapa
Tib. Nob. II	hā-hā-hā-hā	—	—
P.	—	—	—
Hs.	—	—	—
Bl.	ha-ha-ha-ha	—	—
IPP.	ha-ha-ha	mi-bhi-yan	hi-hi-hi-ba-bha
Chin.	ho ho ho	mo-p'o-i-na	his-ti-tī/po-po

Uig.	vačrapani	ana na mama antaravi ta	svaha
Tib. Nob. II	—	—	svāhā
P.	—	—	—
Hs.	—	—	—
Bl.	—	—	—
IPP.	ba-jra-pā-ni	a-ha-ci-ri-ca	svā-hā
Chin.	po-che-lo-po-ni	o-t'ien-chih-ri-ch'a	so-ho

तद्यथा मुनि[२] मुनिंधरे मतिमति (fem. of °मान्) सुमति महामति हाहा-हाहा □ वज्रपाणि ...

Dhāraṇī 20

Next Brahmā announces the dhāraṇī called "Brahma-rule". It gives protection against anxieties, sufferings and sudden death.

Uig.	tadyata	hiri miri	tiri	sinha
Tib. Nob. II	'di-lta-ste	hi-li mi-li	tsi-li	svā-hā
P.	—	—	—	
Hs.	—	—	—	
Bl.	tadya-tha	—	—	
IPP.	tadyathā	hi-li mi-li	dhi-li	svā-hā
Chin.	tan-chih-t'a	hsi-ri mi-ri	ti-ri	so-ho

Uig.	vara hampa puri		vara hampani
Tib. Nob. II	bra-hma-pu-re	svāhā	—
P.	pra-hma-sa-re	svāhā	—
Hs.	pra-hma-sa-re	svāhā	—
Bl.	—		—
IPP.	hrah-ma-bu-re		bra-hma-sva-re
Chin.	po-ro-t'ien-mo-pu-ri		po-ro-t'ien-mo-mo-ni

Uig.	var-a hampa harpi	puspa san satari	svaha
Tib. Nob. II	pra-hma-ga-rbhe	pu-spa-san-sta-re	svāhā
P.	prahma-ga-nba	—	—
Hs.	prahma-ga-nbe	—	—
Bl.	brahma-bi-su-garbhe	pu-spa-sam-sta-re	—
IPP.	bra-hma-ga-rbhe	pu-spa-sam-si-dha-re	svā-hā
Chin.	po-ro-t'ien-mo-chieh-pi	pu-se-po-seng-hsi-tan-ri	so-ho

तद्यथा। हिलि मिलि धिलि स्वाहा। ब्रह्मसारे ब्रह्मस्वरे ब्रह्मगर्भे पुष्पसंधारे स्वाहा।

Dhāraṇī 21

Then Xormuzda (Xormuzda is the name of Indra in Uigur, in Chinese he is called Śakra) claimed that he had a dhāraṇī. He announced the dhāraṇī called Včirasani (Vajrasani, Tib. badzra-śani, Chin. po-chê-lo-shan-ni) which ends all horrors, accidents, sudden death, removes miseries and thus helps the gods and humankind.

Uig.	tadyata	vayri	vayrani
Tib. Nob. II	'di-lta-ste	bi-ni	ba-ra-ni
P.	—	—	—
Hs.	—	ni	ba-rāni
Bl.	tadya-thā	ra-ni	—
IPP.	ta-dya-thā	bi-ni	bi-rā-ni
Chin.	tan-chih-t'a	p'i-ni	p'o-ra-ni

Uig.	vanta nampa tanti	mani niti titi ti	kayri
Tib. Nob. II	ban-dha-ma-dan-de	ma-ti-ti / ti-ti	gau-ri
P.	pan-dha-mā-dan-te	—	
Hs.	band-ha-ma-dan-te		go-ri/
Bl.	ba-ndha / ma-dande	ma-ni-ne-ti / ti-ni /	gau-ri
IPP.	bhan-dha-ma-dha-na-ti	ma-ni-de-di-di-ni	gau-ri
Chin.	pan-t'o / mo tan-chih	mo-ni-ni-chin-ni /	ch'u-ri

Uig.	kantari cantali	mantanggi	pukkasi
Tib. Nob. II	gan-dha-ri / can-dā-lī	ma-tan-gi	pukka-se
P.	—	—	—
Hs.	gan-dha-ni can-dā-li	—	—
Bl.	canda-li	ma-tam-gi	—
IPP.	gan-dha-ri can-da-li	ma-tad-gi	pu-kka-si
Chin.	chen-t'o-ri / chan-ch'a-ri	mo-teng-ch'i	pu-chieh-ssu

Uig.	sara varapi	ninamantu nam a ontarani
Tib. Nob. II	—	—
P.	—	—
Hs.	—	—
Bl.	—	—
IPP.	sa-ra bha-re-bhe	hi-na-ma-tu-ta-ma-on-dha-ra-ni
Chin.	so-ro po-rai-pi	hi-no-mo-ti-ta-mo / wu-to-ra-ni

Dhāraṇī 21 (continued)

Uig.	mantarani	tar a niki	čakir-a-bari
Tib. Nob .II	—	dha-ra-ni-ke	—
P.	—		—
Hs.	—	—	—
Bl.	—	—	—
IPP.	ma-hā-la-ni	—	ca-tra-ba-kse
Chin.	mo-hu-ra-ni	ta-ra-ni-chi	che-chieh-ro-p'o-chih

Uig.	čiv-a lisi-a vari		svaha
Tib. Nob. II	—		svāhā
P.	—		—
Hs.	—		—
Bl.	—		—
IPP.	sa-pa-ri-sa-pa-ri		svā-hā
Chin.	she-fa-ri ch'u-fa-ri		so-ho

Dhāraṇī 22

Afterwards the Four Mahārājas (in Uigur their names are Vaisravani/Vaiśravaṇa, Tartirastitiri Dhṛtarāṣṭra, Virutaki/Virūḍhaka, Virupaksi/ Virūpākṣa) proclaim the magic formula entitled "The one which grants fearlessness to all beings". This protects one from suffering, secures health and happiness, increases one's life span and wards off all the sufferings of diseases and sudden death.

Uig.	tadyata	puspi	supuspi
Tib. Nob. II	'di-lta-ste	pu-spe	su-pu-spe
P.	—	pu-spe-pu-spe-pu-spe	—
Hs.	—	—	—
Bl.	tadya-thā	—	—
IPP.	ta-dya-thā	pu-spe	su-pu-spe
Chin.	tan-chih-t'a	pu-sê-pi	su-pu-sê-pi

Uig.	nantu rupari	nubanantu sani
Tib. Nob. II	dhu-ma-pa-ri-hā-re	—
P.	—	—
Hs.	—	—
Bl.	—	—
IPP.	dhū-ma-pa-ri-hā-re	—
Chin.	tu-mo-po-ra-ho-ri	—

Uig.	ari-a pari susati	santati	mukti aksi
Tib. Nob. II	ā-rya-pra-sa-ste	sān-te	ni-rmug-te
P.	—	—	ni-mug-te
Hs.	—	—	ni-rmu-te
Bl.	a-rya-pu-sa	santa	ni-mu-kte
IPP.	ā-rya-pa-svā-hā	—	—
Chin.	a-ri-yeh-po-ra-shê-hsi-ti	shan-ti	nieh-mu-ti

Uig.	manggal i	sitti	sitti viti	svaha
Tib. Nob. II	man-ga-le	stu-te	sta-bi-te	svāhā
P.	—		sta-pi-te	
Hs.		—	—	—
Bl.	ma-gal-ya	stu-te	—	—
IPP.	—	—		svā-hā
Chin.	mang-chieh-li	su-tu ti	hsi-ch'ê-pi-ti	so-ho

तद्यथा। पुष्पे सुपुष्पे धूमपरिहारे आर्यप्रशस्ते शान्ते निर्मुक्ते मंगल्ये स्तुते स्तविते स्वाहा।

Dhāraṇī 23

The Nāga-kings: Manasi (Skr. Manasvin, Chin. ma-na-si), Anavatapti (Skr. Anavatapta), Baslap (Skr. Vidyujjvāla), and Qamag (Skr. Suraśmi) presented the dhāraṇī Cintāmaṇi. It protects one from accidents as well as from the magic power of demons, it defends one against the kākhordas and vetādas. It defends one from lightning and thunder, horrors, sorrow and diseases, from animals which harm mankind: tigers, wolves, lions, poisonous snakes, mosquitoes, horseflies. It protects all those who hold this dhāraṇī in their mind, write it down, recite it or worship it.

Uig.	tadyata	ančari	amari
Tib. Nob. II	'di-lta-ste	a-tsa-le	a-ma-re
P.	—	ārya-dze	—
Hs.	—	—	—
Bl.	tadya-thā	—	—
IPP.	tadyata	acale	amare
Chin.	tan-chih-t'a	a-chê-ri	a-mo-ri

Uig.	amirti	aksayi	abayi
Tib. Nob. II	a-mri-te	a-ksa-ye	a-bhi-ye
P.	—	—	—
Hs.	—	a-kse-ye	—
Bl.	—	—	—
IPP.	a-mri-te	a-ksa-ye	a-be-ye
Chin.	a-mi-ri-ti	o-ch'a-i	a-pi-i

Uig.	mani karisutti	sarva	
Tib. Nob. II	pu-nya-ba-ryā-ba-te	sarba	pā-pam
P.	parya-ba-ryā-ba-te	sarba	pā-ba
Hs.	pu-nya-pa-ryā-ba	sarba	pa-ba
Bl.	pu-nya-ba-rya-ba-te	—	
IPP.	pu-nya-ba-re-ya-ba-ddhe	sa-rba	pa-ba
Chin.	pên-ni-po-ri-yeh-li-ti	sa-p'ɔ	po-po

Dhāraṇī 23 (continued)

Uig.	prasamari ya	svaha	—
Tib. Nob. II	pra-sa-ma-nī-ye	svāhā	ā-rya-pu-nye
P.	pra-sa-mā-ni-ye	—	a-rya-pu-nya
Hs.	—	—	—
Bl.	—	—	aryabandu
IPP.	pra-sa-ma-ni-ye	svā-hā	arya pu-nya
Chin.	po-ri-chan-ni-i	so-ho	a-li-i pau-tou

Uig.	—	—
Tib. Nob. II	so-bā-kī-ye	svāhā
P.	—	—
Hs.	—	—
Bl.	—	—
IPP.	so-bā-ki-ye	svā-hā
Chin.	su-po-ni-i	so-ho

तद्यथा अचले अमरे अमृते अक्षये अभये पुण्यपर्याबद्धे सर्व-पाप-प्रशमनि स्वाहा। आर्यपुण्ये स्वकीये स्वाहा।

Dhāraṇī 24

The fifteenth chapter is entitled "Worship of goddess Sarasvatī". This chapter has five dhāraṇīs and is one of the oldest parts of the Suvarṇaprabhāsa text. However the Central Asian manuscript found by Mironov, and the Chinese translation of the Sūtra by Dharmakṣema seem to prove the fact that the Sarasvatī chapter was originally very short. Dharmakṣema's version agrees with the beginning of I-tsing's version. Pao-kuei added Jñānagupta's version to Dharmakṣema's translation. The Tib. II version almost fully covers the text of Tib. I, and it agrees with I-tsingš translation. From the caves of Tun-huang many fragments of the Suvarṇaprabhāsa-sūtra were found, and fragments of I-tsing's version. Among the fragments of I-tsing's version the Sarasvatī chapter occurs most often: 36 copies have been found. Some parts of the Uig., Chinese, Tib. III, and text of I-tsing are missing from the Sanskrit version. In this chapter Sarasvatī tells of the importance of the Sūtra. She describes the magical bath which should be held on a day of the Puṣya asterism. Thirtytwo scented drugs (the names of drugs are given in transcription in the Uigur text) are to be obtained in equal proportions and the first dhāraṇī in this chapter has to be chanted 108 times.

Uig.	tadyata	sukarati	krti krt
Skr. Nob.	tadyathā	sukṛte	kṛta
Bag.	tadyathā	sukṛte	—
Tib.	tadya-thā	su-kri-te	kri-ta
C.	—	—	—
P.	—	—	—
Hs.	—	—	—
II Hs.	—	su-te/	kri-te
II Bl.	—	—	—
IPP.	ta-dya-thā	su-kri-dte	kri-dte/kri-kye
Chin.	tan-chih-t'a	su-chi-li-ti	chi-li-ti/chi-li-ti

Dhāraṇī 24 (continued)

Uig.	karmatali	čihu	krti
Skr. Nob.	kamali	jana	karate
Bag.	kara	jāta	bhāge
Tib.	ka-ma-li-na-li	ja-na	ka-ra-te
C.	ka-ma-la ? ici ?	?	ka-ra-te
P.	ma-ma-li-na-li	ja-na	ga-ra-te
Hs.	—	—	—
II Hs.	ka-ma-tā-li/na-li	jā-na	—
II Bl.	ka-ma-ta-li/na-li	dza-na	—
IPP.	ka-ma-hā-le	jna-no	ka-ra-ndhe
Chin.	chieh-mo-tan-li	shanu-nu	chieh-ro-chih

Uig.	sakarti	vi-	čalini
Skr. Nob.	hamkarate	indra	jāli
Bag.	hamsarande	indra	jālamalilaka
Tib.	han-ka-ra-te	in-dra	jā-li
C.	ham-ka-rā-te	—	ja-li
P.	—	—	—
Hs.	—	—	—
II Hs.	han-ka-ra-te	—	—
II Bl.	ham-ka-ra-te	—	ja-li-ni
IPP.	ha-nka-ra-te	in-dra	ja-ri-ni
Chin.	ho-chieh-ra-chia	yin-ta-ro	she-li-ni

Uig.	sankka tiri	prasate
Skr. Nob.	śakaddre	paśaddre
Bag.	—	upasade
Tib.	sa-kad-dre	pa-sad-dre
C.	—	—
P.	—	pa-sad-dri
Hs.	—	—
II Hs.	sa-kad-dre	ba-sād-dre
II Bl.	sam-ka-ra-dre	ba-sad-dre
IPP.	sa-ka-ra-nte	ba-sa-dre
Chin.	shou-chieh-ran-chih	po-she-chih-ri

Dhāraṇī 24 (continued)

Uig.	…. ni
Skr. Nob.	abartaksike/na
Bag.	avatāsike
Tib.	a-brtak-si-ke
C.	—
P.	a-brta-ka-si-ke
Hs.	a-brtag-si-ke
II Hs.	a-barta/ka-si-ke-na/
II Bl.	a-barta-ka/se-ke-na
IPP.	a-pa-rta-ka-si
Chin.	a-fa-ti-chieh-hsi-chi-no

Uig.	kutu kutu	kakavili	karilavili
Skr. Nob. II	kutraku	—	kapila
Bag.	kutra	—	kukala
Tib.	ku-tra-ku	—	ka-pi-la
C.	—	—	—
P.	—	—	ka-bi-la
Hs.	—	—	—
II Hs.	ka-tra-ku	—	ka-pi-la-ka
II Bl.	ku-tra-ku	—	ka-ba-le
IPP.	ku-tu ku-tu	kha-ke-bi-rye	ka-bi-le ka-bi-le
Chin.	chu-tu chu-tu	chiao-chia-pi-ri	chieh-pi-ri chieh-pi

Uig.	kavilamati	—	sandi
Skr. Nob.	kapilamati	śīlamati	sandhi
Bag.	vimalamati	śīlamati	samdhi
Tib.	ka-pi-la-ma-ti	sī-la-ma-ti	san-dhi
C.	—	—	—
P.	ka-bi-la-ma-ti	—	—
Hs.	—	—	san-dhi
II Hs.	bi-ma-la-ti	sī-la-ma-ti/sī-la-ma-ti/sī-la-ma-ti	—
II Bl.	ka-be-la-ma-ti	—	bandhi
IPP.	ka-bi-la-ma-ti	sī-la-ma-ti	sin-dha
Chin.	chieh-p'i-ro-mo-ti	shih-lo-mo-ti	shan-ti

Dhāraṇī 24 (continued)

Uig.	dundumavati	bayati	vanti
Skr. Nob.	dhudhumamabati	—	—
Bag.	budhamati	—	—
Tib.	dhu-dhu-ma-ma-ba-ti	—	—
C.	—	—	—
P.	—	—	—
Hs.	dhu-dhu-ma-ma-pa-ti	—	—
II Hs.	dhu-dhu-ma-ba-ti	—	—
II Bl.	dhu-dhu-ma-ba-ti	—	—
IPP.	dhu-ma-pa-tre	ba-pad-ku	ban-ci-le
Chin.	tu-mo-mo-ti-ri	po-fa-chu	pan-chih-ri ?

Uig.	siri siri	satya sittay e	svaha
Skr. Nob.	śiri śiri	satyasthite	svāhā
Bag.	si siri	satyasthite	svāhā
Tib.	si-ri si-ri	sad-tya-sthi-te	svā-hā
C.	—	—	—
P.	—	—	—
Hs.	—	—	—
II Hs.	—	san-tya-sthi-ti	—
II Bl.	—	—	—
IPP.	si-ri si-ri	sa-dtya-sthi-te	svā-hā
Chin.	shih-ri shih-ri	sa-ti-hsi-t'i-ti	so-ho

तद्यथा। सुकृते कृतकृत्ये कमलि जनकरते हंकरते इन्द्रजालि शंखधरे पाशधरे आवर्तशिखे न कुत्रकु कपिले[२]
कपिलमति शीलमति सन्धि धुधुममवति श्रि[२] सत्यस्थिते स्वाहा॥

Dhāraṇī 25

If a person wishes to have a bath according to the regulations he should make a maṇḍala of eight *hasta*. In a peaceful and quiet place he should think about the things he can see before him and should not divert his thoughts. He should smear this maṇḍala, scatter flowers on it, should fill a gold and silver pot with milk and honey, appoint four men to stand at the four doors of the mandala, also have four boys to stand at the corners of the maṇḍala each with a pot of water. Then he should light incense, play musical instruments, put a big mirror in the maṇḍala, take clean water, make a *sim* a *vaku* (in Chin. circle, in Sanskrit sīmābandha), and repeat the dhāraṇī twentyone times (three times in Chin., seven times in Tib.).

Uig.	tadyata	ankki	nayani
Skr. Nob.	syād yathedam	arake	nayane
A.	—	—	—
BDE.	—	—	—
Bag.	syadyathedam	ane	nayane
Tib.	syād ya-the-dan	a-ra-ke	na-ya-ne
P.	—	—	—
Hs.	—	—	—
II Hs.	sa	—	na-ye-na
II Bl.	syad	—	—
IPP.	ta-dya-thā	an-ra-ke	na-ya-ni
Chin.	tan-chih-t'a	o-ra-chi	no-yeh-ni

Uig.	bili	mili	hili	miri
Skr. Nob.	—	—	hile	mile
A.	—	—	hili	—
BDE.	—	—	hili hili	—
Bag.	—	—	hili	hili
Tib.	—	—	hi-le	mi-li
P.	—	—	—	—
Hs.	—	—	hi-le	—
II Hs.	—	—	—	—
II Bl.	—	—	—	—
IPP.	—	—	hi-li	mi-le
Chin.	—	—	hsi-ri	mi-ri

Dhāraṇī 25 (continued)

Uig.	kiri	kikuli	svaha
Skr. Nob.	gile	khikhile	svāhā
A.	—	khile	—
BDE.	—	khile	—
Bag.	hili	hili	svāhā
Tib.	ki-le	khi-khi-le	svā-hā
P.	—	—	—
Hs.	—	—	—
II Hs.	gi-li	—	—
II Bl.	—	—	—
IPP.	ki-le	khi-khi-le	svā-hā
Chin.	ch'i-ri	ch'i-ch'i-ri	so-ho

स्याद् यथेदम्। अलके नयने हिलि मिलि हिलि मिलि खिखिलि स्वाहा।

Dhāraṇī 26

Before entering the water the purifying dhāraṇī is as follows:

Uig.	tadyata	sami	jasami	sugaravati
Skr. Nob.	tadyathā	—	—	sagaṭe
ABDE	—	—	—	sugate
Bag.	tadyathā	—	—	sugate
Tib. Nob. II	ta-dya-thā	—	—	sa-ga-te
C.	—	—	—	—
P.	—	—	—	—
Hs.	—	—	—	—
II Hs.	—	—	—	sa-ga-ta
II Bl.	—	—	—	sa-ga-de
IPP.	ta-dya-thā	—	—	sa-ga-te
Chin.	tan-chih-t'a	—	—	so-chieh-chih

Uig.	vikrati	vibitatati	svaha
Skr. Nob.	bigaṭe	bigaṭābati	svāhā
ABDE	vigate	—	—
Bag.	vigate	vigatāvati	svāhā
Tib. Nob. II	bi-ga-te	bi-ga-ta-ba-ti	svāhā
C.	—	bi-ga-tā/ba-bā	—
P.	pi-ga-te	bi-ga-tā/pa-tā	—
Hs.	—	bi-ga-tā/pa-tā	—
II Hs.	bi-ka-ta	pi-ga-tā-pa-ti	—
II Bl.	bi-ga-te	bi-ga-ta-ba-ti	—
IPP.	bi-ga-te	bi-ga-ca-ba-ddhe	svā-hā
Chin.	p'i-chieh-chih	p'i-chih-ch'a-fa-ti	so-ho

तद्यथा। सगटे विगटे विकटावति स्वाहा।

Dhāraṇī 27

He should recite this dhāraṇī seven times. When he has had his bath, he should take the water, food and drink which he offered in the maṇḍala and throw it into a pool or a river. After he has bathed, he should put on clean clothes and enter a clean house. He should recite the following dhāraṇī twentyone times (in Chin. three times, seven times, in Tib. twentyone times).

Uig.	tadyata	sami	visami
Skr. Nob.	—	śame	bisame
A.	—	—	—
BDE.	—	—	—
G.	—	—	—
Bag.	—	same	viṣame
Tib. Nob. II	tadya-thā	sa-me	bisame
C.	—	—	—
P.	—	sa-me	pi-sa-me
Hs.	—	sa-me	be-sa-me
II Hs.	—	sa-me	—
II Bl.	—	sa-mo	—
IPP.	ta-dya-thā	sa-me	bi-sa-mi
Chin.	tan-chih-t'a	sa-mi	p'i-sa-mi

Uig.	svaha	sakrti	vikrti
Skr. Nob.	svāhā	sagaṭe	bigaṭe
A.	—	sugate	—
BDE.	—	sugate	—
G.	—	sugate	vigate
Bag.	svāhā	sugate	—
Tib. Nob. II	svāhā	sa-ga-te	bi-ga-te
C.	—	—	—
P.	—	—	—
Hs.	—	—	—
II Hs.	—	—	—
II Bl.	—	—	—
IPP.	svā-hā	sa-ga-te	bi-ga-te
Chin.	so-ho	so-chieh-chih	p'i-chieh-chih

Dhāraṇī 27 (continued)

Uig.	svaha	vikrati vati	svaha
Skr. Nob.	svāhā	sukhatinate	svāhā
A.	—	—	—
BDE.	—	—	—
G.	—	—	—
Bag.	svāhā	—	svāhā
Tib. Nob.II	svaha	su-kha-ti-na-te	svāhā
C.	—	—	—
P.	—	—	—
Hs.	—	—	—
II Hs.	—	—	—
II Bl.	—	bi-ga-de-ba-te	—
IPP.	svā-hā	bi-ga-ca-ba-ddhe	svā-hā
Chin.	so-ho	p'i-chieh-ch'a-fa-ti	so-ho

Uig.	sakara sanputtay a	svaha
Skr. Nob.	sāgarasambhūtāya	svāhā
A.	—	
BDE.	—	
G.	sāgarasamkr(ku?)tāya	svāhā
Bag.	sāgarasambhūtāya	svāhā
Tib. Nob. II	sā-ga-ra sam-bhū-tā-ya	svāhā
C.	sa-ga-ra-sam-bhū-tā-ya	svāhā
P.	sa-ga-ra-sam-bhū-ta-ya	svāha
Hs.	sa-ga-ra-sam-bhu-ta	svāhā
II Hs.	sa-ga-ra-sam-bhu-ta	svāhā
II Bl.	sā-gha-da (na?)/sam-buddhā-ya	svāhā
IPP.	sa-ga-ra-sam-bud-dhā-ya	svāhā
Chin.	so-chieh-ro-san-pu-to-yeh	so-ho

Dhāraṇī 27 (continued)

Uig.	sakanti matay a	svaha
Skr. Nob.	skandamātrāya	svāhā
A.	skandhamārutaya	svāhā
BDE.	skandhamārutaya	svāhā
G.	skandhamārutaya	svāhā
Bag.	skandhamārutāya	svāhā
Tib. Nob. II	skan-da-mā-tā-ya	svāhā
C.	—	
P.	skan-dha-ma-tā-ya	svāhā
Hs.	skan-dha-ma-tā-ya	svāhā
II Hs.	—	
II Bl.	skan-da-mā-tā-ya	svāhā
IPP.	skan-dhā-ma-hā-ya	svā-hā
Chin.	sai-chien-t'o-mo-to-yeh	so-ho

Uig.	nilakantay a	svaha
Skr. Nob.	nīlakaṇṭhāya	svāhā
A.	nīlakarṇāya	svāhā
BDE.	nīlakarnāya	svāhā
G.	—	
Bag.	nīlakanthāya	svāhā
Tib. Nob.II	nī-la-ka-nthā-ya	svāhā
C.	—	
P.	nī-la-kan-thā-ya	svāhā
Hs.	—	
II Hs.	ni-la-kan-tha-ya	svāhā
II Bl.	—	
IPP.	—	
Chin.	ni-lo-chien-t'o-yeh	so-ho

Dhāraṇī 27 (continued)

Uig.	aparačit-a viryay-a	svaha
Skr. Nob.	aparājitabīryāya	svāhā
A.	—	
BDE.	—	
G.	—	
Bag.	aparājitavīryāya	svāhā
Tib. Nob. II	a-pa-rā-ji-ta-bī-ryā-ya	svāhā
C.	—	
P.	a-pa-ra-ji-(?) ta-bi-rya-ya	svāhā
Hs.	a-pa-ra-ji-ta-pa-ryā-ya	svāhā
II Hs.	a-ba-ra-ji-ta-bī-rya-ya	svāhā
II Bl.	a-pa-ra-ji-ta/bi-rya-ya	svāhā
IPP.	a-pa-ra-ji-ta-bī-ryā-ya-	svā-hā
Chin.	a-po-ro-shih-ch'e-p'i-ri-yeh-yeh	so-ho

Uig.	himavanti sanibuttay-a	svaha
Skr. Nob.	himabatasaṃbhūtāya	svāhā
A.	himabatagalaṃbhutāya	svāhā
BDE.	—	
G.	—	
Bag.	himavatasaṃbhūtāya	svāhā
Tib. Nob. II	hi-ma-ba-ta-sam-bhu-tā-yā	svāhā
C.	—	
P.	hi-ma-bā-sam-bhu-tā-yā	svāhā
Hs.	hi-ma-pā-sam-bhu-ta-ya	svāhā
II Hs.	hi-ma-pad-sa-ma-bhud-ta-ya	svāhā
II Bl.	hi-ma-bandha/sam-buddha-ya	svāhā
IPP.	hi-ma-ban-dha-sam-bud-dhā-ya-	svā-hā
Chin.	hsi-mo-p'an-ch'e-san-pu-to-yeh	so-ho

Dhāranī 27 (continued)

Uig.	ani-mira-vakryatay-a	svaha
Skr. Nob.	animilabaktrāya	svāhā
A.	animisatrāya	svāhā
BDE.	animisatrāya	svāhā
G.	anilavaktrāya	svāhā
Bag.	animiṣacakrāya	svāhā
Tib. Nob. II	a-ni-mi-la-bag-trā-ya	svāhā
C.	a-ni-mi-la-bak-tra-ya	svaha
P.	a-ni-mi-la-bag-tra-ya	svāhā
Hs.	a-ni-mi-la-bag-tra-ya	svāhā
II Hs.	i-ni-bi-la-bag-tra-ya	svāhā
II Bl.	animi-la-bak-tā-ya	svāhā
IPP.	a-ni-bi-la-bha-dra-ya	svā-hā
Chin.	a-ni-mi-lo-po-tan-ro-yeh	so-ho

Uig.	—			
Skr. Nob.	namo	bhagabate	brahmaṇe	
A.	namo	bhagvatyai	brahmaṇyai	
BDE.	namo	bhagvatyai	brahmanyai	
G.	namo	bhagvatyai	brahmane	
Bag.	namo	bhagavatyai	brahmanyai	
Tib. Nob. II	na-mo	bha-ga-ba-te	bra-hma-ṇe	
C.	—			
P.	na-mo	bha-ga-ba-te	pra-hma-ne	
Hs.	na-mo	bha-ga-ba-te	pra-hma-ne	
II Hs.	na-mo	bha-ga-ba-te	pra-ma-ne	
II Bl.	na-mo	bha-ga-ba-te	dra-hmā-ne	
IPP.	na-mo	bha-ga-ba-te	bra-hma-ṇe	svā-hā
Chin.	nan-mo	po-ch'ieh-fa-tu	po-ro-t'ien-mo-hsieh	so-ho

Dhāraṇī 27 (continued)

Uig.	namo	sarasvati	divini ya svaha	
Skr. Nob.	namaḥ	sarasvatyai	debyai	
A.	—			
BDE.	—			
G.	—		—	
Bag.	namaḥ	sarasvatyai	—	
Tib. Nob. II	na-maḥ	sa-ra-sva-tyai	—	
C.	—		devyai	
P.	na-ma	sa-ra-svā-tyai	de-byai	
Hs.	na-ma	sa-ra-svā-tyai	—	
II Hs.	—		de-bai	
II Bl.	na-ma	ssa-ra-sva-tya	de-bai	
IPP.	na-mha	sa-ra-sva-te	de-bai	
Chin.	nan-mo	sa-ro-suan-ti		

Uig.	mha divini ya	svaha	sidyantu	mi
Skr. Nob.	—		sidhyantu	
A.	—		—	
BDE.	—		—	
G.	—		—	
Bag.	—		sidhyantu	
Tib. Nob. II	—		sid-dhyam-tu	
C.	—		—	
P.	—		nur-tyan-tu	
Hs.	—		nur-tyan-tu	
II Hs.	—		sid-tyan-tu	
II Bl.	maha-de-byai		si-ddhyantu	mī
IPP.	ma-ha-de-bi-ye	svā-hā	si-dhya-na-tu	
Chin.	mo-ho-t'i-pi'i	so-ho	hsi-tien-tu	man

Dhāraṇī 27 (continued)

Uig.	mantir-a-padi	svaha
Skr. Nob.	matrapadā taṃ	—
A.	—	—
BDE.	—	—
G.	—	—
Bag.	mantrapadāstam	—
Tib. Nob.II	man-tra-pa-dā	—
C.	man-tra-pa-da	—
P.	—	—
Hs.	—	—
II Hs.	man-dra-ba-tā	—
II Bl.	—	—
IPP.	man-tra-ba-dā	svā-hā
Chin.	man-tan-ro-po-t'o	so-ho

Uig.	tiritu ta brahmanu maninta	svaha
Skr. Nob.	brahmānumanyatu	svāhā
A.	brahma namasyantu	svāhā
BDE.	brahma namasyantu	svāhā
G.	—	
Bag.	—	
Tib. Nob. II	taṃ ta-ra-tu	
C.	daṃ	
P.	dam	
Hs.	da-ma	
II Hs.	—	
II Bl.	—	
IPP.	dha-ra-to	
Chin.	tan-ra-tu	

तद्यथा समे विषमे स्वाहा। सुगते विगते स्वाहा। सुखाधिनते स्वाहा। सागर-सम्भूताय स्वाहा। स्कन्दमात्राय स्वाहा। नीलकण्ठाय स्वाहा। अपराजित-वीर्याय स्वाहा। हिमवत-सम्भूताय स्वाहा। अनिमिलवक्त्राय स्वाहा। नमो भगवत्यै ब्रह्मण्यै स्वाहा। नमो सरस्वत्यै देव्यै महादेव्यै स्वाहा। सिध्यन्तु मे मन्त्रपदा: स्वाहा। तरतु ब्रह्मानुमन्यन्तु स्वाहा।

Dhāraṇī 28

Sarasvatī announces the longest dhāraṇī:

Uig.	tadyata	muri čiri	inči
Skr. Nob.	syād-yathedam	mure cire	abaje
A.	—	vire	araje
B.	—	sure	araje
D.	—	sure	araje
E.	—	vire	araje
G.	sa (sam?) yetham	sure	avaje
Bag.	syādyathedam	sure vire	araje
Tib.	syād ya-the-dan	mu-re/tsi-re	a-ba-dze
C.	—	—	—
P.	syad	—	a-ba-dze
Hs.	syad	—	a-pa-dza
II Hs.	sa-ya-thi-dan	mu-ri tsi-ri	—
Bl.	—	—	—
II Bl.	—	—	—
IPP.	ta-dya-thā	mu-re ci-re	a-ba-ddhe
Chin.	tan-chih-t'a	mu-ri chih-ri	—

Uig.	ančuvati	hingguli	mingguli
Skr. Nob.	abajabati	hiṅgule	mingule
A.	arajavati	—	piṅgale
B.	arajavati	—	piṅgale
D.	arajavaji	higule	—
E.	arajavati	—	piṅgale
G.	—	—	piṅgale
Bag.	arajavati	hi-gule	piṅgale
Tib.	a-ba-dza-ba-ti	hiṅ-gu-le	min-gu-le
C.	—	hi ? -	mi ?
P.	—	—	—
Hs.	a-pa-dza-ba-ti	hin-gu-li	—
II Hs.	—	—	—
Bl.	—	—	—
II Bl.	—	mim-gu-le	mim-gu-le
IPP.	a-ba-ja-ba-ti	hing-gu-le	ming-gu-le
Chin.	a-fa-ch'a-fa-ti	hsing-yü-ri	ming-chü-ri

Dhāraṇī 28 (continued)

Uig.	manggulavati	ranggusti	—
Skr. Nob.	piṅgalabati /	maṅguse	marīci
A.	piṅgalabati /	mukhe	—
B.	piṅgalabati /	mukhe	—
D.	piṅgalabati /	mukhe	—
E.	piṅgalabati /	mukhe	—
G.	piṅgalabati /	mutrāṣe	—
Bag.	pingale vati	mukhe	marīci
Tib.	bin-gal-a-ba-ti/	man-gu-se	ma-ri-tsi
C.	bi-ga-la-ba-ti	ma-gu-se	—
P.	—		—
Hs.	—		—
II Hs.	pin-ga	mun-gu-se	mā-ri-tsi
Bl.	—		—
II Bl.	pinga	mingu-se	mā-ri-tsai
IPP.	ming-gu-la-ba-ddhe	mam-gu-se	ma-ri-ci
Chin.	ming-chü-lo-fa-ti/	yang-chü-shih	mo-ri-chih

Uig.	samati	visamavati	agri magri
Skr. Nob.	samati	daśamati	agrīmagrī
A.	sumati	diśamati	—
B.	sumati	disamati	aśrīmasrī
D.	sumati	disamati	aśrī
E.	sumati	disamati	asrīmasrī
G.	svamati	disamati	atrīmatrī
Bag.	sumati	disamati	agrāmagrī
Tib.	sa-ma-ti	da-sa-ma-ti	a-gri-ma-gri
C.	—	—	—
P.	—	—	—
Hs.	—	—	—
II Hs.	svā-ma-ti	di-sa-ma-ti	a-ghri-ta-ma-ghri
Bl.	—	—	—
II Bl.	—	—	a-gri-ta-ma-gri
IPP.	—	—	a-ghri-ma-ghri
Chin.	san-mo-ti	p'i-san-mo-ti	o-chin-ri/mo-chin-ri

Dhāraṇī 28 (continued)

Uig.	taqivi tanačavanti			čiri čiri
Skr. Nob.	tara citara cabati			ciciri
A.	talavi talecabuḍi			viciri
B.	talabuḍi			viciri
D.	talabuḍi			viciri
E.	talabuḍi			viciri
G.	taraci taracavati			ciciri
Bag.	talavi tale ca vaḍi			vicari
Tib.	ta-rat si-ta-ra		tsa-ba-ti	tsi-tsi-ri
C.	—	rep.	rep.	—
P.	rep.	tsi-ti-ri	—	—
Hs.	rep.	tsi-ti-ri	—	—
II Hs.	—	—	—	—
Bl.	—	—	—	—
II Bl.	ta-ra-tsi	ta-ra-tsa-ba-ti		tsi-ri-tsi-ri
IPP.	ta-ra-ci	da-ra-ca-baddhi		ci-ci-ri
Chin.	tan-ro-chih	tan-ro-che-fa-ti		chih-chih-ri

Uig.	miri	mandaddi	mariči
Skr. Nob.	śiri miri	—	marīci
A.	rīmariṇī	—	vīmarini
B.	—	—	mariṇi
D.	—	—	mariṇi
E.	—	—	mariṇi
G.	sirimarisirī	—	—
Bag.	—	—	mariṇi
Tib.	si-ri-mi-ri	—	ma-ri-tsi
C.	—	—	—
P.	—	—	—
Hs.	—	—	—
II Hs.	si-rī-mi-ri	—	mi-rī-tsi
Bl.	—	—	—
II Bl.	—	—	māra-tsyai
IPP.	si-ri-mi-ri	ma-nan-dhi-dam	mi-ri-tsi
Chin.	shih-lo-mi-li	mo-nan-ti-t'an	mo-ri-chih

Dhāraṇī 28 (continued)

Uig.	pay napayravi	loka čisti
Skr. Nob.	pranaye	lokajyeṣṭhe
A.	nipāṇaye	lokahyeṣṭake
B.	—	lokajyeṣṭhake
D.	—	lokajyeṣṭhake
E.	—	lokahyeṣṭhake
G.	viprāṇaye	lokajaiṣṭe
Bag.	praṇaye	lokajyeṣṭhake
Tib.	pra-na-ye	lo-ka-jye-ṣṭhe
C.	—	—
P.	bra-na-ye	lo-ka-jye-sthe
Hs.	pra-na-ye	lo-ka-dze-sthe
II Hs.	prā-na-ye	lo-kā-jā-srē
Bl.	—	—
II Bl.	pra-na-pri-ye	—
IPP.	ba-ran-a-bi-rye	lo-ka-je-sthe
Chin.	pa-ro-na-pi-ri-i	lu-chia-shih-se-chi

Uig.	loka siristi	loka prayi	sitta varti
Skr. Nob.	lokaśreṣṭhe	loka-priye	siddhiprite
A.	—	priya	siddhavrate
B.	—	priya	siddhavrate
D.	—	priya	siddhivrate
E.	—	priya	siddhivrate
G.	lokasriṣṭe	—	siddhavrate
Bag.	—	priya	siddhivrate
Tib.	lo-ka-sre-ṣṭhe	lo-ka-pri-ye	sid-dhi-pri-te
C.	lo-ka-sri-ṣṭhe	—	—
P.	lo-ka-srī ?-ṣṭha	lo-ka-bri-ye	sad-dhi-bri-te
Hs.	lo-ka-sre-sthe	lo-ka-bri-ye	sad-dha-bri-te
II Hs.	lo-ka-sre-sthe	lo-kā-pri-ye	sid-dha-pra-te
Bl.	—	—	—
II Bl.	—	—	si-ddhi-prā-pte
IPP.	lo-ka-sre-sthe	lo-ka-bi-le-ra	si-ddha-bra-he
Chin.	lu-chia-chih-ri-se-chih	lu-chia-pi-ri-i	hsi-to-po-ti-ti

Dhāraṇī 28 (continued)

Uig.	bimba muki	sači suči čari	aprati hari
Skr. Nob.	bhīmamukhi	śuci khari	apratihate
A.	sīmamukhi	śavirī	—
B.	—	śacivari	—
D.	—	śacicari	—
E.	—	sacivari	—
G.	—	suvacari	—
Bag.	bhimamukhi	sacivari	apratihate
Tib.	bhi-ma-mu-khi	su-ci-kha-ri	a-pra-ti-ha-te
C.	—	—	—
P.	bi-ma-mu-khi	—	—
Hs.	bi-ma-mu-khi	—	—
II Hs.	bhri-ma-mu-khi	—	—
Bl.	—	—	—
II Bl.	—	—	—
IPP.	bhi-ma-mu-khi	su-ci-ca-ri	a-pra-ti-ha-te
Chin.	p'i-mo-mu-ch'i	shu-chih-che-ri	a-po-ri-ti-ho-ti

Uig.	aprati hata buddi	namuči namuči
Skr. Nob.	apratihatabuddhi	namuci namuci
A.	—	tamuci muci
B.	—	muci
D.	—	muci
E.	—	muci
G.	apratihatasuddhih	tamuci
Bag.	apratihatabuddhi	namuci
Tib.	a-pra-ti-ḥa-ta-bud-dhi	na-mu-tsi
C.	—	—
P.	—	—
Hs.	—	—
II Hs.	—	na-mu-tsi na-mu-tsi
Bl.	—	—
II Bl.	—	na-mu-tsi/mahā/na-mu-tsi
IPP.	a-pra-hi-ha-ha-bu-dhi	na-mu-ci na-mu-ci
Chin.	a-po-ri-ti-ho-ch'e-p'o-ti	nan-mu-chih nan-mu-chih

Dhāraṇī 28 (continued)

Uig.	mha divi	karti krina tram
Skr. Nob.	mahādebi	pratigṛhṇa
A.	—	pratigṛhṇa
B.	—	pratigrhna
D.	—	pratigṛhṇa
E.	—	—
G.	—	pratigrhna
Bag.	mahādevi	pratigrhna
Tib.	ma-hā-de-bi	pra-ti-gri-hna
C.	—	—
P.	—	bra-ti-gri-ha
Hs.	—	—
II Hs.	mahā	—
Bl.	ma-hā-de-bī	—
II Bl.	ma-hā-de-byi	—
IPP.	ma-hā-de-bī	pra-te-gi-na-gri-ni
Chin.	mo-ho-t'i-pi	po-ra-ti-chin-ri-hun-na

Uig.	namas karana	mam a sukasav an
Skr. Nob.	namaskāram	mama
A.	—	sarvasatvānāṃ
B.	—	sarvasatvānāṃ
D.	namaskāra	sarvasatvānāṃ
E.	—	sarvasatvānāṃ
G.	—	sarvasatvānāṃ
Bag.	namaskāra	sarvasttvānāṃ
Tib.	na-ma-ska-ra-na	—
C.	na-ma-ska-ram	—
P.	—	—
Hs.	—	—
II Hs.	na-ma-skar-na	—
Bl.	—	—
II Bl.	na-ma-ska-rā-na	—
IPP.	na-ma-ska-ra	miṅ-gzug
Chin.	nan-mo-sai-chia-ro	wo-mou-chia-p'o-ti ?

Dhāraṇī 28 (continued)

Uig.	—	buddir aprati bonta
Skr. Nob.	—	buddhir apratihatā
A.	—	—
B.	—	—
D.	—	—
E.	—	—
G.	—	buddhir apratihatā
Bag.	—	buddhirapratihatā
Tib.	—	—
C.	—	—
P.	—	—
Hs.	—	—
II Hs.	—	—
Bl.	—	—
II Bl.	—	—
IPP.	bud-dhi-dra-sa-hi	buddhi a-pra-ti-ha-ta
Chin.	ta-ri-she-hsi	p'o-ti ? a-po-ra-ti-ho-ch'e

Uig.	bavatu	čerirmi	visuda yatu
Skr. Nob.	bhavatu	—	vidya me sidhyatu
A.	bhavantu	—	vidya me siddhyantu
B.	—	—	—
D.	—	—	—
E.	—	—	—
G.	bhavanti	—	vidya me siddhyantu
Bag.	bhavatu	—	vidyā me siddhyatu
Tib.	—	—	—
C.	—	—	—
P.	—	—	—
Hs.	—	—	—
II Hs.	—	—	—
Bl.	—	—	—
II Bl.	—	—	—
IPP.	bha-du	si-bha-me	bi-sud-dhi-to
Chin.	p'o-po-tu	shih-p'o-mi	p'i-shu-chih-tu

Dhāraṇī 28 (continued)

Uig.	šastar-a-šaloka-mantar
Skr. Nob.	śāstraślokatantra
A.	śāstralokatantra
B.	śāstralokatantra
D.	śāstralokatantra
E.	śāstralokatantra
G.	śāstraloke/tatra
Bag.	śāstralokatantra
Tib.	—
C.	—
P.	—
Hs.	—
II Hs.	—
Bl.	—
II Bl.	—
IPP.	sa-stha-so-lo-ka man-tra
Chin.	she-hsi-tan-ro-shu-lu-chia/man-tan-ro

Uig.	pitaka tiv a dasi	tatyata
Skr. Nob.	piṭakakāvyādiṣu	tadyathā
A.	—	—
B.	—	—
D.	—	—
E.	—	—
G.	—	—
Bag.	piṭakākadyādiṣu	tadyathā
Tib.	—	tad-ya-thā
C.	—	—
P.	—	—
Hs.	—	—
II Hs.	—	—
Bl.	—	—
II Bl.	—	—
IPP.	bi-dhi-ka ka-bi-ya-dhi-so	ta-dya-thā
Chin.	pi-te-chia-chia-pei-yeh-ti-shu	tan-chih-t'a

Dhāraṇī 28 (continued)

Uig.	mha prabavi	hili mili hili	mili
Skr. Nob.	mahāprabhāve	hili hili/mili	mili
A.	—	hili hili	mili
B.	—	hili hili	mili
D.	—	hili hili	mili
E.	—	hili hili	mili
G.	mahāprabhavo	—	
Bag.	mahāprabhāve	hili hili mili	mili
Tib.	ma-ha-pra-bha-be	hi-li-hi-li/mi-li-mi-li	
C.	—	—	
P.	—	—	
Hs.	ma-ha-pra-bhā-pa	—	
II Hs.	ma-hā-pra-bhā-ba	—	
Bl.	ma-hā-pra-bhā ?	—	
II Bl.	—	he-li-he-li mi-li-mi-li	
IPP.	ma-hā-pra-bha-ba	hi-li-mi-li hi-li-mi-li	
Chin.	mo-ho-po-ra-p'o-pi	hsi-li-mi-li hsi-li-mi-li	

Uig.	vičarantu mam a bottir ayan naman ya a	
Skr. Nob.	vicaratu mama	
A.	vicatu mama vicaratu me māyā	
B.	vicavatu mama vicaratu me māyā	
D.	vicavatu mama vicaratu me māyā	
E.	vicavatu mama vicaratu me māyā	
G.	+ sarvasatvānām ca	
Bag.	vicaratu mama vicaratu me maya sarvasattvānāṃ ca	
Tib.	—	
C.	—	
P.	—	
Hs.	—	
II Hs.	—	
Bl.	—	
II Bl.	—	
IPP.	bi-ca-ra-to bi-bud-dhi min-gzug bud-dhi-bi-sud-dhe	
Chin.	p'i-che-ra-tu	mi p'o-ti

Dhāraṇī 28 (continued)

Uig.	bagavatina	sarin tiyan
Skr. Nob.	bhagavatyā devyāḥ	sarvasatyā anubhāvena
A.	—	—
B.	bhagavatyah	—
D.	bhagavatyāh	—
E.	bhagavatyāh	—
G.	devyā	sarvasvatyā nubhāvena
Bag.	bhagavatyā devyāḥ	sarvasatyā anubhāvena
Tib.	—	—
C.	—	—
P.	—	—
Hs.	—	—
II Hs.	—	—
Bl.	—	—
II Bl.	—	—
IPP.	bha-ga-bad-tyam be-ba-yam	sa-ra-sa-tya
Chin.	—	sa-lo-suan-tien

Uig.	karate vi	—	qyrt mamati
Skr. Nob.	karate	keyūre	keyūrabati
A.	kadarke	—	yuvati
B.	kadarake	—	yuvati
D.	kadarake	—	yuvati
E.	kadarake	—	yuvati
G.	karade ?	—	—
Bag.	karadake	—	yuvati
Tib.	ka-ra-te	ke-yū-re	ke-yū-ra-ba-ti
C.	—	—	—
P.	—	—	—
Hs.	—	—	—
II Hs.	ka-ra-de	—	—
Bl.	—	—	—
II Bl.	ka-ra-te	—	—
IPP.	ka-ra-dhe	ke-yu-re	ke-yu-ra-ma-te
Chin.	chieh-ro-chih	chi-yu-ri	chi-yu-ro-mo-ti

Dhāraṇī 28 (continued)

Uig.	hili mili hili mili	—
Skr. Nob.	hili mili/hili mili	hili hili
A.	hili mili hi	—
B.	hili mili hili	—
D.	hili mili hili	—
E.	hili mili hili	—
G.	hili mili	—
Bag.	hili mili	—
Tib.	hi-li mi-li hi-li mi-li	hi-li-hi-li
C.	—	—
P.	—	—
Hs.	—	—
II Hs.	hi-li mi-lī	—
Bl.	—	—
II Bl.	—	—
IPP.	hi-li mi-li	—
Chin.	hsi-li mi-li hsi-li mi-li	—

Uig.	atahayami	mana divi	budda satyena
Skr. Nob.	āvāhayāmi	mahādevīm	buddhasatyena
A.	—	—	—
B.	—	mahādevi	—
D.	—	mahādevi	—
E.	—	mahādevi	—
G.	—	—	—
Bag.	āvāhayāmi	mahādevi	buddhasatyena
Tib.	—	—	—
C.	—	—	—
P.	—	—	—
Hs.	—	—	—
II Hs.	—	—	—
Bl.	—	—	—
II Bl.	—	—	—
IPP.	a-ba-ya-mi	ma-ha-de-be	bud-dha-sa-tyan
Chin.	a-p'o-ho-yeh-mi	mo-ho-t'i-pi	p'o-t'o-sa-ti-no

Dhāraṇī 28 (continued)

Uig.	darm a satyena	sangga satyena
Skr. Nob.	dharmasatyena	saṃghasatyena
A.	—	—
B.	dharme satyena	—
D.	—	—
E.	—	—
G.	—	—
Bag.	dharmasatyena	—
Tib.	—	—
C.	—	—
P.	—	—
Hs.	—	—
II Hs.	—	—
Bl.	—	—
II Bl.	—	—
IPP.	—	sam-gha-sa-tyena
Chin.	ta-mo-sa-ti-no	seng-ch'ieh-sa-ti-no

Uig.	indinan satyena	varuna satyena
Skr. Nob.	indra satyena	varuṇasatyena
A.	—	—
B.	—	varuṇa satyana
D.	—	—
E.	—	—
G.	—	—
Bag.	indrasatyena	varuṇa satyena
Tib.	—	—
C.	—	—
P.	—	—
Hs.	—	—
II Hs.	—	—
Bl.	—	—
II Bl.	—	—
IPP.	in-dra-sa-tyan	ba-ru-na-satyan
Chin.	yin-ta-ro-sa-ti-no	—

Dhāranī 28 (continued)

Uig.	ye loke satyena
Skr. Nob.	ye loke satyavādinaḥ santi teṣāṃ satyavādināṃ
A.	—
B.	—
D.	—
E.	—
G.	—
Bag.	ye loka satyavādinaḥ santi tesa
Tib.	—
C.	—
P.	—
Hs.	—
II Hs.	—
Bl.	—
II Bl.	—
IPP.	ye lo-ke sa-tya
Chin.	i lu-chi sa-ti-p'o-ti-no

Uig.	vādira	tisan satyena vacatina
Skr. Nob.	satyavāditi	teṣāṃ satyavādināṃ satyena
A.	—	—
B.	—	—
D.	—	—
E.	—	—
G.	—	—
Bag.	—	teṣāṃ satyavacena
Tib.	—	—
C.	—	—
P.	—	—
Hs.	—	—
II Hs.	—	—
Bl.	—	—
II Bl.	—	—
IPP.	sad-tyena	te-sa-ma sad-tyan sad-te-ba-ca-ni-ni
Chin.	—	ti-shan sa-ti-no sa-ti-fa-che-ni-no

Dhāraṇī 28 (continued)

Uig.	avahayami	mandir	tadyata
Skr. Nob.	āvāhayāmi	mahādevīm	tadyathā
A.	—	—	—
B.	—	mahādevī	—
D.	—	mahādevi	—
E.	—	mahādevi	—
G.	—	—	—
Bag.	āvāhayami	mahādevi	—
Tib.	—	—	tad-ya-thā
C.	—	—	—
P.	—	—	—
Hs.	—	—	—
II Hs.	—	—	—
Bl.	—	—	—
II Bl.	—	—	—
IPP.	a-ba-ha-ya-mi	ma-hā-de-vi	—
Chin.	a-p'o-ho-yeh-mi	mo-ho-t'i-pi	—

Uig.	hili	hili mili hili mili
Skr. Nob.	hili hili	hili mili hili mili
A.	—	hili mili
B.	—	hili hili mili
D.	—	hili hili mili
E.	—	hili hili mili
G.	—	hili sili
Bag.	—	hili hili mili
Tib.	hi-li hi-li	hi-li mi-li/hi-li mi-li
C.	—	—
P.	—	—
Hs.	—	—
II Hs.	hi-li mi-li	—
Bl.	—	—
II Bl.	—	—
IPP.	—	hi-li mi-li hi-li mi-li
Chin.	—	hsi-ri mi-ri/hsi-ri mi-ri

Dhāraṇī 28 (continued)

Uig.	vičarantu mam a	buttir	namo kagavati
Skr. Nob.	vicaratu mama		namo bhagavatyai
A.	—		—
B.	vicalantu mama		—
D.	vicalantu mama		mantratoyani sarvasatvānāṃ
E.	vicalantu mama		—
G.	—		—
Bag.	vicarantu mama		namo bhagavatyai
Tib.	—		—
C.	—		—
P.	—		—
Hs.	—		—
II Hs.	—		—
Bl.	—		—
II Bl.	—		—
IPP.	bi-ca-ra-to	bud-dhe	na-mo bha-ga-ba-ti
Chin.	—		nan-mo po-ch'ieh-fa-ti

Uig.	sarasvati mana divi
Skr. Nob.	mahadevyai sarvasatyai
A.	—
B.	—
D.	—
E.	—
G.	mahadevyai svatyai
Bag.	sarasvatyai
Tib.	—
C.	—
P.	—
Hs.	—
II Hs.	—
Bl.	—
II Bl.	—
IPP.	ma-hā-de-ba sa-ra-sa-ti
Chin.	mo-ho-t'i-po sa-ro-svan-ti

Dhāraṇī 28 (continued)

Uig.	sidrantu mantir-a prta
Skr. Nob.	sidhyantu mantrapadā me
A.	siddhyamtu mantrapadā me
B.	—
D.	—
E.	—
G.	sindhyantu mantrapadā me
Bag.	siddhyantu mantrapadāḥ
Tib.	—
C.	—
P.	—
Hs.	—
II Hs.	—
Bl.	—
II Bl.	—
IPP.	si-dhyan-tu man-tra-pa-dā-ni
Chin.	hsi-tien-tu man-tan-ro-po-t'o-mi

Uig.	namo gagavati	svaha
Skr. Nob.	namo bhagavatyai	svāhā
A.	—	—
B.	—	—
D.	—	—
E.	—	—
G.	—	—
Bag.	—	svāhā
Tib.	—	svāhā
C.	—	—
P.	—	—
Hs.	—	—
II Hs.	—	—
Bl.	—	—
II Bl.	—	—
IPP.	—	svā-hā
Chin.	—	so-ho

Dhāraṇī 28 (continued)

Those who wish to recite this dhāraṇī should pay homage with flowers of the season and scented incense. They must pay homage with scented powder to the Buddha and Sarasvatī.

They should recite the above dhāraṇī twentyone times (Tib. twentyone, Chin. three times for seven days). If a person does not give up what he craves for, and strives for, for three months, six months, nine months or a year, then he will attain it.

Some of the passages concerning the last instructions of the last dhāraṇī are missing from the Uigur and the Tibetan versions.

तद्यथा। मुरे चिरे। अवजे अवजवति। हिंगुले-मिंगुले मिंगुलवति। मंगुषे। मारीचि। समति विसमति ० अग्रि-मग्रि। तरचि तरचवति। चिचिरि शिरि मिरि मारीचि। प्राणप्रिये लोकज्येष्ठे लोकश्रेष्ठे लोकप्रिये सिद्धव्रते बिम्बमुखि (vl. भीममुखि)शुचि-चरि अप्रतिहते अप्रतिहत-बुद्धि नमुचि[२] महादेवि प्रतिगृह्ण नमस्कारम् अमुकस्य। मम बुद्धि दर्शिहि। सर्व-सत्त्वानां बुद्धिर् अप्रतिहता भवतु। शिवं मे विशुध्यतु शास्त्र-श्लोक-मन्त्रपिटक-काव्यादिषु।

तद्यथा। महाप्रभावे हिलि-मिलि हिलि-मिलि। विचरतु मे बुद्धिर् अमुक-बुद्धि-शुद्धिः भगवत्यां देव्यां सरस्वत्याम्। करटे केयूरे केयूरमति हिलि-मिलि हिलि-मिलि। आवाहयामि महादेवि बुद्धसत्येन धर्मसत्येन संघसत्येन इन्द्रसत्येन वरुणसत्येन। ये लोके सत्यवादिनः तेषां सत्येन सत्यवचनेन आवाहयामि। महादेवि हिलि-मिलि हिलि-मिलि। विचरतु अमुक-बुद्धिः। नमो भगवति महादेवि सरस्वति। सिध्यन्तु मन्त्रपदा मे। स्वाहा।

Dhāraṇī 29

The next dhāraṇī 29 is in the seventeenth chapter of the eighth tegsinč or chüan of the Uigur and of the Chinese text of I-tsing. The sixteenth and seventeenth chapters of the Uigur text basically agree with the Chinese chapters under the same number. They are devoted to Goddess Śrī, and these two chapters agree with the eighth chapter of the Sanskrit text (chapter 9 in Sanskrit is a sort of introduction to chapter 10). The chapter exists in Dharmakṣema's and Pao-kuei's versions.

In the beginning of the chapter Śrī describes her abode in the town of Vaisravani called Danavati (Chinese translates it, Skr. Aḍakāvatī), in the garden called Supuspi Skr. Puṇya-kusumaprabhā. Then Śrī gives instructions as to what a person should do who wants to increase his fortune. He should clean his house, smear his body with cow-dung. He should get a painting of Śrī made and decorate it. He should bathe his body and get his body massaged with scents. Then he should step into the house and pay homage to the Buddha Ratnapuspi (in Skr. Ratnakusumaguṇasāgaravaiḍūryakanakagirisuvarṇakāñcanaprabhāsaśrī), then say the name of this Sūtra. He should take incense and various costly foods and drinks, flowers, light incense and should pay homage to Śrī's picture. Then he should pay homage to the different Buddhas of the three times (Uig. Ratnasiki/ Skr. Ratnaśikhin, Suvarnandivači, Prabangkosi, Mahadivači, Aksobi, Ratnamiti, Abita, Dundubiš, Somadivači, Kančanaprbi, Kančanakosi, Nirvnu, Somakisimi, Ratna Vitači etc.). After paying homage to all the Buddhas and Bodhisattvas he should call the goddess Śrī and all the things that he has wished for will be fulfilled.

Dhāraṇī 29 (continued)

Uig.	tadyata	namo siri mahadivini
FWK.M.	—	namo siri mahadivini
Skr. Nob.	—	—
A.	—	—
B.	—	—
C.	—	—
D.	—	—
E.	—	—
F.	—	—
G.	—	—
Bag.	—	—
Tib.	—	—
C.	—	—
P.	—	—
Hs.	—	—
II Hs.	—	—
Bl.	—	—
II Bl.	—	—
IPP.	—	na-mo sri-ma-hā-de-bi
Chin.	—	nan-mo shih-ri-mo-ho-t'ien-nu

Dhāraṇī 29 (continued)

Uig.	tadyata	priti purna čari
FWK.M.	tadyada	priti purnančari
Skr. Nob.	syād yathedam	pritipūrṇapare
A.	—	pratipūrṇṇapare
B.	—	pratipūrṇṇapare
C.	saryya yathedam	partipūrṇṇapare
D.	—	pratipūrṇṇapare
E.	—	pratipūrṇṇapare
F.	syad yathyadam	pratipūrṇṇavale
G.	samghayathedam	pratipūṇṇapare
Bag.	syād yathedam	pratipūrṇavare
Tib.	syā-dya-the-dan	pra-ti-pur-na-pa-re
C.	—	—
P.	—	pra-ti-pur-na-ba-re
Hs.	sya-bya-the-dam	—
II Hs.	sa-ya-the-dan	pra-ti-pu-ra-na-ca-re
Bl.	—	—
II Bl.	syad-ya-thi-dam	pra-ti-pur-na-ca-re
IPP.	ta-dya-thā	pra-ti-pu-rna-ca-re
Chin.	tan-chih-t'a	po-ri-pu-ru/na-che-ri

Dhāraṇī 29 (continued)

Uig.	samanta darsi	maha vihar a gati
FWK.M.	samanta dirdirsani	maha hara gati
Skr. Nob.	samantadarśane	mahābihāragate
A.	samantagate	—
B.	samantagate	—
C.	samantagate	—
D.	samantagate	—
E.	samantagate	—
F.	samantagate	—
G.	samantadarsanena	mahāvihāragati
Bag.	—	—
Tib.	sa-man-ta-dar-sa-ne	ma-ha-bi-ha-ra-ga-te
C.	—	
P.	—	ma-ha-bi-ha-ra-ga-ti
Hs.	—	ma-ha-pi-ba-ra-ga-ti
II Hs.	—	—
Bl.	—	—
II Bl.	sa-man-tā-dar-sa-ne	ma-ha-bi-ha-ra-ga-ti
IPP.	sa-ma-nta-dha-ra-sa-ne	ma-ha-bi-ha-ra-ga-te
Chin.	san-man-to-ta-ra-she-ni	mo-ho-p'i-ho-ro-chieh-ti

Dhāraṇī 29 (continued)

Uig.	samanta vitimpari	maha karaniy a
FWKM.	samanta vrdipani	maha karaniy a
Skr. Nob.	samantabedanagate	mahakarya
A.	—	mahakaya
B.	—	mahakaya
C.	—	mahakaya
D.	—	mahakaya
E.	—	mahakaya
F.	—	mahakaya
G.	samantavimanante	mahakaya
Bag.	samantagate	mahakarya
Tib.	sa-man-ta-be-dan-a-ga-te	ma-ha-ka-ryam
C.	—	—
P.	sa-man-ta-bi-da-na-ga-te	ma-ha-karya
Hs.	sa-man-ta-bi-da-na-ga-te	ma-ha-karya
II Hs.	sa-man-ta-bi-mā-na-ga-te	ma-ha-ka-rya
Bl.	—	—
II Bl.	sa-man-tā-bi-ma-na-ga-ta	ma-ha-ka-rya
IPP.	sa-ma-nta-bi-ta-ma-ma-ni	ma-ha-ka-li-ye
Chin.	san-man-ch'e-p'i-t'an-mo-ni	mo-ho-chia-ri-yeh

Dhāraṇī 29 (continued)

Uig.	sarva artasadani supratipuri
FWK.M.	sarvarta sadani supratipuri
Skr. Nob.	sattvaarthasamantānuprapure
A.	satvārthasamatānuprapure
B.	satvārthasamatānuprapure
C.	satvārthasamatānuprapure
D.	satvārthasamatānuprapure
E.	satvārthasamatānuprapure
F.	satvārthasamatānuprapupure
G.	satvārthasamatvānuprapure
Bag.	sattvārthasamatānuprapure
Tib.	satva-artha-sa-mam-ta-nu-pra-pu-re
C.	—
P.	satva-artha-sa-ma-ta-nu-pra-pu-re
Hs.	satva-artha-sa-ma-ta-nu-pra-pu-re
II Hs.	svaha/a-rta-sa-ma-ta-nu/pu-pu-re
Bl.	—
II Bl.	satva-artha-sa-ma-ta-nu-pra-bu-ne
IPP.	sa-rba-a-rtha-sa-dha-ni su-pa-ri-te-bu-re
Chin.	sa-p'o-o/t'a-so-tan-ni/su-po-ra-ti-pu-ri

Dhāraṇī 29 (continued)

Uig.	aray a darnata maha vigupiti
FWK.M.	ayina darmata maha vigipidi
Skr. Nob.	āyānadharmata mahābhogine
A.	āyānadharmmita mahābhāgino
B.	āyānadharmmita mahābhāgino
C.	āyānadharmmita mahābhāgino
D.	āyānadharmmita mahābhāgino
E.	āyānadharmmita mahābhāgino
F.	āyāmidharmmata mahābhāgine
G.	āyānadharmamta mahakopit?e bhopi? te
Bag.	āyānadharmita mahābhāgine
Tib.	a-ya-na-dha-rma-ta ma-ha-bho-gi-ne
C.	—
P.	a-ya-na-dha-rma-ta ma-ha-bho-gi-ne
Hs.	a-ya-na-dha-rma-ta ma-ha-bho-gi-ne
II Hs.	a-ya-yan-dha-rma-ta ma-ha-pho-gi-ne
Bl.	—
II Bl.	a-ya-na-dha-rma-ta ma-ha-bho-ge-ne
IPP.	a-ya-na dha-rma-ta ma-ha-bho-gi-ni
Chin.	a-yeh-no-ta-mo-to mo-ho-p'i-chu-pi-ti

Dhāraṇī 29 (continued)

Uig.	maha maitrapa upa sanhiti
FWK.M.	maha maitrupa sansiti
Skr. Nob.	mahāmaitriupasaṃhite
A.	mahātejopasaṃhite
B.	mahāmaitriupasaṃhṛte
C.	mahāmaitriupasaṃhitam
D.	mahāmaitriupasaṃkrte
E.	mahāmaitriupasaṃhrte
F.	mahāmaitriupasaṃhitaṃ
G.	—
Bag.	mahatejopamamhite
Tib.	ma-ha-mai-tre-u-pa-san-hi-te
C.	ma-ha-mai-tre-u-pa-sam-hi-te
P.	—
Hs.	—
II Hs.	ma-ha-mai-tro-pa-san-hi-te
Bl.	—
II Bl.	ma-ha-mai-tri/su-pa-san-ti
IPP.	ma-ha-mu-tre-u-ba-sam-hi-te
Chin.	mo-ho-mi-tu-ru-wu-po-seng-hsi-ti

Dhāraṇī 29 (continued)

Uig.	maha hinarasi	su sangire hiti
FWK.M.	mha huhusi	susan gire sidi
Skr. Nob.	hitaisi samgrihite	samgrihite
A.	rsisamgrhite	—
B.	rsisamgrhite	—
C.	rsisamgrhite	—
D.	rsisamgrhite	—
E.	rsisamgrhite	—
F.	rsisamgrhite	—
G.	ihetersisamgrihite	—
Bag.	—	rsisamgrhite
Ṫib.	hi-tai-si	sam-gra-hite
C.	—	—
P.	hi-te-si	san-gra-hi-te
Hs.	—	san-gra-hi-te
II Hs.	hi-tai-se	san-gri-hi-te
Bl.	—	—
II Bl.	—	—
IPP.	ma-ha-kri-na-si	su-sam-gi-ri-hi-te
Chin.	mo-ho-chieh-ri-shih	su-seng-chin-ri-hsi-ti

Dhāraṇī 29 (continued)

Uig.	samanta ratna	anu paliti	svaha
FWK.M.	samanta ratna	anupalandi	svaha
Skr. Nob.	tesamartha	anupalani	—
A.	samaya	anupalena	—
B.	samaya	anupale	—
C.	samaya	anupalane	—
D.	samaya	—	—
E.	—	—	—
F.	samaya	anuparanya	—
G.	samaya	anupalane	—
Bag.	samaya	anupalane	—
Tib.	te-sa-mar-tha	a-nu-pa-la-ni	svāhā
C.	—	—	—
P.	—	a-nu-pa-la-na	—
Hs.	te-sa-mra-tha	—	—
II Hs.	—	a-nu-pa-la-te	—
Bl.	—	—	—
II Bl.	—	a-nu-ba-la-ni	—
IPP.	sa-ma-nta-ti	a-nu-pa-ri	svāhā
Chin.	san-man-to-o-t'a	a-nu-po-ra-ni	so-ho

Dhāranī 30

The same chapter is among the Central Asian fragments of the Suvarṇaprabhāsa-sūtra published by F.W.K Mueller in 1908.

After a person has recited this formula, he should take a morning bath for seven days, pay homage to the innumerable Buddhas with flowers and incense, and repent his sins in the afternoon. Then he should tell of his wishes, of what concerns him and other people. And what he wishes for will be fulfilled. He should either clean his house, or go to the forest or to a lonely place and draw a maṇḍala with cowdung, burn sandal-incense and pay homage to Śrī. He should decorate the maṇḍala, recite the dhāraṇī, and wait for the goddess Śrī to come. Then the goddess will surely come, enter his house or sit down by him. She will satisfy his wishes: gold, silver, gems, fortune, cows, lambs, corn, drink, food and clothes. If he wants to have rich crops he should pay homage mainly to the three gems and also to Śrī, sacrifice drink and food, incense and flowers. After he has paid homage to Śrī, he ought to take the remains of the food of sacrifice and exchange it for fresh food which he should again offer in sacrifice. Thus the Goddess will stay with such a person, and see to it that he does not suffer any lack for all his life.

The eighteenth chapter in the eighth tegsinč or chüan in the Uigur, Chinese and Tibetan versions has three dhāraṇīs. This chapter agrees with the tenth chapter of the extant Sanskrit text, but at the same time a part of this chapter (homage to the Buddhas) is in the ninth chapter in the Sanskrit text[15].

The title of the chapter in the Uigur text is "Worship of Vasundharā (Vasintari), the Goddess of the Earth". The Sanskrit, Chinese and Tibetan versions give the name Dṛḍhā instead of the name Vasundharā. In this chapter the Goddess of the Earth proclaims a dhāraṇī which helps human beings and gods to have health and happiness. "That person who wants to see my real body should keep in his mind this dhāraṇī and then I will satisfy him according to what he wishes. If he wants a secret fortune of jewels, or if he wants supernatural knowledge, or if he wants drugs to ensure a long life, or if he wants to defend against his enemies, or if he wants to liquidate other doctrines, he should clean his house, perform a bodhimaṇḍa, bathe his body, put on clean clothes, and sit down on a place covered with grass. He should burn incense in front of the picture of the Buddha (which has the relics of B.) or besides a stupa (which has the relics of Buddha). He should scatter flowers and sacrifice food and drinks. There he should recite this calling formula on the eighth day of the white month (with moonlight) under the puṣya asterism".

Dhāraṇī 30 (continued)

Uig.	tadyata	čiri čiri	čuru čuru
Tib. Nob. II	tadya-thā	ci-li ci-li	cu-ru cu-ru
P.	—	—	—
Hs.	—	—	—
Bl.	—	—	cu-lu cu-lu
IPP.	ta-dya-thā	ci-ri ci-ri	cu-ru cu-ru
Chin.	tan-chih-t'a	ciri ciri	chu-ru chu-ru

Uig.	kuru kuru kuru	kutu kutu	tutu tutu
Tib. Nob. II	ku-ru ku-ru	kut-u ku-tu	to-tu to-tu
P.	—	—	—
Hs.	—	—	—
Bl.	—	ku-tu ku-tu	—
IPP.	ku-ru ku-ru	ku-tu ku-tu	to-tu to-tu
Chin.	chu-ru chu-ru	kou-chu kou-chu	tu-chu tu-chu

Uig.	yana yana	visay-a visay-a	svaha
Tib. Nob. II	ba-ha ba-ha	pa-ri-sa pa-ri-sa	svāhā
P.	—	—	—
Hs.	—	—	—
Bl.	—	sa-ba-ri sa-ba-ri	—
IPP.	bha-ha bha-ha	pa-sa pa-sa	svā-hā
Chin.	fu-ho fu-ho	fa-she fa-she	so-ho

Dhāraṇī 31

"When somebody has recited this magic formula 108 times and has invited me with that, then I will come to him. And when somebody wants to see me in person and wants to speak to me he should follow the previously announced method and recite the following formula":

Uig.	tadyata	ačani	kirasani	sasi a dari
Tib. Nob. II	tadya-thā	an-ca-ni	kya-lig-ka-ni	si-si-dha-ri
P.	—	—	—	—
Hs.	—	—	—	—
Bl.	—	—	kya-li-ksa-ni	—
IPP.	ta-dya-thā	a-ncu-ne	ki-khe-ksa-ne	si-si-dha-ri
Chin.	tan-chih-t'a	o-che-ni	chieh-li-ch'a-ni	shih-ni-ta-ri

Uig.	h-a h-a hi hi	kuru yari čiri	svaha
Tib. Nob. II	ha-ha/hi-hi	ku-ru ba-re	svāhā
P.	—	—	—
Hs.	—	—	—
Bl.	—	su-ru ba-re	—
IPP.	ha-ha hi-hi	ku-ru ba-re	svā-hā
Chin.	ho-ho hsi-hsi	ch'u-ru fa-ri	so-ho

Dhāraṇī 32

"When somebody has kept this dhāraṇī in his mind, he should recite it 108 times and then recite the following dhāraṇī. Then I will surely show myself in my bodily form and what he wishes will be granted. This is the magic formula for the protection of the body".

Uig.	tadyata	nisiri	varsakati
Tib. Nob. II	tadya-thā	ni-ri-si-ri	pā-sa-ka-ti-ta-ti
P.	—	—	bā-sa-ka-ti-ta-ti
Hs.		—	— —
Bl.		—	— —
IPP.	ta-dya-thā	ni-si-ri	pā-sa-ka-ti
Chin.	tan-chih-t'a	ni-shih-li	mo-she-chieh-chih

Uig.	tarta kuti kuti	buti li	titi viti
Tib. Nob. II	ku-ti	bū-de-re	ti-ti/pa-ti
P.	—	—	—
Hs.	—	—	—
Bl.	—	—	—
IPP.	na-ki-ku-dti	pu-ti-pu-de-ri	di-ti-bi-ti
Chin.	na-chih-chu-chih	p'o-ti-p'o-ti-ri	pei-chih-pei-chih

Uig.	kukuti	kav-a čire	svaha
Tib. Nob. II	ku-ku-ti/	ka-ba-ci-li	svāhā
P.	—	—	—
Hs.	—	—	—
Bl.	—	—	—
IPP.	ku-ku-ti	ka-ba-ci-li	svā-hā
Chin.	chu-chu-chih	chu-p'o-chih-li	so-ho

When he recites this dhāraṇī he should take a thread of five colours, recite the formula twentyone times, make twentyone knots on the thread, bind the thread on the left forearm, and then under the protection of the formula what he was afraid of will not occur.

Dhāraṇī 33

The thirtythird dhāraṇī is in the 19th chapter in the eighth tegsinč, or eighth chüan. This chapter agrees with the eleventh chapter of the Sanskrit text, but in the Sanskrit text (as in the previous chapter) the dhāraṇī part is missing[16].

The title of the chapter is "Worship of the leader of the gods Saṃjñāya" in Uigur, in Sanskrit "On Saṃjñāya", in Chinese "Saṃjñāya the leader of Yakṣas", the Tibetan title agrees basically with the Chinese title. Saṃjñāya proclaims a dhāraṇī in the chapter.

Uig.	namo budday-a	namo darmay a
Tib. Nob. II	namo bud-dhā-ya	namo dha-rmā-ya
P.	—	—
Hs.	namo bu-dha-ya	—
Bl.	namo bu-dha-ya	namo dha-rma-ya
IPP.	na-mo bu-ddha-ya	na-mo dha-rmā-ya
Chin.	nan-mo fo-t'o-yeh	nan-mo ta-mo-yeh

Uig.	namo sanggay a	namo brahmay a
Tib. Nob. II	na-mah san-ghā-ya	namo bra-hmā-ya
P.	na-mah san-gha-ya	—
Hs.	na-mah san-gha-ya	—
Bl.	na-mah sam-gha-ya	—
IPP.	na-mha sam-ghaya	na-mo bra-hmā-ya
Chin.	nan-mo seng-ch'ieh-yeh	nan-mo po-ro-han-mo-yeh

Uig.	a namo indir-a-ya
Tib. Nob. II	na-mah in-drā-ya
P.	—
Hs.	—
Bl.	na-mo in-dra-ya
IPP.	na-mo in-drā-ya
Chin.	nan-mo yin-ta-ro-yeh

Uig.	namo čatur maharančanan
Tib. Nob. II	na-mah ca-tur-nām mahā-rā-jā-nam
P.	na-mah ca-tur-nām/mahā rā-jā-nām
Hs.	na-mah ca-tur-nā-ma/mahā-rā-jā-na-ma
Bl.	na-mah ca-tur mahā-rā-jā-nan
IPP.	na-ma-sca-tur-nām ma-hā-rā-jā-nam
Chin.	nan-mo che-tu-nan mo-ho-ro-she-nan

Dhāraṇī 33 (continued)

Uig.	tadyata	hari hari	mala mali
Tib. Nob. II	tadya-thā	hili-hi-li	mi-li mi-li
P.	—	—	—
Hs.	—	—	—
Bl.	—	—	—
IPP.	ta-dya-thā	hi-li-mi-li	mi-li mi-li
Chin.	tan-chih-t'a	hsi-ri-hsi-ri	mi-ri mi-ri

Uig.	kuru kuru	maha guru	gantari
Tib. Nob. II	gau-ri	maha-gau-ri	gan-dha-ri
P.	gu-li	—	—
Hs.	gu-li	—	—
Bl.	—	—	—
IPP.	—	ma-hā-gau-ri	gan-dha-ri
Chin.	ch'u-ri	mo-ho-ch'u-ri	chieh-t'o-ri

Uig.	maha kantari	antar-a miti
Tib. Nob. II	maha-gan-dha-ri	dri-mi-dir
P.	—	dri-mi-dri
Hs.	—	dri-mi-dri
Bl.	—	—
IPP.	ma-hā-gan-dha-ri	dra-mi-ti
Chin.	mo-ho-chien-t'o-ri	ta-lo-mi-chih

Uig.	maha antar-a miti	danta kukuti
Tib. Nob. II	maha-dri-mi-di	dan-ta khu-khun-tē
P.	mahā-dra-mi-di	dan-dā khu-khun-te
Hs.	mahā-dra-mi-di	dan-dā khu-khun-te
Bl.	—	—
IPP.	—	dha-nta khu-gun-dhe
Chin.	mo-ho-ta-ro-mi-chih	tan-ch'a ch'u-ch'uan-ti

Uig.	ha ha ha ha ha	hi hi hi hi hi
Tib. Nob. II	ha-ha-ha-ha-ha	hi-hi-hi-hi-hi
P.	—	—
Hs.	—	—
Bl.	—	—
IPP.	ha-ha-ha-ha-ha	hi-hi-hi-hi-hi
Chin.	ho-ho-ho-ho	hsi-hsi-hsi-hsi-hsi

Dhāraṇī 33 (continued)

Uig.	hu hu hu hu hu	huu arutami karutami
Tib. Nob. II	hu-hu-hu-hu-hu	ha-lo-dha-me/gu-dha-me
P.	—	—
Hs.	—	—
Bl.	—	—
IPP.	ho-ho-ho-ho-ho	ha-lo-dha-me ku-rba-be
Chin.	hu-hu-hu-hu-hu	han-lu-t'an-mi-ch'u-t'an-mi
Uig.	ča ča ča ča ča	či či či či či
Tib. Nob. II	ca-ca-ca-ca-ca	ci-ci-ci-ci-ci
P.	—	—
Hs.	—	—
Bl.	—	—
IPP.	ca-ca-ca-ca	ci-ci-ci-ci
Chin.	che-che-che-che	chih-chih-chih-chih
Uig.	čü	čanta si-a bra
Tib. Nob. II	cu-cu-cu-cu	can-dē-sva-ra
P.	—	—
Hs.	—	—
Bl.	—	can-de-sva-ra
IPP.	cu-cu-cu-cu	ca-nte-sva-ra
Chin.	chu-chu-chu-chu	chan-ch'a-che-po-lo
Uig.	sakara bra sakra	kuru tistari
Tib. Nob. II	si-kha-ra/si-kha-ra	—
P.	—	—
Hs.	—	—
Bl.	—	—
IPP.	sigra si-gra	—
Chin.	shih-chieh-ro shih-chieh-ro	—

Dhāraṇī 33 (continued)

Uig.	utistari	bagavan
Tib. Nob. II	ud-ti-sthā hi	bha-ga-bān
P.	u-ti-sthā hi	bha-ga-ban
Hs.	u-ta-sthā hi	bha-ga-ba-na
Bl.	utthistha he	—
IPP.	u-ti-stha ti	bha-ga-bā-na
Chin.	wu-ti-se-ch'a hsi	po-ch'ieh-fan

Uig.	čanačavi y a	tadyata
Tib. Nob. II	san-din-jnā-ya	tadya-thā
P.	—	—
Hs.	—	—
Bl.	sam-bdi (bid?)-jnā-ya	—
IPP.	sam-ram-jna-ya	ta-dya-thā
Chin.	seng-shen-erh-yeh	tan-chih-t'a

"One who keeps this dhāraṇī will be looked after for a life time with medicines, drink and food, clothes, flowers, fruits, and rare stones. And whatever he wishes: men, women, boys and girls, gold silver, jewels, necklaces I will secure all of them for him. For this formula has such a great power, that when he recites this formula I will go to him and see to it that he will get everything according to his thoughts. He should know the way to recite this dhāraṇī. He should get four or five feet high picture of Saṃjñāya painted, holding an axe in his hand. He should make a maṇḍala for this picture, and then he should draw four full circles with water mixed with honey, or water mixed with sugar, scented oil, scented powder, incense, flowers and garlands. Further he should put a fireplace in front of the maṇḍala on the earth and in that make a fire from charcoal. He should burn oil and mustard seeds in that fireplace and recite the above magic formula. Then Saṃjñāya will come himself and ask the people who recited the magic formula: "Tell me what you want". Then according to their wishes he will bring gold if they want gold, or silver or secret jewels. If they want to have the knowledge of the eye of the gods, or if they want to know what another man's mind holds (what is going on in another's mind), or if they want plenitude of power, or to liquidate the sufferings of other beings, everything will be perfectly fulfilled".

This dhāraṇī is the last in the Uigur text. The Chinese text of I-tsing has some more magic formulas in the twentyfifth chapter. The Tibetan and Uigur versions do not have dhāraṇīs in the twentyfifth chapter.

The picture which emerges from the comparison of the dhāraṇīs is very complex. On some points the Uigur version has kept parts which are not retained by the Sanskrit version. In the 28th dhāraṇī all the versions give the word *bimamuki*, only the Uigur version has kept the word which is suited for the context. In the 27th dhāraṇī the arrangement of the words is unique: two words appear earlier than in the Sanskrit, Tibetan and Chinese versions. The 31st dhāraṇī has extra words compared to the other dhāraṇīs. In the 28th dhāraṇī there is also the second person pronoun *tvam* which are not retained by any other version. In the 24th dhāraṇī the Uigur word *vičalini*, meaning 'moving', which corresponds to the Tibetan and Sanskrit *indrajalini*, gives the impression that the Uigur text might go back to a different Sanskrit tradition from the dhāraṇīs in other versions

On some points dhāraṇīs in the Tibetan version of the texts of the Imperial Palace of Peking (IPP) and the Uigur dhāraṇīs show similar features. An example of this is in the 28th dhāraṇī where the Uigur *manggulavati*, corresponds to IPP *ming-gu-la-ba-ddhe*, and Chinese *ming-chu-la-fa-ti*. These forms are probably derived from Sanskrit *maṅgalavati*. The Sanskrit and Tibetan words occurring here probably go back to the word *pingalabati*. Some other examples show that the Uigur and other Tibetan versions bear more similarity to each other. In the 9th dhāraṇī the Uigur *mantr-a padani* correlates with Tibetan *man-tra-pa-dā-ni*, and at the same time IPP gives *man-tra-pa-te*.

These facts indicate that the dhāraṇīs of the Uigur text are not directly derived from any of the extant versions, but probably are from such a Sanskrit version which was used also by the authors of the Ming Tripiṭaka.

The Tibetan version shows more similarity to the Sanskrit of the manuscripts and blockprints published by Nobel and Bagchi.

The aim of the present work was not to give Sanskrit reconstructions. At the present stage of research, when only a few dhāraṇīs have been reconstructed, it would bring doubtful results. To pave the way for further research first a corpus of dhāraṇīs from different versions and languages is needed. Such a collection will make it possible for a researcher acquainted with the history and development of Sanskrit, Prakrit and Dravidian languages a reconstruction of the dhāraṇīs.

11. SOME REGULAR LINGUISTIC CORRELATIONS BETWEEN THE SANSKRIT AND UIGUR PRESENTATION OF THE DHĀRANĪS

For a linguistic comparison in this part three dhāraṇīs, which had the corresponding Sanskrit were chosen for examination, two from chapter 15 devoted to Sarasvatī (26th and 28th), and one from chapter 17th which is devoted to Śrī. The last dhāraṇī is represented by two Uigur versions: by the version of Radloff-Malov's edited text, and by the text found in Turfan and published by F.W.K. Mueller. The three dhāraṇīs give considerable material: dhāraṇī 26 consists of approximately 7 words, dhāraṇīs 28 consists of 67 words, and the third dhāraṇīs has about 17 words. This material, even if it does not give an overall picture of the correlations of Sanskrit and Uigur phonemes, gives an idea about the basic trends of correlations.

The Uigur script, which originated from the Sogdian, does not have a full set of signs for the representation of all the phonemes. It has only fourteen basic graphemes.

The *first* grapheme  denoting both Uigur *a* and *e* phonemes represent in initial position long Sanskrit *ā* and *a* and *e* also, but initial Skr. *e* did not occur in our examples. In the middle of the word this grapheme represents Skr. *a*, long *ā* and *e*. One example occurred when this grapheme corresponded to Sanskrit *-ha-* in the middle of the word, and in three examples this grapheme represented Sanskrit *-i-* in the middle of the word (Skr. piṭakakāvyādiṣu/ Uig. pitakadiudasi). At the end of the word this grapheme represents Skr. *-ā*, *-e* and *-a*.

The *second* grapheme  looks similarly as the preceding (1), but it denotes *n* and because of this it can be distinguished from the first grapheme especially in cases when the following vowel is marked. In initial position only Skr. *n* correlation was met with in the three dhāraṇīs. In the middle of the word it represented in the above mentioned dhāraṇīs *n*, *ṅ*, *ṇṇ*, *y*, *r* and *b* in one case for each, and *h* in two examples (for example: Skr. *mahādevyai* in Uigur is *mana divi*). In the aforesaid dhāraṇīs there were some cases when final Uigur *n* represented Sanskrit *ṃ* (for example: Skr. *namaskaraṃ* Uig. *namaskarana*).

The *third* grapheme  represents Uig. *i*, *ï* and *y* phonemes. In initial position the correlating Sanskrit phonemes were *a*, *i* and *y* and each of them were represented by one example each. In the middle of the word this grapheme occurred much more often. The correlating phonemes were *i*, *ï*, *y* in a number of cases it corresponds with Skr. *a* (for example Skr. *taraci* Uig. *tahivi*), with *e* (Skr. *lokajyeṣṭhe* Uig. *lokačisti*), in a number of cases with *v* (Skr. *āvāhayāmi* Uig. *ayāhayāmi*). Single cases of correspondences of the grapheme with Sanskrit *h* and *t* also occurred. The third phoneme in final position correlates to the mentioned material with Sanskrit *i* and *e* sounds (Skr. *lokaśreṣṭhe* Uig. *loka siristi*). In three cases Skr. *ai* diphthong correlates with the third Uigur grapheme.

The *fourth* Uigur grapheme denotes three Uigur phonemes *o*, *u*, *ö*, and *ü*. In initial position this grapheme did not occur in any of the three dhāraṇīs. In the middle of the word this grapheme replaces Sanskrit *u* or *ū* phoneme, it correlates in a number of cases with *a* (Skr. *abjavati* Uig. *ančuvati*). In a single case this grapheme correlates with Sanskrit *v* in the middle of the word. In word-ending position regular cases of *o* and *u* correlations were observed.

The *fifth* Uigur grapheme represents Uigur *p* and *b* phonemes. In initial position the fifth grapheme correlates with Sanskrit *bh*, *b* and *p*. (In these dhāraṇīs initial *ph* does not occur). In the middle of the word the same correlations occur. In the three dhāraṇīs there was no case of the fifth grapheme in the final position.

The *sixth* grapheme denotes the *v* phoneme. In the middle of the word this phoneme correlates with Sanskrit *v*, and in a number of cases with Skr. *b* (for example: Skr. *mahabiharagate* = *mahāvihāragate/* Uig. *mha vihar a gati*, Skr. *prāṇaye/* Uig. *pay payravi*). In initial and final positions Uigur *v* did not occur in the aforesaid material.

The *seventh* grapheme denotes the Uigur *q*, *ğ* and *h* phonemes. In initial position this grapheme correlates with Sanskrit *h* and *k*, in the middle of the word this grapheme occurs only in correlation with the Sanskrit *h* phoneme, and in one case Sanskrit r correlates with it.

The *eighth* grapheme denotes *k* and *g* phonemes. In the three dhāraṇīs the Sanskrit correlating sounds were in initial position *k*, *bh* and *p*. The *bh* occurred in two, *p* in one case (examples: Skr. *bhagavatyai/* Uig. *gagavati*, Skr. *pratigṛhṇa/*Uig. *karti grin na*). In the middle of the word this grapheme correlates with *g*, *gh*, *k*, and in a single case with *v* (Skr. *sarvasatvānām/* Uig. *sukasy an*). In word-ending position this phoneme does not occur in the aforesaid dhāraṇīs.

The *ninth* grapheme represents Uigur *t* and *d* phonemes. In the initial position it has two Sanskrit correlating phonemes *dh* and *d*, in the middle of the word it has *ṭ*, *d*, *ṭh* and *dh*. Sanskrit *b*, *v* and *s* are represented by this grapheme (one case each): Skr. *āvāhayāmi/* Uig. *atahayami*. In word-final position this grapheme does not occur.

For the *tenth* grapheme denoting *ž* and *z* there was no example in the three dhāraṇīs.

The *eleventh* grapheme denoting *l* occurs in initial position and in the middle of the word, in both positions correlating with Sanskrit *l* phoneme. In final position it is not found in any of the three dhāraṇīs.

The *twelfth* grapheme denoting *m* phoneme, occurs in initial position, correlating with Sanskrit *m*, and in the middle of the word correlating with Sanskrit *m*. In one case only in the middle of the word the grapheme denotes *m* correlated to Sanskrit *b* (in Nobel's edition: Skr. *keyūrabati* = *keyūravatī*/Uig. *qeyurta mamati*).

The *thirteenth* grapheme denotes Uigur *r* phoneme. It occurs only in one case in the initial position, correlating with Sanskrit *m* (Skr. *maṅ-gu-ṣe/* Uig. *ranggusti*). In the middle of the word it correlates with Sanskrit *r*, with Sanskrit *t* and *y* in two cases, and with Sanskrit *a* in one case (Skr. *apratihate/* Uig. *aprati hari*, Skr. *praṇaye/* Uig. *pay payravi*, Skr. *sidhyantu mantrapadā me/*

Uig. *sidrantu mantir a prta*). In final position it correlates with Sanskrit *r* and in one case with Sanskrit *m* (Skr. *mahadevīm/* Uig. *manadir*).

The *fourteenth* grapheme / denotes Uigur *s* and *š* phonemes. In initial position this grapheme correlates with Sanskrit *s* and *ś*. In the middle of the word it correlates with *s*, *ṣ*, *ś*. In the final position this grapheme does not occur.

The *fifteenth* grapheme denoting Uigur *č*, occurs in three dhāraṇīs in an initial position or in the middle of the word. In the initial position it correlates with Sanskrit *c*, *ś* and *kh* (Skr. *śivam me* Uig. *čerirmi*, Skr. *khari/* Uig. *ceri*). In the middle of the word the Uigur grapheme correlates with Sanskrit *-jy-* and *-j-* and *c* (Skr. *lokajyeṣṭhe/* Uig. *loka čisti*, Skr. *abje/* Uig. *inči*).

A close study of the regular deviations might reveal a good deal about the peculiarities of the manuscript from which these dhāraṇīs were taken.

12. CONCLUSION

As the translation of the Uigur Suvarṇaprabhāsa-sūtra and its continuous use through many years among the Uigurs in Kansu can not be viewed without a study of the history of Uigur Turks and their society and also their long-lasting association with Buddhism, we have devoted the first part to the geographical and historical background of Uigur society.

A study of the historical background of Uigur society was also necessary because till now no such study has been done exploring the important events of the history of Uigur Turks. Our investigation makes it clear that the Uigurs were originally a part of a 'nomadic empire'— the First Turkish Empire on the Orkhon (546-658). In the 8th century before settling down on the Turkish area the Uigurs came into contact with Sogdian priests, became acquainted with Manicheism and took over the Sogdian script.

It seems that for the cultural history of the Uigurs this was a major turning point. By acquiring a 'modern' script they were able to join the international transport of intellectual production.

Though the ruling stratum of Turkish society (according the Chinese sources) got to know Buddhism much earlier, this early contact did not leave much trace in Turkish literature.

After a Qirgiz attack in the 8th century the Uigurs shifted from the area of Altai towards the Turfan Bisbaliq area, and in the direction of Kansu. In the area of Turfan, Buddhism was professed for a long time. Indian traders lived there and Sanskrit was a revered language among others.

By then other nomads had already come into contact with the Buddhist culture of the Central Asian settlements. It was a speciality of Uigurs that they adjusted themselves to the material and spiritual culture of their sedentary neighbours. It is necessary to emphasize here that unlike their nomadic predecessors they did not go towards grazing lands but towards the settled areas. They established the Uigur kingdom in the area of Turfan and Kansu and adjusted themselves to the traditionally accepted agriculture of the area. The religion of the state was Buddhism but the manuscripts show that besides Buddhism Manicheism and Nestorianism coexisted.

The Uigur documents published by L.N. Gumilyov, S.E. Malov, W. Radloff support the fact that Buddhism became the most important religion in the Uigur State. The power of the Buddhist Church was secured by the fact that monasteries became big landowners, villages with all their population belonged to them and the peasants of these villages were in socage to them. The names of the Kocho, Yar, Lukchun and Murutluk monasteries occur most often in the documents. They were also important centres of the translation of literature. The documents published by S.E. Malov make it clear that the monks knew Sanskrit, Chinese and Tibetan languages. Uigurs were famous for being excellent scribes. After the fall of the Uigur Kingdom in the 13th century they became scribes at the courts of Cinggis Khan and their script was adopted for Mongolian and Manchu languages. After the 13th century Kansu was mainly under Chinese supremacy. During this time the position of monasteries in Kansu and in the whole of China was strengthened.

The fifth chapter describes the origin and formation of Uigur language and literature. It is the language of this special group of Old Turkish manuscripts. The Uigur language — as the text of the Suvarṇaprabhāsa-sūtra also shows — still kept some of the Proto-Turkish consonants, but it began the process of labial and illabial assimilation of vowels. The Uigur language has two dialects *ṅ* and *y* dialects and the Suvarṇaprabhāsa-sūtra shows features of the *y* dialect.

With regard to the literary value of the Old Turkish and Uigur manuscripts, it is worth noting that many features of genuine folk poetry and literature crept into them. The fifth chapter makes it evident through examples that Old Turkish inscriptions in Runic script show simple poetic forms based on parallelisms. The existence of lyric songs is not in question but till the eleventh century lyric songs had not been written down. Buddhist texts incorporated tales, which were very popular among the Uigurs. Hymns and poems show such features of poetry which were later retained by Osman literature.

Among the sūtras, which were specially favoured materials for rendering into Uigur, the Suvarṇaprabhāsa-sūtra is the most extensive extant text.

It is generally accepted (by Ş. Tekin, A. Gabain, W. Radloff, S.E. Malov, P. Zieme) that the Suvarṇaprabhāsa-sūtra is a translation from the Chinese version of I-tsing, made by Sinku Seli Tutung. The colophons cited in the sixth chapter do not all agree with this generally accepted fact. According to the first colophon the translation was done from the Tibetan by Kumgan Tutung, while other colophons confirm that it is a translation from the Chinese.

From the investigation of the texts of the different versions in the seventh chapter an even more complex picture emerges. Among the different versions (Sanskrit, Tibetan and Chinese) the Uigur text is the closest in its division, contents of chapters and so on to the Chinese version of I-tsing, but in certain minor features there are differences, like addition of a word, slightly different way of giving back a term and in such cases the Uigur text is unique or it agrees with the third Tibetan translation made by Chos-grub.

Since the material was very extensive and we could not go into the differences in each and every case, the dhāraṇīs were chosen for the purpose of research. Previously on the basis of the opinions of scholars like Max Mueller, Winternitz, etc. it was generally believed that the mantras and dhāraṇīs as found in various texts were nothing but combinations of meaningless syllables. Recent researches in the field have approached this question differently and the role of mantras in the initiation and the yogic exercises has been stressed and at the same time the need for examination of the language of the dhāraṇīs has been expressed by scholars like A. Wayman, M. Eliade, F. Bernhard, Lokesh Chandra, S.C. Banerji and others. We felt that the dhāraṇīs, as they have to be pronounced similarly in all the versions, and do not follow other changes of the text provide a good material for comparison. For this comparison all the 35 dhāraṇīs of the Uigur version have been collected, transcribed and collated word by word with the corresponding Sanskrit, Tibetan and Chinese dhāraṇīs in the ninth chapter. The collection and transcription of the dhāraṇīs reveal a great deal about the proper reading of the Uigur dhārāṇīs as the scope for marking Uigur phonemes is not very precise. By comparison with the Chinese and Tibetan wording, in some cases the Uigur text seems to have preserved a more archaic version than the comparatively late Sanskrit manuscripts. Words and expressions of the dhāraṇīs are translated in the Tibetan and Chinese, but Uigur has kept the Sanskrit words. In some cases the dhāraṇīs of the Uigur version and the dhāraṇīs of the Ming Tripiṭaka show similarities. It seems that the dhāraṇīs or the whole text of the Uigur Suvarṇaprabhāsa-sūtra go back to an earlier Sanskrit version, which might have been also the model or close to the model of the Ming Tripiṭaka. As is shown in this chapter the proper names also show a different tradition from the other texts.

The dhāraṇis and proper names in some Uigur texts used to be marked also in Brahmi script, as in the text of Tišasvustik.

It is possible that a special list of names and dhāraṇīs was transmitted along with manuscripts which are extinct now. However, it is also probable that the copyist often compared the text with other manuscripts similar to modern philological methods.

The collection of dhāraṇīs with the result of investigations of regular changes from rules of correlations among Sanskrit and Uigur phonemes may render help in the restoration of the original Sanskrit forms.

With reading other Uigur texts the number of dhāraṇīs incorporated in these texts is striking. A closer examination of the dhāraṇīs in other texts could throw some light on the tradition of transmission of dhāraṇīs among the Uigurs.

The examination of the Uigur Suvarṇaprabhāsa-sūtra shows that the Uigurs were in constant touch with Sanskrit, Tibetan and Chinese sources. The examination of Uigur texts may contribute to a better understanding not only of Central Asia but also of other connected cultures and their interactions.

13. BIBLIOGRAPHY

V.S. Agrawala, *India as Known to Pāṇini*. Lucknow 1953.

R.R. Arat, *Eski Türk Şiiri* (in Turkish: Old Turkish Poetry). Ankara 1965.

H.W. Bailey, *Khotanese Texts*. Cambridge 1963.

W. Bang & J. Marquart, *Codex Cumunicus*. Göttingen 1914.

S. Bagchi, *Suvarṇaprabhāsasūtra*. Darbhanga 1967.

W. Bang & A. von Gabain, *Der grosse Hymnus auf Mani* (in German: Mani's Great Hymn), TT III 1930.

W. Bang, *Türkische Bruchstücke einer nestorinaischen Georgspassion* (in German: Turkish fragments of a Nestorian George-passion). Museon 1926 pp. 41-75.

Samuel Beal, *Travels of Hiouen Tsang*, 1951.

Ö. Beke, Türkische Einfluss in der Syntax des finnisch-ugrischen Sprachen (Turkish influence on the syntax of the Finno-Ugrian languages), *KSz* XV pp. 1-77.

Lóránd Benkö, Samu Imre: *The Hungarian Language*, Budapest 1972.

H. Berberian, La Litterature Armeno-Turque (in French: The Armenian-Turkish Literature). Fnd.II pp. 809-81.

F. Bernhard, Zur Entstehung einer Dhāraṇī (in German: On the genesis of a dhāraṇī), *ZDMG*, 1969, pp. 148-168.

A. von Le Coq, *Kökturkisches aus Turfan* (in German: Inscriptions of the Kok Türk from Turfan). XI. Berlin 1909.

A. von Le Coq, Chuastuanift, ein Sündenbekentniss der manicheischen Auditores (in German: A confession prayer of the Manicheist believers), *ABAW* 1910.

G.B. Cressey, *China's Geographic Foundations*, New York and London 1934.

K. Czeglédy, Gardizi on the Uigurs, *AOH* 1973 p. 264.

J.A. Dabbs, *History of the Discovery and Exploration of Chinese Turkestan*. The Hague 1963.

Sarat Chandra Das and Pandit Sarat Chandra Shastri, *Suvarna Prabha*. Calcutta 1898.

S. Ch. Das, *Contributions on the religion and history of Tibet*. New Delhi 1970.

Sarat Chandra Das, *A Tibetan-English Dictionary*. Delhi 1973.

S. Dasgupta, *Obscure Religious Cults*. Calcutta 1962.

S.B. Dasgupta, *An Introduction to Tantric Buddhism*. Calcutta 1974.

F. Edgerton, *Buddhist Hybrid Sanskrit Grammar and Dictionary*, Vol. II Dictionary, Delhi-Varansi-Patna 1977.

G. Bethlenfalvy, *A Catalogue of the Urga Kanjur*. New Delhi.

Agehananda Bharati, *The Tantric Tradition*. New York 1975.

B. Bhattacharya, *Buddhist Esoterism*.

V.A. Bogoslovskiy, *Ocherk istorii tibetskogo naroda* (in Russian: An essay on the history of the Tibetan people). Moscow 1962.

L. Boulnois, *The Silk Road*. London 1966.

C. Brockelmann, *Mitteltürkischer Wortschatz—Mahmud al-Kāšġari: Dīvān Lûgāti-Türk* (in German: Middle-Turkish vocabulary—Mahmud al-Kāšġari Dīvān-i Lûgāt-i Türk). Budapest-Leipzig 1928.

Ahmet Caferoğlu, *Turk dili tarihi* (in Turkish: The history of Turkish language), vol. 1. Istanbul 1970.

E. Chavannes, La version ouigour de l'histoire des princes Kalyāṇaṃkara et Pāpaṃkara (in French: The Uigur version of the story of the Princes Kalyaṇāṃkara and Pāpaṃkara). *Toung Pao* 1914 pp. 492-494.

Wang Chun Heng, *Simple Geography of China*. Peking 1958.

G. Clauson, The name Uygur, *JRAS* 1963 pp. 141-160.

A. von Le Coq, *Chotscho, Königliche preussische Turfanexpedition* (in German: Kocho, The Prussian Turfan Expedition). Berlin 1913.

W. Eichhorn, Koloniälkampfe der Chinesen in Turkestan während der Ch'ien-lung (in German: Colonial wars by the Chinese in Turkestan during Ch'ien-lung). *ZDMG* p. 262-266.

M.Eliade, *Yoga, Immortality and Freedom*. New Jersey 1973.

R.E. Emmerick, *The Sūtra of Golden Light*. London 1970.

E. Esin, The Turkish Bakši and the Painter Muhammad Siyāḥ Kalam, AO 1970 pp. 81-114.

E. Esin, *Islämiyetten önceki Türk Kültür ve Islâma giriş* (in Turkish: Turkish culture before Islam, and introduction of Islam). Istanbul 1978.

J.A. Farquhar, *An Outline of the Religious Literature of India*. Delhi-Patna-Varanasi 1967 p. 25.

D. Fuchs, Übereinstimmungen in der Syntax der finnisch-ugrisch und türkischen Sprachen (in German: Correlations in the syntax of the Finno-Ugrian and Turkish languages). *FUF* XXIV pp. 292-322.

A. von Gabain, Das Alttürkische (in German: The Old Turkish language). *Fnd.* I pp. 21-45.

W. Bang & A. von Gabain, Bruchstücke eines Wahrsagebuches. TT1.

A. von Gabain, Alttürkische Schreibkultur und Druckerei (in German: Old Turkish manuscripts and prints). *Fnd.* II pp 171-192.

Annamarie von Gabain, Historisches aus den Turfan-Handschriften. *AO* 1970 pp. 115-124.

A. von Gabain, Das Leben im uigurischen Königreich von Qočo (850-1250) (in German: Life in the Uigur Kingdom of Qočo). Wiesbaden 1973.

A. von Gabain & G.R. Rachmati, Das buddhistische Sūtra Säkiz Yükmäk (in German: The Buddhist Sūtra Säkiz Yükmäk). TTVI SBAW 1934 pp. 93-192.

Annemarie Gabain, Die Alttürkische Literatur (in German: Old Turkish Literature). *Fnd.* II pp. 211-243.

A. von Gabain, Die Uigurische Übersetzung der Biographie Hüen-tsangs. Bruchstücke 5. Kapitels (in German: The Uigur translation of the biography of Hsuen-tsang. Fragments of chapter V). *SPAW* 1935.

A. von Gabain, *Alttürkische Grammatik* (Old Turkish grammar). Leipzig 1950.

L. Giles, Dated Chinese Manuscripts in the Stein Collection. *BSOS* vol. 9.

R. Grousset, *Rise and Splendour of the Chinese Empire*. London 1952.

A. Grünwedel, *Bericht uber archeologische Arbeiten in Idikutschari und Umgebung im Winter 1902-1903* (in German: Report on the archaeological work in Idikutshari and its surroundings). 1906.

L.N. Gumilyov, *Drevnie t'urki* (in Russian: Old Turks). Moscow 1967.

Herbert V. Guenther, *The Life and Teaching of Nāropa*. Oxford 1963.

G. Györffy, *Autour du Codex Cumanicus* (in French: The author of the Codex Cumanicus). Budapest 1942.

E. Haenisch, *Altan Gerel. Die westmongolische Fassung des Golglanzsutra* (in German: Altan Gerel. The Kalmuck or West-Mongolian version of the Sutra of Golden Light). Leipzig 1929.

J.R. Hamilton, *Les Ouighours* (The Uigurs). Paris 1955.

J.R. Hamilton, *Le cont bouddhique du Bon et du Mauvais Prince en version ouigoure* (in French: A Buddhist Story of the Good and Bad Prince in the Uigur version). Paris 1971.

G. Hazai, *Fragments eines uigurischen Blockdruck Faltbuches* (in German: Fragments of an Uigur blockprint folding book). Berlin 1963.

G. Hazai & P. Zieme, Zu einigen Fragen der Bearbeitung Türkischer Sprachdenkmäler (in German: Some remarks on the research on Old Turkish literary records). *AO* 1970 p. 125-140.

G. Hazai & P. Zieme, *Fragments der uigurischen Version des "Jinganjing mit den Gāthās des Meister Fu"* (Fragments of the Uigur version of the Jinganjing with the gāthās of Master Fu). Berlin 1971.

A.F.R. Hoernle, *Manuscript Remains of Buddhist Texts Found in East-Turkestan*, Vol. I. Oxford 1916.

H. Idzumi, *The Suvarṇaprabhāsa-sūtra: a Mahāyāna Text Called The Golden Splendour*. Kyoto 1931.

G. Kara, Aranyfény Sutra (in Hungarian: The Sūtra of Golden Light). Budapest 1975.

G. Kara & P. Zieme, *Fragments tantrischer Werke in Uigurischer Übersetzung* (Fragments of Tantric works in Uigur translation). Berlin 1976.

H. Kern, *Manual of Indian Buddhism*, Delhi 1974.

Klong-čhen rab-'byams-pa, *Kindly Bent to Ease us*, translated from the Tibetan and annotated by Herbert V. Guenther. Emeryville 1975.

J. Kolmas, *Tibet and Imperial China*. Canberra 1967.

F. Köprülü, *Edebiyat Araştirmalari* (Research on literature). Ankara 1966.

E.I. Kychanov, *Gosudarstvo Si Sya* (982-1127) (in Russian: The Hsi Hsia State 982-1127). Moscow 1962.

M. Lalou, *Inventaire des manuscripts tibetains de Touen-houang (Fonds Pelliot tibetain) nos. 1-49* (in French: A Catalogue of the Tun-huang manuscripts of the Pelliot Collection). Paris 1939.

F.D. Lessing & A. Wayman, *Introduction to the Buddhist Tantric Systems*. Delhi 1978.

Lokesh Chandra, *Sanskrit Texts from the Imperial Palace at Peking*. New Delhi 1966.

Lokesh Chandra, *Nīlakaṇṭha Lokeśvara as the Buddhist Apotheosis of Hari-Hara*. New Delhi 1979.

Lokesh Chandra, *Oḍḍiyāna: A New Interpretation*. New Delhi 1979.

C. Mackerras, Sino-Uighur Diplomatic and Trade Contacts. *CAJ* 1962 pp. 215-240.

S.E. Malov, *Talasskie epigraphichesskie pamyatniki* (in Russian: Epigraphic monuments from the Talas river). Leningrad 1936.

S.E. Malov, *Pamyatniki Drevn'e turkskoy Pismennosti* (in Russian: Old Turkish records). Moscow-Leningrad 1951.

L. Maspero, *Les documents chinois* (in French: Chinese documents). London 1953.

Liu Mau Tsai, *Die Chinesische Nachrichten zur Geschichte der Ost-Turken (T'ü-küe)* (in German: Chinese sources about the history of the Eastern Turks/T'ü-küe). Wiesbaden 1958 Vol. I-II.

J.J. Mikkola, *Die Chronologie der türkischen Donaubulgaren* (in German: The chronology of the Turkish Danube-Bulgars). *JSFOu* XXX pp. 1-25.

V. Minorsky, Tamim ibn Bahir's Journey to the Uyghurs. *BSOAS* 1948 pp. 225-305.

Monier Williams, *Sanskrit English Dictionary*. Oxford 1899.

F.W.K. Mueller, Uigurica IV. *SBAW* 1931.

F.W.K. Mueller, Uigurica. *SBAW* 1908.

F.W.K. Mueller, Uigurica II. *ABAW* 1910.

A.M. Scherbak, *Drevn et urkskiy slovar* (Old Turkish Dictionary). Leningrad 1969.

A. Caferoğlu, *Eski Uygur Türkcesi Sözlüğu* (Old Turkish dictionary). Istanbul 1968.

J. Nobel, *Suvarṇaprabhāsottamasūtra: Das Goldglanz-Sutra ein Sanskrittext des Mahāyāna-Buddhismus. Die Tibetischen Übersetzungen mit einem Worterbuch* (in German: Suvarṇaprabhāsottamasūtra. The Sutra of Golden Light. A Sanskrit Text of Mahāyāna Buddhism. The Tibetan Translations with a Dictionary). Leiden 1944.

J. Nobel, *Suvarṇabhāsottamasūtra. Das Goldglanz-sūtra* (in German: Suvarṇabhāsottamasutra. The Sūtra of Golden Light). Leipzig 1937.

J. Nobel, *Suvarṇaprabhāsottamasūtra. Das Goldglanz-Sutra, ein Sanskrittext des Mahāyāna-Buddhismus. I-tsing's chinesische Version und ihre Übersetzung* (in German: The Sūtra of Golden Light. A Sanskrit Text of Mahāyāna Buddhism. I-tsing's Chinese version and its translation). Leiden 1958.

J. Nobel, *Suvarṇaprabhāsottama-sūtra. Das Goldglanz-Sutra. Ein Sanskrittext des Mahāyāna-Buddhismus. Die Tibetischen Ubersetzungen mit einem Worterbuch* (in German: Suvarṇaprabhāsottama-Sūtra. The Sūtra of Golden Light. A Sanskrit text of Mahāyāna Buddhism. Tibetan translation with a dictionary). Leiden 1944.

S.F. Oldenburg, *Russkie Archeologicheskiye Issledovaniya Vostochnom Turkestane* (in Russian: Russian archeological excavations in East Turkestan). 1921.

H.N. Orkun, *Yenisey yazitlari* (in Turkish: Inscription from the Yenisey river). Ankara 1939.

Suniti Kumar Pathak, Tibet, Mongolia and Siberia, *The Cultural Heritage of India,* Calcutta 1970.

P. Pelliot, Kao-Tchang, Qoco, Houo-tcheou et Qara-khodja, avec une note additionele de R. Gauthiot (in French: Kao-Tchang, Qočo, Houo-tcheou and Kara-khoja with a note of R. Gauthiot). *JA* 1911 pp. 579-603.

L. Petech, *China and Tibet in the early 18th century*. Leiden 1950.

N. Poppe, *Vergleichende Grammatik der altaischen Sprachen* (in German: Comparative grammar of the Altaic languages). Wiesbaden 1960.

N. Poppe, *Der altaische Sprachtyp* (in German: The Altaic type of language), Handbuch der Orientalistik V. 1964 pp. 1-16.

O. Pritsak, Von den Karluk zu den Karachaniden (in German: From the Karluks upto the Karakhanids). *ZDMG* 1951 pp. 270-300.

W. Radloff & S.E. Malov, *Suvarṇaprabhāsa-sūtra. Tekst Uygursko redakcii* (in Russian: Suvarṇaprabhāsa-sūtra: text of the Uigur version). Petrograd 1917.

W. Radloff, *Suvarṇaprabhāsa (Das Goldglanz-sūtra) aus dem Uigurischen Übersetzt* (Suvarṇaprabhāsa, The Sutra of Golden Light: a German translation of the first fourteen chapters from the Uigur). Leningrad 1930.

W. Radloff, Die *Alttürkische Inschriften der Mongolei* (in German: Old Turkish Inscription from Mongolia). St. Petersburg 1894, 1895, 1897.

W. Radloff, *Uigurische Sprachdenkmäler* (in German: Uigur documents). Leningrad 1928.

W. Radloff, *Kutadku bilig des Yusuf Hass Hajib*. Petersburg 1891-1910.

W. Radloff, *Chuastuanift ein Bussgebät der Manicheer* (in German: Chuastuanift, a confession prayer of the Manicheists). Petersburg 1909.

W. Radloff, *Tišasvustik, ein in turkischer Sprache bearbeitetes Buddhistisches Sūtra* (in German: Tišasvustik, a Buddhist Sutra in Turkish). Bibliotheca Buddhica Vol. 12, Petersburg 1910.

W. Radloff, *Kuan-ši-im Pusar*. Petersburg 1911.

Ram Rahul, *Politics of Central Asia.* 1974

Ram Rahul, *Himalaya as a Frontier*, New Delhi 1978.

G.J. Ramstedt, Zur Frage nach der Stellung der Tchuwassischen (in German: About the position of Chuwash language). *JSFOu* XXXVIII.

G.F. Ramstedt, *Über die Geschichte des Japanischen* (in German: On the history of Japanese). Helsinki 1942.

J.N. Reuter, Some Buddhist Fragments from Chinese Turkestan in Sanskrit and Khotanese. *JSFOu* XXX p. 7-17.

W. Samolin, East Turkestan to the Twelfth Century. *Central Asiatic Studies*. The Hague 1964.

R. Sankrityayana, *History of Central Asia*. Calcutta 1964.

Schraeder H.H., Die islamische Lehre vom volkommenen Menschen ihre Herkunft und ihre dichterische Gestaltung (in German: The Islamic teaching of the perfect people, its origin and its poetic formation). *ZDMG* 1925 pp. 192-268.

D. Sinor, *Orientalism and History*. Bloomington 1970.

D.L. Snellgrove, *The Hevajra Tantra: A Critical Study*. London 1959.

M.A. Stein, *Ancient Khotan*, Oxford 1902.

M.A. Stein, *Innermost Asia: Detailed Report of Explorations in Central Asia and Westernmost China*. Oxford 1928.

M.A. Stein, *Serindia*. Oxford 1921.

M.A. Stein, *The Thousand Buddhas: Ancient Buddhist Paintings from the Cave Temples of Tun-huang on the Western Frontier of China*. Recovered by Sir Aurel Stein, with an Introductory Essay by L. Binyon. London 1921.

S. Tekin, *Maytrisimit (Burkancilarian mehdidi Maitreya ile bulusma uygurca iptidai bir dram)* (in Turkish: Maitreya, the Messiah of the Buddhists, a primitive drama). Ankara 1976.

D.I. Tichonov, *Chosyaystvo i obsestvenniy stroy uygurskogo gosudarstav, X-XIV vv* (in Russian: Economy and social system of the Uigur State in the 10-14th centuries). Moscow-Leningrad 1966 p. 60.

F.W. Thomas, *Tibetan Documents Concerning Chinese Turkestan*. 1930.

E.J. Thomas, *The Life of Buddha as Legend and History*. London 1975.

V. Thomsen, Dr. M.A. Stein's Manuscripts in Turkish Runic Script from Miran and Tun-huang. *JRAS* 1912 pp. 181-227.

V. Thomsen, Ein Blatt in Türkischer Runeninschrift (in German: One page in Turkish Runic Script). *Sitz. d. K. Preuss. Akad. d. Wiss. Phil.-hist Klasse* (SPAW) 1910 vol. XV pp. 296-306.

V. Thomsen, *Turcica*. Helsingfors 1916.

V. Thomsen, Alttürkische Inschriften aus der Mongolei (in German: Old Turkish inscriptions from Mongolia). *ZDMG* Vol. 78. Leipzig 1924.

Tsong-kha-pa, *Tantra In Tibet, The Great Exposition of the Secret Mantra*, translated and edited by Jeffrey Hopkins, London 1977.

G. Tucci, *Tibetan Painted Scrolls*. Roma 1949.

L.A. Waddell, *The Buddhism of Tibet or Lamaism*. Cambridge 1971, pp. 159-164.

H. Winkler, *Japaner und Altaier* (in German: Japanese and Altais). Berlin 1894.

Winternitz, *A History of Indian Literature*, Vol. II, Delhi 1972.

A. Zajanczkowski, Die Karaimische Literatur (in German: The Qaraim literature). *Fnd.* II pp. 793-801.

P. Zieme, Ein uigurisches Turfan-fragment der Erzählung vom guten und vom bösen Prinzen (in German: An Uigur Turfan fragment of the Good and Bad Princes). *AOH* 1974 pp. 263-269.

P. Zieme, Singqu Seli Tutung: Übersetzer Buddhistischer Schriften ins Uigurische (in German: Singqu Seli Tutung—translator of Buddhist works into Uigur). *Tractata Altaica*. Wiesbaden 1976.

P. Zieme, *Ein Uigurisches text über die Wirtschaft Manichaischer Kloster im Uigurischen Reich* (in German: An Uigur text about the economy management of affairs of Manicheist monasteries in the Uigur Empire). Researches in Altaic Languages, 1975 pp. 331-338.

P. Zieme & G. Kara, *Ein Uigurisches Totenbuch* (An Uigur Book of the Dead). Budapest 1978.

E. Zürcher, *The Buddhist Conquest of China* Vols. I-II. Leiden 1972.

......